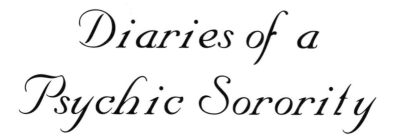

Diaries of a
Psychic Sorority

Diaries of a Psychic Sorority

TALKING WITH THE ANGELS

"God's thoughts, as angels, have come to guide us."
In love, Lily 3-1-98

KIMBERLY LILITH PHELPS

TERESA McMILLIAN

BARBARA LEE WITH

& ALL OUR HEAVENLY GUIDES

Diaries of A Psychic Sorority

TALKING WITH THE ANGELS

© 1997 Synergy Alliance
P.O. Box 24326
Edina, MN 55424

E-mail: SynergyAll@aol.com
http://www.angels4peace.com/synergy

McMillian, Teresa
Phelps, Kimberly Lilith
With, Barbara Lee
Diaries of a Psychic Sorority:
Talking With the Angels
Library of Congress Catalog Card Number
97-91160

Cover: Susan Abbott

Printed in the United States of America

This book is dedicated to all the people in our lives
who we *thought* caused us so much pain
that there was nowhere to go but up.

TABLE OF CONTENTS

ACKNOWLEDGEMENTS FROM THE ANGELS

We would like to thank those who have participated in the listening of the voices for your hearts and your minds and your spirits. We would like to thank the original triad, who were brought together for the purpose of dictation (but you know the funny thing about that). We would like to thank those who are skeptical, because skeptics help to strengthen those with faith. We would like to thank the ones who come to send this out to every corner of the world. We would like to thank the ones who supply the time and means and resources to make this dream come into complete fruition. But most of all, we would like to thank the channel who spent many countless hours, not only learning this art, but also delivering the messages with her voice that we find so soothing.

So begins a new era...an era where you can truly watch and be amazed.

ACKNOWLEDGEMENTS FROM THE TRIAD

We would like to thank God
in all of your various forms
(and you know the funny thing about that).

PROLOGUE

Life is difficult? Life is terrifying!

If you think of all the terrible things that could happen in your life, you might be tempted to go straight to bed with the covers pulled over your head. Between war, famine, drive-by shootings, car accidents or the death of someone dear, you might never leave your house again.

But if you think about only good things, about all the miracles that happen every single day, you risk being called a cockeyed optimist, in deep denial, or unrealistic. Society says it's okay to reach for a little taste of happiness, but don't set yourself up for failure by dreaming too big. The higher you reach, the farther you fall, after all.

Just for a moment, allow yourself to toy with a possibility: What if our fear is actually *causing* the violence in the world, not the other way around? What if just by healing our own inner fear we could actually heal the entire planet?

This is the true story of three strong, ordinary women from the Midwest who were brought together by their angels to be taught how to teach the world such a mission.

Every day, every hour, every sleeping and waking moment the Earth is surrounded by angels. Call them guides, call them the Higher Power. Call them anything you want, but don't say they haven't been trying to talk with all of us.

People see them as shadowy figures, angels of death, old friends, the light at the end of the tunnel, and Christ Jesus. Each angelic description is the result of some kind of cooperation between the human mind and the divine beings. In other words, everyone may not see angels in the same way, but the power behind each and every vision remains unchanged.

Let's say that you could actually call up your angels on your own divine communication lines. It would be pretty handy having their voices speak to you about anything you want. Why save your conversation with angels for when, say, the plane is going down, or the tornado hits? Why not ask for help when you're late, and you're trapped in the express lane at the grocery store and the lady in front of you has (gasp) eleven items in her cart, and is using food stamps to boot? What would the angels say about that?

And what if the angels, talking so clearly through us, could guide us with step-by-step instructions for bringing peace into the world? Not just the global peace we all pray for, but the peace that begins within each of us.

For how can we bring peace to the planet if we can't even settle the conflicts we have with our neighbors, families, co-workers, strangers, or within our own minds?

And what if, by hearing the voices of the angels in human form, something within us is so deeply moved that we begin to make these changes in total disregard of what our conscious minds think?

We have been instructed to tell our story. Some voices are our individual views, some are the collective thoughts of the three of us, and some are written by the pen of the angels. This is, after all, "a beautiful dance of great cooperation."

How do we begin to tell this story? It seems like fiction, but we know what follows is fact.

You don't need to believe anything you read. You don't have to be religious, spiritual, politically-correct or pass a stress test. You only need to read the book, give it time to sink in, and then, as the angels are so fond of telling us, "simply watch and be amazed."

☆ ────────────────────────────

PART ONE

---

*Congratulations,
You're Dying*

CHAPTER ONE
The Psychic Sorority

BARBARA

February 28, 1994

As the wheels of the plane fold back into the belly of the 10:40 a.m. flight to Honolulu, the thought crosses my mind that flying is something I might soon be doing without the help of a plane. After what I've just been through, anything seems possible.

The events of the past two-and-a-half months stretch beyond the ability of my conscious mind to comprehend them. On the other hand, so many miracles occurred within that period, I'm beginning to think these unusual events are the norm.

For example, I know for a fact that Gary and I will be getting married on this trip we're taking to Kaua'i, even though our wedding is planned for July in northern Wisconsin. Last night, sitting at my mother's kitchen table, I had a vision. I "saw" our wedding on the island, surrounded by exotic flora, waterfalls and the songs of the whales. It was like a scene out of Eden. And there was no doubt in my mind that it was real.

Was this the reason Gary won those two round-trip tickets in that United Way contest at work in December? And is Teresa's last minute windfall enabling her to unexpectedly join us in a few days so that she can be my maid of honor? And then there's Luddy, one of our dearest friends living on Maui who is also flying over. Is he to be best man?

I leapt up from the kitchen table and called Teresa. "Oh, my god, Teresa, I think … I mean … I think I'm getting married in Hawaii! Better bring something fabulous to wear!"

I tried to sound casual. In actuality, I sounded like I'd just swallowed a few dozen canaries. I couldn't believe what I was saying, and yet, all the training I've been through has taught me to recognize a vision when I *see* one. It's a feeling in the body, not just a thought process that passes through the mind. It's like your body is in two places at once: having the vision, and being in the vision.

The flight attendant brings lunch and as I pick at the foil wrapper of my miniature salad dressing, I think about how masterfully the angels have taught me to recognize a vision.

I've dubbed one of their training sessions the "Purple Jacket Day." One morning on the ski trail, the angels asked me to deliver a message to the woman "in the purple jacket" about her estranged brother. "They" identified her only by the color of her jacket. A complete stranger, I approached her with a message from her angels, and she wasn't even shocked. "It would be an answer to my prayers," she said almost sheepishly, after I told her their message.

Flying over the Pacific, blasting westward at 600 miles an hour, the sun begins to slip below the horizon. The aura of the earth glows a warm dark red, transforming before my eyes into a vivid orange.

All I can do is stare out the window and think about Kim and Teresa: complete strangers to me, bosom buddies to each other, all of us brought together coincidentally by personal crisis, in one way or another.

I am so moved by Teresa's sensitivity, and how easily she is touched so deeply. And Kim's quest for understanding and articulation has challenged and enlightened me every step of the way. Although I've only known them for a little over four months, the ties that bind us are more like those of very old and trusted friends.

For some yet-to-be-revealed reason, Kim is staying behind in the Midwestern winter while we're off to frolic in the South Pacific. For the first time since the beginning of our association she will be separated from us. What will be in store for her while we are romping beneath the volcano?

Reflection brings questions: How did this whole thing begin? For that matter, how far back into the past does this reach? I mean, have the angels been planning this from our respective childhoods?

☆ ───────────────────────────────────────

Where did these two women come from, and why did they walk into my life at this time? Why am I gifted with this art of talking to the angels? And now they're doing it, too. Is making the voices available for anyone who would listen the kind of healing "they" have been training us to do?

But the most mysterious question of all: Where is it leading us?

Spinning toward the horizon, helpless through space, the sun slips over the edge of the world, and instantly it is night.

"We are sailing on a ship
That's bound for muddy waters
But we are together.
We'll guide her clear of reefs and rocks
And we'll anchor in the harbor of my soul"

"Sailing on a Ship" © 1971 Barbara With

The angels first officially began talking to me when I was seventeen. My friend Mike told me his mom gave "readings." When pressed for an explanation, he simply said, "Just have one."

So, one Saturday morning I went to his mother's third floor walkup with a loaf of my father's fresh baked sourdough bread and my best friend Gayle to take notes.

Junice, a gentle forty-year-old woman, emanated an extraordinary peace. Her apartment smelled like frankincense, and on the wall hung a famous picture of Jesus, all aglow in the warmth of his halo. She explained that she was going to go into a trance and "they" would speak. When I inquired where she went during this, she said she felt like she was floating around somewhere in space and when she came back, she would have no memory of what was said.

At seventeen, I was, to put it mildly, a raging cynic. My parents had divorced after years of verbal and physical abuse. My specialty was throwing tantrums in public and not speaking to my family for weeks at a time. With my father finally gone, and my mother working sixty hours a week to keep the family afloat, life was fairly confounding.

Since the age of thirteen I had been writing moody, introspective music, but I didn't understand what many of the songs meant or where they were coming from. It was easy to escape into that private, solitary world inside me to write music. To me, that process felt like what I imagined outer space would feel like. So when a strange woman told me she was going to be "floating around in space," this was something I could relate to. This was something I wanted to see.

☆ ――――――――――――――――――――――――――――――――――

She lit a candle and closed her eyes. Instantly the room seemed to fill with a subtle, fluorescent light. Suddenly she, or "they," began to speak. Their voice was kind and lyrical. Referring to themselves as "we," they said my life would change so dramatically it would be like the opening of a door that I would walk through and become a completely different person. They described my emotional and psychological state so precisely, I cried. Their words were lasers, cutting straight into my heart as they used actual phrases I had thought or said verbatim.

Then they spoke about a past life I had lived as a painter. My paintings are apparently hanging today in museums. I lived during the first part of this century somewhere in Europe and my work focused on the suffering of the common people. My husband was in the service of the people. They spoke in great detail without ever giving me the name of the painter.

Then they told me later in this life I would find out who I had been. After that solitary spring afternoon, life was never quite the same again.

When I left her apartment, I walked around for hours trying to digest this. How did she, or they, know so much about me? Could I actually see and touch something, a painting, I had done in another life that survived through time? Why would it be brought to me again in this life?

Aside from Mike and Gayle, there really wasn't anyone to talk to about this. Certainly the foyer of high school wasn't an appropriate place for a round table discussion of former lives and talking with angels. I don't think Jeff, the burly football player I had a crush on, would have understood my excursion into the ethers.

And this other life I had lived? How could ... how does it all work? And how would I find out who I had been?

I continued to see Junice about twice a year. Each and every reading spoke of traveling the world, healing through music. They described in detail the clothing I would be wearing, the large audiences, and the power of my music to help heal people. Ever since I was old enough to hold a hairbrush and sing along to "Heat

Wave" I firmly believed I was destined to be a star. These sessions in the afternoons in her apartment only confirmed it.

And I watched as the things "they" told me came to pass. My music developed from entertaining at weekend high school parties to performing in public at local coffeehouses. I began to develop a following, and soon became one of the top draws of the local music scene. Local newspapers were writing about me, I began winning local music awards. It appeared everything was right on schedule.

But I gripped my interpretation of the prophesies of the angels for dear life. I fully believed that anything less than what *I thought of* as success—tons of money, international recognition, record contracts and lunch with The Boss—meant I was a failure. Even though I truly was on my way to achieving the very predictions I so longed to see unfold, because they didn't look like *I* thought they should, I felt like I was going nowhere.

But unbeknownst to me, these sessions weren't just to prepare me for some kind of rock super-stardom. They were the beginning of a unique apprenticeship of hearing the angels through a human voice and studying the prophesies as they unfolded. I had no idea how much I was learning.

My life became one long highway. I traveled the country singing my original music wherever anyone would have me. At first I played only coffeehouses and concert halls at the local colleges. I swore I would never play in bars. All my concentration was lost in the noise and smoke, and my introspective songs only served to depress the people looking for a jolly time. But that's where the steady money was. So I bit the bullet, learned music people could recognize and tried my best to make a living as a musician.

I played supper clubs in Colorado and gay bars in Palm Springs; I did happy hours at country western bars in Texas and off-nights at rock clubs throughout northern Wisconsin. I would drive virtually anywhere someone would hired me to perform.

The difference between the prophesies of healing the world with music and the reality of being a human jukebox was searing. I began to turn more and more to alcohol and drugs, readily available for easing the pain of being ignored by the drunken patrons more interested in hearing something they could sing along to than my original work. Drinking took the edge off, and made me forget the beautiful dream I thought I had lost. At night after the gigs, alone in all those cheap little motel rooms, I often thought of staying home and trying to be "normal," but this was the only life I knew how to live.

Nine years after my first reading, at a party where I knew no one but my date, the hostess handed me a book she said she thought I'd enjoy. I couldn't figure out how she deduced this after knowing me only twenty minutes. On the cover was a drawing that looked eerily similar to one I had drawn when I was young. As I read about this artist's life, a strange feeling crept over my body. A warmth started in my solar plexus and spread into my limbs and throat.

The details of her life fit perfectly the past life description "they" had given me all those years ago. This artist had lived in Germany through both World Wars. Her paintings captured the strife of the people of the time. Her husband had been a doctor. Picture after picture bore a supernatural resemblance to the sad, shadowy faces I had drawn as a teen.

This was perhaps my first lesson in vision: I was sitting at the party, but I was equally physically present in this woman's memory, the memory of my past life. I was also connected to that afternoon in 1972 when I first heard the angels speak to me through a human voice and tell me about this eventual moment.

For nine years I'd wondered how in the world I would ever find out who I had been in that life. There I sat, weeping openly in the dining room at a cocktail party full of strangers.

After that, I read everything about her I could get my hands on. The descriptions of her life were uncommonly parallel to mine. She grew up crying her way through life, as I did. She fell painfully, secretly in love with almost everyone she met. So did I, except I exposed my feelings to the point of embarrassment to the objects of my affection. She constantly did self-portraits. From an early age, I used to sit in front of the mirror and sketch my eyes. Her poetry contained almost the identical phraseology as mine.

And the drawings.

☆

I checked books of her work out of the library, dug out my old sketches and compared them to hers. Stroke for stroke, style for style, the same. Incredible.

Now, the purpose of telling this story is not to convince you I had been a great artist in another life. It's to draw pictures of the experiences that were the fertile ground into which the angels planted the seeds that grew into the life I live today, a life of talking with the angels.

How many times have you felt the hand of God nudge you this way or that? Seemingly split-second decisions led to situations beyond your wildest dreams. A car that could have arrived a second earlier would have killed you. You think longingly of someone and they miraculously appear.

Don't be fooled into thinking these are mere coincidence. It's those angels, hanging around every step of the way. How am I so sure?

They told me.

They speak to me in my left ear. They guide, suggest, advise, make corny jokes and generally carry on conversations all day long. In the beginning, it was quite distracting. In fact, they hounded me for weeks to begin this book. They started dictating it to me at the most inopportune times until I finally sat and started writing.

Angels aren't distant, virginal, silvery creatures who only come in times of great need. They are funny, warm, individual beings with distinct personalities. How many are there around us? I'm not sure, but it seems like a whole host. And they love the human race with the most divine and unconditional love imaginable.

But I'm getting ahead of myself. How did I go from an raging cynical teenager to a faith-filled woman who lets the angels speak through her? And how did they guide Teresa and Kim to me? How has this heroic mission of theirs unfolded through their words and our voices?

Synchronicity.

"How can the spirit that made the mountains
Have taken him from you?
Well, gaze into the night sky
He's probably better off than you or I.
He's giving to us what God gave him.
It's a gift for his survival,
Part of his Master Plan."

"Master Plan" © 1986 Barbara With

The angels first began speaking through me in 1987, shortly after the death of my beloved friend and mentor, Morton. He was the first person close to me to die. If, as the angels tell us, pain is the fertile ground that prepares us for revelation, then those days after his death were certainly making me ready for *something*.

We met in northern Wisconsin one summer in the late seventies. He was an exceptionally eccentric English teacher who I imagined, in his younger days, to be like the teacher from "Dead Poet's Society." In the winter he taught English, and in the summer he came north and became the local garbageman of the resort community we lived in. As writers, we relished our correspondences, and he mentored me with my writing, particularly my poetry.

Many hot summer evenings we'd barbecue fresh lake trout pulled that morning from Lake Superior, and he'd challenge me to write a poem in sixty seconds, or recite my latest ode to yet another bad relationship. We'd do crossword puzzles with the Brewers' game on his old radio and dream about the year I'd finally have the means to build my house, right next door to his, on the parcel of land he'd sold me.

One spring night in 1985, after a few too many gin and tonics, Morton drove his truck off the road and onto the beach. It was the same beach young Philip Linehan landed on when he missed the turn and drove his Harley into a tree, discovered dead the next morning, neck broken.

Although Morton wasn't seriously injured, his excursion onto the beach put him in the hospital for three weeks and scared him straight. No more butts or booze. But being clean for six months made him aware of a persistent sore throat. Further examination revealed throat cancer.

After the shock wore off, he made arrangements to move into my mother's home for a few months while receiving treatment at the Vet's hospital. After radiation, he'd sneak off to the local tavern to smoke and drink, then come home and pretend to be sober. As if he was fooling any of us.

Radiation bought him nine or ten more months, but when he checked in again at the end of 1986, they found the cancer had spread. One of my last memories of Morton is of him in his tiny room at the VA, silently acting out a Greek tragedy he was relating to my love life at the time, his vocal chords removed, gesturing with sweeping arm movements and melodramatic facial expressions. Like a fading Shakespearean actor putting his all into his last big role, Morton mimed the terrible tale so fancifully I ached from the laughter.

A few weeks later he left for the East to be near his daughter at the end. As we stood in line at the airport, I held on tight to him, choking back my tears. And in a rare moment of pure tenderness, he told me he loved me. When we stepped away, we knew we would never see each other again in this life. It was small surprise when his daughter-in-law called the next month to tell me he had passed on.

At his memorial service many people told me of his special love for me. As I sat at the piano in the little country church on the shore of Lake Superior, I mustered the courage to sing for him one last time, "Over The Rainbow," his favorite song in my repertoire. I managed to deliver the performance of my life, but as soon as the song ended I began to cry, and did not stop for anything for a very long while.

One spring afternoon not long after the funeral, during a rare respite from the weeping, I began writing an ironic letter to my friend about how "bad it is to make judgments." In the middle of the second paragraph my hands suddenly became independent of my conscious thinking. Something seemed to take control of what I was typing. I read the words for the first time as they appeared on the paper, instead of hearing them in my brain. The pronoun "we" was being used. "They" continued on with the thoughts I had about judgments:

> *The channel where the emotions flow, like the wind through a tunnel, is narrowed, as in your rush hour, and nothing gets through but a small trickle of what really is. Open up, the universe is waiting for your arrival.*

I was shocked. This was not me writing. But, if it wasn't me, who was it? I typed the question, "Where am I?"

> *Taking a back seat. You have always known you were a channel, and have been channeling for many years. You sang. When you sang you removed yourself from your body. Have you not always said you felt as if someone else was coming through you, as if you weren't writing the song?*

It was true. From the time I was thirteen and started composing music, I'd describe the process by saying the songs were already written, and someone else was telling me what to write.

> *You sent yourself away by intense hypnosis, listening to the music from the inside out. When you were young you were sheltered from being exposed to certain lifestyles and emotions so as to allow you to unfold them at this particular time.*

> *Everything was divinely timed for you to have just the right attitude of innocence. That is another power. In divine order, all things can only be timed perfectly. It is not for you to decide what is perfectly.*

> *You have a painful habit of thinking you have "arrived" some- where, when actually the journey continues far beyond where you*

imagine you have landed. Preconceived notions of how everything will happen only hinder the work of it.

Okay, then who are you?

We are sound waves. We have worked closely with you for as long as you can remember and beyond. You will now use this information to formulate a newer and much bigger picture of you, the eternal soul. Find peace within and you will create peace from without. We will come sooner and more often. Everything will move along faster now as the class begins to pick up momentum.

They went on to speak extensively about my past, re-framing it from a perspective of unconditional love and acceptance. Those painful years of playing music in bars weren't wasted. According to the angels, even though my ego wasn't being fulfilled, apparently the music was still doing its miraculous healing work, in spite of what my conscious mind was thinking. And the reason I drank was to medicate my pain so I could go on and do the work. They said if I had understood how powerful I was at the time, my ego would have destroyed me. I knew that was true.

It was like re-writing the past, healing it, coming to terms with my shameful and shame-filled behavior. They infused a sense of divine purpose even in something that appeared to be so destructive. It eased my mind for the moment, but I didn't know at the time it would take years of lessons before I could understand it with my heart.

We talked for three pages. They assured me they would come again. For days after, I swore I heard Morton's voice in my left ear. He was saying, "So you think I helped you on the Earth … just wait and see how I can help you from here!"

☆

"Mama said, 'Child, give it up,
Let the well run dry.
Everybody's got their crocodile tears to cry,
Give it up, let it go, learn to say goodbye,
Turn around, take a step you might learn to
Let go, let go, let go, let go, let go now.
Say goodbye, learn to say goodbye.'"

"Let Go" © 1987 Barbara With

As I continued to write, strange things happened to my body. "They" described it as preparing my body to receive their transmissions, which were a higher frequency than I was used to. For two solid weeks I had dreams consisting of nothing more than millions of numbers being poured into my head. I woke up exhausted. I couldn't sleep despite being constantly tired. It took about a month to adjust to the changes.

After that, I began to invite my friends to talk to "them." The person would sit on my left side and I would write freehand. It was a tedious task. I'm not sure why I didn't think of speaking sooner, because of my experiences with Junice. Perhaps it was part of the divine timing they are always talking about.

I did this writing for about a year. I often asked questions in my journals and "they" would answer. Once I asked, "Why aren't you incarnating now?"

There is a vast area of knowledge, communication and love on "invisible" planes. You are designed, as incarnates on the planet, to touch, taste, smell, see and hear. You also have a beginning awareness of just how complex the scheme of things is. But you are merely scratching the surface of how much of life is mind power, concentration, discipline, order.

We were incarnate as humans on the earth for many years. But we became aware of the rest of ourselves—the power of the dream world, meditation, the power of kindness and love—we found the door to the higher understanding of what the mind can do. We saw that three dimensions were only a small part of the entire picture, and, as we have learned to live in the fourth, fifth, sixth [dimensions] and so on, we slowly left the game of the earth plane. We outgrew the lessons. We passed through various stages of form and began moving faster. Now we are up to the speed of sound. Soon we will evolve into pure light. There will be no room for verbs. It will be osmosis. Think of lying soaking up the sun. You are drinking in God in its purest but most disguised form.

They were persistent in nudging me to speak their words. Finally, at a party one evening, a group of us were discussing my new-found psychic abilities. Someone suggested I speak the voices for the group. Everyone was game, except for one skeptical guy in the corner. I assured him he didn't have to believe it, but asked if he'd have the courtesy to keep it to himself. He agreed.

I shut my eyes. Suddenly I felt a wind blowing through me, like the rush of wings moved from the bottom of my feet to the top of my head. I still couldn't tell if anything was happening. Then I started to speak.

We didn't record that first time, but the skeptical guy in the corner asked the most in-depth questions about the nature of reality. "They" spoke at length about the soul and past lives, and then proceeded to address people individually.

When I finally opened my eyes, a number of people were in tears. Others' mouths were agape. I had no idea how powerful the experience had been, but judging by the look on people's faces, something miraculous had taken place. Even the skeptical guy in the corner admitted he, too, was amazed.

My God, was this a fascinating, mysterious process! I wanted to do more. To begin, I gave sessions to two dear friends, Jane and Bruce, and asked them, if they were satisfied, to refer others to me. Everything that has come to pass is directly related back to those two readings. The only advertising I ever did was word of month.

During these beginning readings, I found myself having many doubts. When I'd speak the voices, my own ego voice would go on and on, saying, "You can't tell them that, you don't even know them! You're a fake. They're never going to believe this crap! And you're taking their money on top of it! What a charlatan!"

When it got so bad I could hardly hear through the din, I asked "them" what I could do about this. They suggested giving my ego a *little* place where it could sit and rant and not disrupt the readings.

I developed a ritual to do before each encounter, not only to help quiet the ego, but to ask for only the purest energy to come through me. I'd first imagine a little ledge, approachable by a small ladder, with a tiny rocking chair and an oriental rug. I'd watch my ego-self climb onto the little loft and get into the little chair and rock and complain, trying to fill my head with doubt. Picturing it outside myself weakened it's power and visualizing everything in miniature also reduced the size of its voice.

Then I'd close my eyes and repeat:

> *I now surround myself with pure, white light,*
> *The pure Christ-line light of my own Christ consciousness.*

That created something of a cavern within me. Now there was more room for "them" to enter that space within me. When they entered it felt like putting on a glove: They were the hand and I was the glove.

Sometimes I saw a flow of words, like the Times Square message board. Mostly, I saw pictures that formed analogies describing someone's life. They were big on metaphors, parables and speaking figuratively. And they loved a good play on words.

Requests to hear them speak were infrequent at first. I'd read for three or four people a month and then none for a few months. Strangers called and came and went and came again, usually in six month intervals. I was always amazed at the repeated requests because I still had doubts about the process.

It appeared to me that most people were satisfied with the sessions and they were often moved to tears. The process seemed to open them up to themselves and help them find a key within to unlock some of the mysteries that comprised their lives. Human spirit naturally seeks answers, while human beings sometimes flounder in the questions. This appeared to be a way to help the two parts connect consciously, if only for the hour or so the session would last.

All of these experiences inspired me to spend more time in the place where the voices spoke. I began going there in my meditations. While I could reduce my doubts, I couldn't rid myself of them completely, but even that didn't stop me from hearing their voices. I had many a long conversation with the angels in those meditations. They answered every question I posed about the events of my life.

One question frequently asked was about my love life. "Train Wrecks-R-Us" had been my credo when it came to long-term relationships. If someone was giving out medals, I certainly would have brought home the gold in the "Sheer Volume" division. By the time "they" started speaking about this remarkable man I was going to meet, I had been through so many men and thought each and every one was Mr. Right, I ignored the forewarnings about this new guy.

Gary and I met in 1989. To get over my latest broken heart, I convinced myself that I should learn to date as many guys as I could at one time. Just be painfully honest and let the chips fall where they may. No more getting involved. So I ran an ad in the personals.

"Preternatural, untamed redhead seeks gorgeous gutsy swain for philanthropy..." I lied about my age. Gary answered with the most sincere letter and a "really-nice-but-not-*too*-nice guy" picture. He lied about his height. On our first date, he told me he was a journalist. I told him I was a psychic. In an informal display of my talent, I asked him for the name of someone in his life, whom I obviously wouldn't know, and offered to describe him sight unseen. I captured his boss's personality to a tee, and also promised Gary that he'd get a raise and promotion in August. Since his annual review always came in March, it would be unusual for him to get a raise in August.

"Well," he replied in his best skeptical journalist's voice, "If I get a raise in August, you can have half of it."

Later that summer, after he got it, I tried to collect, but he claimed he never agreed to such a deal.

☆————————————————————————

Being a Virgo and therefore a natural master of detachment, he possessed something I'd always longed for: a center of balance. He also had the equilibrium of a strong, loving family and a sense of duty and discipline. But, as we are all prone to do, he sometimes had a hard time accepting the very things I admired about him.

We worked our way through five years together. We bought a home and began our gardens. He easily gave me the sense of continuity and stability I longed for, and in return I coaxed him out of his Virgo order and helped reconnect him with his wildhood.

Gary was not what you might call a believer. He was always mildly amused by the strange voice coming out of the back room on nights I'd give readings. He called it my "alter-ego." But through a series of difficulties in his own life, he was drawn to the warmth of the messages. I mean, how long can someone live under the same roof with a host of angels and not be lured into their tender trap?

For some reason, swimming, which I did year round, became a regular place I could hear the voices without much difficulty. In early 1993, while doing laps at the club, a large group of angels appeared before me. This was new. In most pool meditations, I'd never sensed more than two or three at a time. This appeared to be an entire host.

They told me I was to begin working with this new group of angels. Apparently, things were going to start happening faster now, in almost every aspect of my life, including my music.

This was good news. Shortly after Morton died, I sold all my musical equipment and checked into treatment. Weary from driving from tavern to supper club, playing in wedding bands, not even doing my original music anymore, I was lonely, afraid, addicted, and tired of dreaming that my purpose was to heal the world. How could I heal the world if I felt so sick myself? I was bitter, cynical and in desperate need of other job skills besides playing music.

With my hunt and peck typing I registered at temporary secretarial agencies and learned word processing. I got my first "real" job at age thirty-four as secretary to the president of an advertising agency. That only lasted nine months but in that time I taught myself desktop publishing. Then I worked for a video producer as his gal

Friday. Even fewer hours and a more contemporary atmosphere felt like a short chain to a woman who had roamed freely for the first seventeen years of her adult life. That lasted two years.

Finally, after much consideration, I decided to sing again. Only this time, I would do it with serious, sober intent. Piece by piece I would build my career from the ground up, however long it would take and whatever I had to do. I began by recruiting two other women to sing harmonies, and started performing around town as an acoustic trio. We worked once a month, made no money, but it was original and it was from the heart and it was good. Of course, I immediately fell into thinking about the prophesies of my youth and the dreams of being a "star."

Now the angels had appeared to me in the pool and told me it was all going to change, and quickly. I, of course, expected the next guy to swim by would be a record producer and sign me right there. A few days after the pool visit, when nothing seemed much different, I forgot their message and fell back into the daily grind of the three-dimensional world.

More and more people were coming to hear the voices. One night, shortly after meeting this new group of angels, a woman called and said she had been referred by one of my regular clients who was a temp where she worked. She wanted to make an appointment for a reading. She didn't mention her last name. I remembered her first name, Teresa, and that her husband was a musician.

On the day of her appointment, a stunningly beautiful woman appeared at my door. She could have been a model or an actress and had an air about her that spoke of an unpretentious regality. She didn't appear to be in crisis, but was obviously in pain. After the session, she seemed genuinely moved. We exchanged a few words, I got her address for my mailing list and she left.

Often times referrals called and said they were a friend of so-and-so. When they'd call again six months later, I usually didn't remember who they were. Unlike Junice, I would remember what was being said during the reading, but only for a short time. And rarely did I remember what had been said in a previous session.

But when Teresa came back that autumn, I remembered exactly who she was.

☆ ───

TERESA

March 4, 1994

Standing at the Northwest ticket counter, the clerk cheerfully checks my bag and asks if I prefer window or aisle. I want to tell him I'll ride on the wing if I have to.

It's pretty crazy how this whole trip to Kaua'i came about. When I think about it, there were certainly a fair number of coincidences involved.

In the early planning stages of their trip, when Kim and I still barely knew Barbara, she offhandedly suggested that we join her and Gary in Hawaii. They were renting a huge house from a friend of Gary's sister, and there was plenty of room. We teased her, saying, "We're sure Gary wants to spend this romantic vacation in a tropical paradise with all three of us." She assured us that he really wouldn't mind, as long as it was only for part of their trip.

Later, after giving it some thought, I turned to Kim and said, "Boy, I really feel like I'm going. Do you?" She just looked at me and said, "No."

Some weeks passed. Despite the fact that business was slow and I was totally broke, I couldn't get the notion that I was going to Hawaii out of my head. Of course, meditating and finding myself high up on a cliff overlooking the ocean, watching the whales as a beautiful waterfall tumbled by—or—describing a dream I had to Barbara about Ryan O'Neal and her telling me I perfectly described her friend Luddy, who was also going to be there, didn't help matters any.

Then one night Kim, our good friend Lee and I went to hear Barbara sing. On the break, as Barbara talked about her trip, I started whining about wanting to go along. When Lee asked why I would go, I told her about the invitation, the free place to stay, the dream and the meditation. I told her about no money and no way to get there.

Without hesitation, Lee offered me her newly-acquired frequent flyer ticket! I couldn't believe it! She must have sensed my intense emotion about wanting to go. Suddenly, one of the biggest obstacles was eliminated. I still didn't have any spending money, but things certainly were looking up.

The very next morning my husband called to say he had just gotten a royalty check for some commercials he had played on and just happened to be putting $700 into my bank account. I hung up the phone and sat there dumbfounded. A free place to stay. A free plane ticket. Money in my bank account. Visions. Dreams. Gee, should I go? I could have sworn I felt the angels laugh.

So, here's me…just waiting to board the plane. I cannot believe I am going to Hawaii! How in the world did I get here?!

I'm a southern girl. I grew up in North Carolina. My family didn't have much money, and my father was an alcoholic. These days much light has been shed on the effects of alcoholism on a family, but back then those experiences left me in the dark.

I'm the youngest of three girls. On some level, I always knew the significant people in my life loved me. But today when I try to remember what growing up felt like in my family, all I can recall is the feeling of "just being there."

I loved my Daddy more than anything. Although he drank a lot, he was not the usual boisterous drunk who screamed and yelled and beat up everyone. When he was drunk, he was introverted and quiet. I didn't understand why my Mom yelled at him like she did. I always felt sorry for him.

Sometimes he would take me with him and sneak down to the corner store for a beer. I was only two or three, and I remember standing on the seat beside him as he drove down the road in our green '63 Oldsmobile 98, my arms around his neck, loving on him all the way. He would sit drinking his beer in the parking lot of the store and say, "Now, don't you tell your Mama I had this beer." And I never did. Heaven only knows what keeping those secrets for him did to me as I watched my mother suffer through a pain I couldn't possibly have understood.

Mom was the tornado. She reacted to my father's drinking by running around the house ranting and raving most of the time. I have to say, though, she never directed her anger at me. It was her life that made her crazy—the messy closets, the empty liquor bottles hidden around the house, the bills she couldn't pay. I remember many times going with her to my daddy's office to pick up his pay for the week. Mom would come out crying because there were only a few dollars left. My dad took advances all week to drink on, and even though he had a wife and three daughters to support, the company he worked for let him. You see, his boss was his own brother. More dysfunction.

Practically every Sunday Mother would pack our bags because we were moving out. Leaving him. We never did. She couldn't do it. Instead she sought solace in her family. Most weekends we'd drive to the mountains and spend some time with Grandma and Grandpa so she could get away from it all, just for a little bit.

I have a sister ten years older than me. I realize now how hard she tried to give me the attention I didn't get from my parents. When I was young, she'd tell me stories about whatever adventure she was having at the moment, and believe me, there were some doosies! I remember listening rapt as she shared her cool grown-up secrets with me. Unfortunately, some of those secrets really hurt my mom, and consequently, my family. So, at eleven years old, I was still keeping other people's secrets and watching my mom suffer.

I have another sister three years older than me. Growing up, we were practically invisible to each other except, of course, to fight. At a time in our lives when we should have clung to each other for support, we instead chose to totally ignore each other.

There is good news in all of this. When I was fourteen years old, my Dad went to church one Sunday and found something to believe in besides the booze. He never touched another drop of alcohol the rest of his life. After we girls were grown and out of the house, Mom and Dad had some really good years together before she became terminally ill with cancer. My dad stood right beside her through that long painful illness to the day she died. Her death was very hard on him. It took him two years before he could go through the house and pack up her things. I'm so thankful their life together didn't end in that chaos. Instead, they found a deep and abiding love for each other that had been hiding under all that insanity.

My dad passed away ten years after my mom. In the absence of both our parents, my two sisters and I regrouped and bonded ever so tightly. We vowed never to lose that closeness again in our lives. I thank God everyday for their never ending love and support.

While I was growing up, though, that love and support mostly came from my best friend, Dawn. We met in the third grade and since the age of seven we've continued to nurture our very special friendship. Through the years, we've shared everything—our fears, our hopes, our dreams, our dysfunctional families. Together we learned about boys, alcohol, drugs, driving, friends, love, and now, marriage and children.

One of the many reasons I'm grateful for knowing Dawn all my life is the different perspective she has on my family. Although she saw the havoc alcoholism wreaked on us, she also remembers the tender side of my family life I seem to have forgotten, like the sweet way my mother would talk to me and always call me "Baby." I wish I could remember that.

Another reason Dawn was so important in my life in those early years was from a spiritual perspective. When I was very small, my mom sometimes took me to church, but we didn't go on a regular basis. After Dawn and I became friends, I went to Baptist church with her family every Sunday. Somehow, with Dawn's family it was expected of me. Maybe it was because Dawn and I were so close and her mom treated me like I was her own. Even if the two of us didn't spend Saturday night together, they would drive to my house on Sunday morning and pick me up so I could go.

I realize now how important that spiritual base was. At the time, I think I went simply because it was the right thing to do. Dawn and I would study our Sunday School lesson on the way there. What was difficult when I got to church, though, was being told that there were questions I shouldn't ask—about God, the Bible and such. I was told not to question, so I didn't. This left a lot of holes in my thinking about the place I'd hoped to find peace. Somehow it only made me feel bad—you know, a sinner.

I remember one Sunday of revival week when I felt compelled in my heart to walk down to the front of the church while the invitation was being given. The choir was singing "Just As I Am," and I was scared to death that if I didn't give my life to Jesus I would be damned to an eternity in hell. At only thirteen years old I wondered

☆

what I could have possibly done to have sealed such a fate for myself. Yet, there I was, crying and telling the preacher I wanted to accept Jesus so I could have eternal life. I thought *that* was the missing link to finding peace in my life. It wasn't.

I have now come to believe my soul is eternal. I feel closer to God than I ever did in those days. I understand the teachings of Jesus and believe He was delivering the same messages the angels teach us every day—*Love yourself*. No one ever mentioned that back then.

I believe many people find their peace in whatever religion they choose. And isn't that just what religion should do—give us a sense of peace in our hearts? I understand my religious upbringing had an important place in my life. It was a step in the right direction. I just didn't find true peace until now.

When I was twenty years old, I was hired as a flight attendant by a major airline and transplanted from North Carolina to Minneapolis. I loved my new job. Shortly after moving to Minneapolis, I met my future husband, Randy, who was a musician. We fell madly in love. Even after several years of marriage people teased us about how sickening it was to watch us together—always holding hands and kissing. We couldn't keep our hands off each other.

Because of the nature of our two occupations, we spent a lot of quality time with each other. It was the perfect set-up. We had a wonderfully carefree lifestyle, flying all over the country, going on great trips. Both our schedules were so flexible, sometimes we'd jet off to Acapulco for the night, or hop down to New Orleans for a week. Other times I would simply go watch him play his music. I would sit and stare at him, hearing those familiar songs for the millionth time thinking how much I loved this man. The interesting thing was, even with the insecurity and low self-esteem built-in from my upbringing, I never questioned or doubted how much he loved me. He always made sure I knew. No one had ever done that in my life before. It was a dream come true.

Five years after we were married, we were pregnant with our first child. It wasn't the best timing in our unsettled lives, but given the depth of our love, I knew it would be fine. So I was naturally crushed when I told him about the baby and he asked, "Are you sure it's mine?" There was absolutely no reason for him to question that. A few weeks later I happened upon an article that said many men ask that question. It wasn't that he doubted me, but somehow he doubted himself and his ability to be a father. I was so relieved to read this, I was able to let it go and we moved through the pregnancy with tremendous excitement and happiness, preparing for the advent of this symbol of our love.

We started Lamaze class near the end of my term. That's where I met Kim. She chatted with us throughout the classes, but not any more than anyone else. I'm sure I wouldn't have talked to her at all if she hadn't been so outgoing and approached me first. I was still very shy because of my own insecurities. Then, after the last class, as Randy and I were backing out of our parking space, she ran up to the car, gave me her phone number and said, "Call me when you have your baby!" A couple seconds later we would have missed each other completely. It seemed odd to me that she did that. I looked at Randy after we pulled away and said, "That was weird."

Two weeks later my beautiful daughter was born. Since I wasn't working, Randy had to work a day job and play in the band at night to make ends meet. The day after Sarah was born he wasn't able to come to the hospital at all. I was hungry for someone to share my precious new baby with, so I called that strange woman from the Lamaze class. To my surprise, Kim came to the hospital that day and even brought a gift and flowers. I thought, "Who is this woman?" I couldn't believe she extended herself to me like that. After all, I was certainly nobody special.

I had planned to stay home with Sarah for a few months, but money was definitely tight. Kim and I continued to stay in touch. I knew she was going right back to work and had not yet arranged for daycare, so I offered to watch her new baby, Katie. Every morning she'd bring Katie over and we'd sit for at least an hour getting to know each other over coffee. Our friendship deepened on levels even we didn't understand.

By all appearances, Kim had the perfect life—money, a career, a beautiful home, a husband with a normal job and now a beautiful new baby. I remember wondering why this incredible woman seemed to love being with me so much. I didn't think I had anything to offer her and knew she'd figure that out sooner or later.

☆————————————————————————

It was wonderful to be home with the girls. Since they were only a month apart, it was like having twins. They seemed to always want to eat at the same time, so I took turns holding Sarah at one feeding and then Katie at the next. It was odd to me that I loved both of these babies like my own.

A few months later, money was really tight and I knew I had to go back to work. Obviously, I wasn't going back to the airlines, so I prepared to take a job I swore I'd never have—working in an office. I knew someone had to give up a career traveling to give this child some stability. I automatically assumed it had to be me.

Within a few months, my life started going downhill. I was confined all day in an office at a job I never wanted, I was still trying to adjust to being a new mother, and now it felt like I had two children—Sarah and Randy. It wasn't that Randy expected me to take care of him, but I didn't know how *not* to. I mean, that's what you do when you love someone, right? Caretake them at the expense of your own needs, whether they expect you to or not. After all, that was the model I learned from my mom.

I became a wreck and cried all the time. I didn't understand what I was feeling or why, and I certainly couldn't see the effect that growing up in a dysfunctional family was having on me now. I only knew I had these two people in my life and I was somehow responsible for their happiness and well-being. I was at a total loss.

It's obvious to me now my transformation started in an effort to give Sarah something I never felt—a feeling of being unconditionally loved and cherished. I couldn't bear to think of this precious child, who I loved more than life itself, growing up feeling the same way I did—like she's "just there" or not important, and sacrificing herself thinking that it would make people love her. Somehow I had to make it different for her. Somehow I had to show Sarah how much I cherished her.

Then it hit me like a ton of bricks. I could say the right things to help build her self-esteem, but when push comes to shove, if she doesn't know how to really love herself, it won't matter. And how do you teach someone self-love? You have to show them that *you* love *yourself.* Children mirror their parents. They take their cues from us. I didn't have a clue where to start because I had never known that kind of self-love. I didn't know what to do.

☆

What I didn't realize was what started as a journey for the benefit of my child became a journey back to myself.

Kim encouraged me to see a therapist. She really loved hers and suggested I see him. She even gave up her own appointment so I could get in faster, instead of having to wait the usual three to four weeks required of a new patient.

God bless Dr. McKee. With his help, I did a lot of healing work on my dysfunctional past. It was a major feat. I don't fool myself into thinking I'm cured. I know I will be working this process the rest of my life. I'm thankful now for all those years and hard lessons. They made me into the person I am today. Once co-dependent people learn to moderate their behavior, the caring and nurturing they overdid in their extremes become a healthier kindness and compassion, qualities we could use more of in this world of ours.

After years of therapy, I finally found some ground to stand on. But there was still that missing peace.

We decided to move back to North Carolina to be near my family. Randy and I were drifting apart. With his band traveling all the time, my life was very much that of a single parent. While he was on the road for five or six weeks at a time, I held down the home fort: caring for Sarah, paying the bills, taking care of our three cats and working a full-time job. When he came home, usually for just a week or so, it took the entire time to reconnect. About the time we'd get settled in, he'd leave again. This continued for three years.

Somehow in all that time apart, we managed to create baby number two. Even though things were rocky, we pulled ourselves together. Nine months later we had a beautiful baby boy. When Austin was six months old, we moved back up north by Randy's family, bought our first house and Randy joined a local band that didn't travel. Everything seemed to be falling into place in my life, but over the next three years I "went away" emotionally. I didn't know who I was or what I wanted anymore.

I thought my marriage was the problem. Randy played in the band every weekend, partied after playing, and didn't get home until the wee hours of the morning. I was home every weekend with our two small children. The distance between us grew.

☆ ──

I see now how I was waiting for him to do something to change my life. It was beyond my comprehension that I was creating my own unhappiness. And now, after thirteen years of marriage, more than ever it felt like we weren't going to make it. I was desperate for some answers.

After pouring my heart out to a friend one day, she offered me the number of a psychic with whom she consulted and found helpful. I guess I always believed in psychic abilities, but at that time had no personal experience with anything like that. In an attempt to find some kind of peace and hope, I called her. The reading was filled with many details about things that were going to transpire and the names of people I would meet. Throughout the year, I watched as many of her predictions unfolded just as she said. Still, they were just details and not much peace was found.

The crisis continued, and later that fall, Randy and I separated. I was devastated. Even though I was the one who left, I knew it wasn't because I didn't love him. So why did I do it? Something deep within me had to change or I felt like I would literally die of heartbreak. Apparently, the only way it would unfold was if I was alone and, on some level, I must have known that. I persevered through the pain.

At work one day, a temp in our department overheard me telling a co-worker about my experience with the psychic. She joined in the conversation and told me of another psychic, Barbara, she had been seeing for a number of years. She assured me that this woman could help me find perspective underneath all that pain I was feeling.

I took down Barbara's number, anxious to call her. Being on my own now, money was really tight, so I had to wait. In the meantime, I told two other friends, Lee and Janice, about her and they both went for readings before me. Each of them was moved to tears by the messages the angels delivered through this woman.

The depth of their emotion about their individual experiences convinced me it was time to see Barbara. I arrived at her door, a little nervous, but expecting this reading to be like the other one I had the year before, with lots of detail about people and events in the future. No one could have prepared for how different Barbara's reading would be.

☆

The voices explained what was happening in my life from a higher perspective. They said I was about halfway through a five-to-six-year cycle and by the time it's over, a complete transformation will have taken place.

They described my personality precisely and explained the facade I put up so others could only see the good things about me. And they were right. I always figured no one would like me if they saw the not-so-pretty things, like being angry, or having to say "no," or revealing someone's secrets.

The angels told me that in a past life I was very much in contact with angels and spirits. Due to the religious customs and beliefs of the time, I was unable to let anyone, including my family, know I had the ability to communicate with the ethereal world. I was very small for my age and was often picked on by the bigger kids, so I would go off and be alone with these voices that brought me so much peace. Evidently, the pain created by having to keep such a magnificent thing so secret led me to vow on some deep level that, in another life, I would integrate what was inside me with what I showed outside. Apparently this is that life, where I can now live fully from the true essence of who I am and learn I don't have to keep anyone's secrets—not even my own.

The angels who spoke through Barbara also helped me understand where I was in relation to the big picture of my life. Their words helped me see the influences that got me to this very painful place, but most importantly, they assured me I would find an inner peace and heal the pain of the past. The very thought that I could actually heal these wounds made me weep. Of course, I didn't have any idea *how* I was going to do this, but there was hope and that was more than I'd had for a very long time.

They told me I had three guardian angels watching over me and that, no matter how alone I felt sometimes, I was never really alone. This brought me a great deal of comfort, since Randy and I had separated and he was seeing another woman. Many nights I would sit alone on my sun porch with such intense aching in my heart, and then I would remember my angels. I would talk to them about my pain and just sob. It made a difference knowing someone was there listening, and soon I began to actually feel their presence.

☆

About six months after my reading, Kim reached a crisis point in her life. I encouraged her to see Barbara by talking of the peace it brought to me. I reassured her that she could find it, too, if she opened herself up to the possibility. She was skeptical, to say the very least.

I won't begin to tell her story. Suffice it to say, she went.

KIMBERLY LILITH

March 5, 1994

So here I sit. Alone. Teresa and Barbara are flying around having some kind of wonderful appointment with power in Hawaii. Why am I the one who gets to stay behind? The angels say that in order to learn this lesson I must be alone. They call it the "Barren Plane." Oh great. Thank you very much. I feel like I've been fired!

What strikes me, though, is the realization that, in order to be fired by the angels I must be *employed* by the angels. What does that mean? How does a person like me wake up one day and realize that I am now on a spiritual path? I never expected to be in service to the angels or to humankind. How did I get here?

Being a very mainstream type of person, I often described myself as being so conservative I bordered on boring. According to society's standards I was a very accomplished young woman. I appeared to have everything I ever thought I wanted.

Acceptance came from living my life in a box. In my little tailored suit and matching pearl earrings and necklace, I went off to work every day. I had the perfect husband and together we made lots of money and lived in a pleasantly affluent part of town. At that time my idea of doing something controversial was getting wire-rimmed glasses. I never would have considered seeing a psychic. I didn't want to know about the future. And I didn't believe in reincarnation, so there wasn't anything to tell about the past. So why did I finally go to see Barbara in the fall of 1993?

Twenty years of crisis.

I finally began to get to know myself when I left my first husband. The turning point came with the birth of our daughter, when I began to realize that I would, in large part, form this tiny baby into the person she would become. I would use the sum of my life experiences and insight to do that shaping. I would teach her to be like me. Then the realization came crashing down—I had the word "doormat" written across my forehead! Why in the world would I want her to be like me?!

I had spent the better part of the last ten years trying to convince myself and everyone around me that I was happy. I did a pretty decent job of living in denial for a very long time. Looking at my precious little girl, it came rushing all over me. I basically flipped out. I quit eating, didn't sleep, worked constantly and fell into a deep depression.

Teresa had moved to North Carolina again in one of her attempts to find answers in her life. When I lost it, she wasn't around to hold on to. So one day, in the depths of my illness, I packed thirteen pairs of underwear, a Bible and, for some unknown reason, an ovulation chart and booked a flight to North Carolina.

I never made it to North Carolina. Instead, I spent a week in a psych ward, where I began to put the pieces back together.

In the hospital I discovered that I was basically killing myself one day at a time. Living my life in high gear day after day, I was taking excellent care of everyone else's needs, totally ignoring my own and doing nothing to nourish myself emotionally. I labored many years under the dysfunctional notion that my husband should save me, thereby building up resentment toward him for something he was incapable of doing. I didn't understand that no one could save me but myself.

When I got out of the hospital I was given the name of a psychologist who I started to see immediately. God bless Dr. McKee. This was the first time in my life that someone I perceived as an authority figure told me that I had needs and those needs deserved to be met. This idea was simultaneously exciting and confounding. Part of me thought it was high time that someone pay attention to my needs. At the same time, I began to realize that I had no idea what my needs were.

I had been unhappy for so long. I spent most of my life trying to please everyone else, never considering what I needed. The box I lived in didn't say anything about self-acceptance. It said, "The more you love someone, the more you do for them and the more you hide your own needs." And it said, in what I thought was my Daddy's voice, "No matter how much you do, you'll never be good enough, but keep trying!" So I kept trying, always looking outside myself for answers. Somebody else had to tell me I was good enough because I couldn't believe that for myself.

☆

It never entered my mind that I was creating the box in the first place, and that I was writing all the rules, which were impossible to live up to. All I needed was to be needed. I thought someone else could fill me up and make me feel whole. Since no one could do this for me, I blamed them for my unhappiness.

Three weeks after I got out of the hospital, scared to death, I left my marriage. I just knew it was the right thing to do. It was my turn now, but my turn for what? The next three years in therapy were spent working out the pain from the past and trying to create a healthy new life.

By the time I met my present husband, Clay, I had learned a great deal but still had many self-defeating behaviors that would again cause me trouble. In less than two years Clay and I fell in love, moved in together, got married, quit our jobs, started a business and had our first child. Not too much stress for what's supposed to be the honeymoon period of a marriage!

Shortly after the birth of our second child, I knew our marriage was in serious trouble. I think the term for this is "Two-time Loser!" I felt like a complete failure, so for a long time I worked very hard to save it. Then, for some reason, I just gave up and announced I was "checking out" of the marriage. This decision was based on the words in the prayer, "God, grant me the serenity to accept the things I cannot change." I finally gave up the idea that I could change Clay. Ha! Little did I know, it was my perception that needed a serious shift!

In order to fill the void my marriage left, I threw myself, heart and soul, into my work. I'm not sure how I was able to do this successfully since Clay and I still worked together. We were in the same building all day and the same house all night. Still I separated myself from what was going on—I removed myself emotionally from the situation without removing myself physically. No wonder the stress increased dramatically. It was always intense, but for these last two years it was intolerable.

In an effort to revitalize our relationship, we talked many times about one of us leaving our business and getting a regular job, but neither of us wanted to be the one to go. One day in March, he suddenly made the decision to leave the business and a week later he started a new job. I was both shocked and relieved. I hoped this would be the catalyst for saving our marriage.

Clay's abrupt departure left many gaps in the internal structure of the company. Our only employee, David, had been with us for eighteen months. Since he worked more closely with Clay, I didn't know him very well, except that he was industrious and good at his job, and he wanted more responsibility. In Clay's absence, he and I regrouped, laying out a game plan for the reorganization. It went amazingly well. Keeping focused on my business helped me stay sane.

Throwing myself into my work, I continued to deny the ongoing decay in my marriage. Business was good, which helped increased the avoidance at home. As time went on I actually began to enjoy this life I was building, with its focus on *me* instead of Clay and our marriage problems. As we spent more and more time apart, we each began to get to know ourselves in a way we never had before, as individuals examining our respective parts in the destruction of our marriage. While the fighting didn't stop completely, we began to, instead of always blaming each other, think about the direction our lives were taking, individually and together. David was a big help at this time. Because he was so close to both Clay and me, his insight helped me see both sides of our situation.

In the end, these efforts toward independence would prove to be the healthiest steps I could have taken.

With a newfound and growing sense of internal strength, I kept my focus on my prospering business. Teresa came to work with us in May. By the end of summer, David, Teresa and I had become a well-oiled machine: She and I designed and sold all the jobs and handled administration, and David supervised the work and the sub-contractors. In early September, we landed the biggest job in the company's history—a high-end kitchen and bath remodeling project for a terrific young couple. It was the kind of job we had dreamt of and had worked very hard to get.

Then the bomb was dropped. Citing personal reasons, David gave his two-week notice, leaving me with the biggest job of my career laying in pieces on the drawing board. Thousands of dollars in cabinets had been ordered, walls were being ripped out and I didn't even know how to hire an electrician.

☆

I shut down. I started crying and didn't stop for weeks—literally. I didn't care about anything and was afraid to even try. The loss of this trusted friend and co-worker revealed the gaping hole in my personal life that I had been busying myself to avoid facing. Now the business was in trouble, too.

I'm not sure what held Clay together at this time, but his strength really came to the surface. I came home from work everyday crying, "What am I going to do?" Clay was amazing. Even though we were still at odds in our marriage, he was somehow able to rise above all of it and support me through my time of crisis. He held steadfast to statements like, "I know you can do it. The business will be fine. You haven't been abandoned. David is just doing what he believes is best for his life."

I was sure that I couldn't go on, not only because I was afraid my business would fail, but because I had become so attached to David. I needed him to hold the business *and* me together.

I now realize how I set myself up for the big crash by relying so heavily on him. I didn't see until it was too late that I had repeated the old co-dependent pattern of moving from one outside source of solace to another. When my marriage fell apart, I turned my focus to my business and the people there who might be able to "feed me."

Clay assured me he would do anything he could to help me get through this. Of course, based on our history of fighting endlessly about the problems and never finding solutions, I didn't believe him. But even if he was only giving me lip service, at least he was being supportive.

Was this the perfect set-up for the angels to swoop in and teach me about self-love, or what? Here I was with my life in the toilet again. I had built myself another box that had begun closing in on me just like before. Why did I keep setting myself up like this? Why did my life continue to accelerate out of control no matter how hard I tried to moderate things?

It's strange, but even as a very small girl I was already constructing a box filled with other people's expectations. Growing up, our household was often on the brink of divorce. I knew I was loved, but was also sure that I must perform well. Love seemed to depend on behavior.

☆ ─────────────────────────────

As the oldest of four children, I grew up fast and found my place early. Since Mom was depressed a lot, I was frequently put in the role of adult, even as early as nine years old. She often confided in me about issues she was having with my dad, which made me Mother's Best Friend. At the same time, I was Daddy's Little Girl, a special but demanding position which probably created resentment in my siblings. I felt trapped *between* my mom and dad, which certainly created resentment in me, as I tried hard to live up to the expectations of the opposing positions. It was fairly confusing.

I had a recurring childhood dream about the grownups as members of two opposing teams about to clash in battle; it was sort of like full-scale war was about to break out on a football field. In my pretty little dress and carrying a small white flag, I walked out onto the battlefield and entered the huddle of adults. I said something to them: short, simple, the basic truth of a child. The grownups would then stand up straight and, looking somewhat astonished, they would leave the battlefield, slowly, almost reverently, as they reflected on the wisdom that this small, innocent child was able to bring to them in order to help them heal their conflicts.

We weren't involved in religion as a family, but for some reason church was very important to me individually. As a child in Cincinnati, I would get on the little bus that came to my street every Sunday morning to take me to Baptist church. Even though my parents didn't go to church, I somehow thought they would love me more if I did. After all, good little girls go to church, don't they?

I always loved God and I knew that God loved me, but by the time I reached adolescence, I didn't seem to fit in anywhere in the church. I asked too many questions, finding myself at odds, not with God, but with religion. The song said, "Yes, Jesus loves me," which brought comfort, but the church said I was a sinner and would always fall short of the glory of God. I didn't consciously see the parallel between this and my belief that I could never be good enough.

A close family friend taught me about Judaism, which I grew to love and took as my own. It kept me close to God, and held family and community as strong priorities. Rather than focusing on salvation and trying to work my way into heaven, the emphasis was put on making a positive difference in the world for the benefit of the future generations. These things were very important to me.

But I always missed Jesus. I hadn't figured out yet that nobody owns Truth and I didn't have to give up Jesus.

Still searching for answers, I majored in religious studies in college. I wondered how this course of study would manifest itself in my life. I was not to know the full answer to this question for almost twenty years.

Back to the crisis. Past experience told me it was time to go back to therapy. It worked so well before. While I waited the many weeks for my appointment, Teresa suggested I reconsider seeing a psychic. Under the circumstances, it wasn't such a bad idea. I was going downhill and it was getting scary.

I had become such an angry and bitter woman. The only voices I listened to were the bad ones—the ones that told me I wasn't good enough. I had a lot of pain and was terrified of facing it. If this psychic could build one ounce of credibility with me and give me something to hold onto in this mess I called my life, I'd be satisfied. I expected to come away with nothing more than some amusing little quips about where my life was heading which I would use to lift my spirits until the therapy kicked in.

In that first meeting with Barbara, the angels spent a lot of time explaining the many misconceptions I had about myself that were going to change in the course of this large transformation that was coming for me. (And I thought they meant I was going to start wearing funky clothes!) Instead, I was going to learn about my own abundance, which I had always doubted. This was the start of the journey back to myself, the beginning of finding a new woman, with a new voice, who would go after a different dream. I could not understand that through the pain would come the opportunity for my transformation.

I was shocked by the amazing peace that came over me in the few weeks after that first session. I had never felt real peace before in my life. The fact that it came after a long period of pain and unhappiness made it even more powerful. The contrast only added to the magic.

I cancelled the appointment with the therapist.

". . . and the wisdom to know the difference"

"The Serenity Prayer"

Barbara: Before reading for Kim that first time, I put my ego in its little chair and recited my usual prayer of protection. Suddenly an exceptionally heightened energy level filled up the spaces within. I had never before seen with such clarity. "They" started talking in double time. The images came fast and furious. I couldn't seem to talk fast enough.

Afterward, I commented about this new intensity. I didn't think at the time it had much to do with her. I understand now that it had everything to do with her. They told her she was in a phenomenal period of transition. When she asked me when she should come back, I suggested, because of the incredibly rapid changes taking place in her life, to come again in a month or so.

I had no idea ...

Kim returned in six weeks to tell me she had not only listened to her tape constantly, but had actually transcribed it. I was shocked. No one I knew had ever studied their reading so intensely. She practically had it memorized. The next reading had the same intensity level as the first, but didn't leave her feeling quite as peaceful.

I spoke with her the following week. She was mad, she said. She felt she had been told she was doing something wrong. She hadn't listened to her tape at all. All she could think about were the circumstances of her life that had brought her to me in the first place. I laughed and tried to assure her that someday those words that now infuriated her would become a box of jewels for her to draw from.

Meanwhile, Teresa and Kim has been talking about their experiences with the angels to some of their women friends. One by one, Patti, Janice, and Lee arrived at my door. And eventually Kelly, Dawn, Nanette and Ellen.

Kim and Teresa: Whenever we talked with any of our friends who had been to Barbara to hear the voices, the conversation always came around to discussing those experiences. So much excitement was created when we got on that subject that Janice suggested we all get together at her house some night, drink a little wine and share our feelings and the information from our sessions.

Barbara: One night, Kim, Teresa and Lee came to see me sing. On my break, we began talking about how these concepts fit into our lives. I was energized by their intense curiosity and our lively discussions about how these readings were affecting them in positive ways. I could hardly tear myself away to return to the piano.

I began to realize, in all the years of speaking the voices, I'd had little real contact with the people who came for this service. Suddenly, here was a group of women, eager to talk and listen more. They brought new life to an old process.

Still I wasn't making a conscious connection about Kim and Teresa. I remember the very moment when the angels started telling me about our future relationship. I was driving down the freeway. It was an exceptionally sunny winter day. An angel whispered in my ear, *"You will teach them to speak our voices."*

I will? Why?

You have a great mission to accomplish together. They will be a part of group sessions.

A mission? What mission?

You will create centers where many will come to hear the voices.

"I don't want to teach anyone anything," I argued. "I am not a good teacher by nature, nor do I have the ability to know how to teach someone else to speak the voices." The angels reminded me that they would be doing the teaching, so I wouldn't have to worry.

On the other hand, I'd tried to do a group session six months earlier, but none of the old friends I invited seemed very enthusiastic. Maybe these new women would be interested, since there were so many of them anxious to learn.

After this message on the freeway, I called Kim and Teresa to propose getting together and seeing what the voices had to say.

☆ ──────────────────────────

Before I could ask them, Kim told me they were planning a little gathering to continue the pursuit of these ideas.

"Great!" I said. "Would you be interested in having me come and speak the voices?"

"Yes!" Kim practically shouted. "We wanted to invite you to this, but we didn't want to impose! We figured this was old hat to you."

"Are you kidding?" I shot back. "It's so exhilarating to talk with you about this stuff. Most people in my life are so used to the fact that I do this, I've forgotten how amazing it can be."

"And what a coincidence that we were all thinking about this group thing at exactly the same time!" Kim sounded genuinely awestruck.

I was dumbfounded.

And so began our psychic sorority.

We picked a date for the first group and invited about fifteen people. Eight of us gathered at Teresa's home that first night, sitting on the hardwood floor in the middle of winter. It was below zero outside. The eight of us together created an energy level none of us had experienced before. Out of the darkness came a familiar voice, and each time "they" spoke of the past life we had all lived together in the far north, we swore we felt a wind blow through the room, chilling and real.

Some of "them" were apparently new to delivering messages to a group. Initially, we had difficulty following what they were saying. But as we all became comfortable with each other, angels and humans alike, their words began to flow, and we settled in for a long winter's night.

What follows are the transcripts from that first group. It was the start of something bigger than we could ever have imagined. It was the beginning of the "mission," and we didn't even know it.

☆

THE ANGELS
December 14, 1993

"Culture"

We are gathered in a place where all paths have come together. We see a scene of sitting together in tribal fashion. Imagine the beat of the drum and darkness and fire light. Feel yourselves enveloped in a circle of power that is served by each individual energy, as well as the collective consciousness of all energies as one.

This is the purpose behind the gathering of like minds. It is powerful when one is capable of opening one's viewpoint, removing one's lens cap, perhaps, and viewing the universe from the eternal self. When two or more people come together with such intent, it is like a high-powered microscope, or, equally applicable, a high-powered telescope. You look in both directions and into infinity at one time. This is the purpose behind all of the energies here at this time.

You have all been brought together to begin an understanding. This understanding is not an earth-shattering revelation never heard before. Contrary, it's a common, everyday occurrence that is taken for granted. If the lessons each of you individually has undergone could be written down, each of you would nod and say "Ah, yes, that's for me." What is different is the external circumstances. You all are undergoing the same instruction. If we were to speak to one over here, the same lesson would be applicable over there.

We have come together to speak of not only the nature of reality as you know it, but also the nature of personal reality in correlation to each other. You will begin to see the world as individual souls all learning the same lesson. If you were to share information from your experiences speaking to us individually, you would see an obvious repetition of lessons. It's not that Barbara is trying to pull the wool over your eyes. A skeptic could come into the room and say that the same thing was said to everyone and, therefore, it is invalid. The true nature of those similarities is that every individual is going through the same lessons.

☆ ——————————————————————————————

To picture the true nature of reality, in terms of three dimensions and five senses, and time and space, see the soul as a sphere. Around that sphere is a film of all the different lives that you have lived. Contained within it are all the memories you accumulate living the many lives you have engaged in on the Earth plane.

What is making you conscious of who you are at this time is a thin thread that runs from the soul to the surface of the film called "awareness." The idea for reincarnating is to become adept at expanding your awareness. Learn to open the lens and spread the awareness so you begin to recognize and accept the presence of the other lives being lived simultaneously. This concept is outside the realms of time and space. All the lives you have lived in the linear sense on the Earth plane are actually being lived simultaneously.

This thin thread of awareness is focused on Kim, on Teresa, on Patti, on Chris, on Kelly, on Lee, on Janice. Each thread is, at this time in your development, very slim, so the only focus you see is this life. The only focus you see with your eyes is this room.

In your awareness somewhere is a memory of a time when you all sat together before the fire and the drums played, and the night grew deep and long, and you talked, and you listened and you exchanged parts of self together on a magical plane to create a bigger magic.

This life was lived in the far northern reaches of where you reside today, perhaps in Canada or what is now Alaska. It was a cold weather climate with a very large population. A certain magic existed in day-to-day life, far different than how you perceive your lives today as a daily grind with interruptions of inspiration.

In this life you all lived together, each of you was given a particular holy task and a magical purpose. You proceeded to live under this purpose every day. When you came together at night and participated in sharing and opening up that lens, a mighty power was created. You did this through various methods of calling the magic to you, through dancing, with the drums before the fire, with the painting of the bodies and the chanting.

As you sit here in the Earth plane in December 1993 superimposed upon that, can you not feel the essence of that other life?

When you call that life up and collectively create that image and memory from your individual bodies, you expand that thread of awareness. Then you are sending another thread from your eternal place, from your soul, into this other life. It feels superimposed, as if you can feel the leather and the furs that kept you warm at that time. You feel the difference of the comfort of this particular home as opposed to living out in the open air.

This is why we often speak to you of past lives. All of these memories are stored in your body. As you physically remember, you take one more thread that expands your awareness until eventually, in an evolutionary way, your awareness becomes so broad and so inclusive of all you truly are you then transcend the need to participate in the Earth plane. That is when you ascend into a greater level of consciousness.

We do not mean ascend in an upward motion because there isn't an up or down. It is fuller, deeper, broader. It is the difference between being a child with your limited point of view of the Earth plane and being adult with your expansive point of view of the Earth plane. It is the difference between the psychology that goes on between human beings and the political nature of power situations. That is the evolutionary process.

What happens when you are not able to broaden your perspective is your view of your world is diminished. Then you judge things in your world view as either bad, something that shouldn't have happened, or a mistake. When you judge an event, person or piece of self, you close down your ability to see a bigger picture, like a camera lens. That is why it is essential to be aware of the judgments you cast upon your experiences. Judgments affect your ability to see broadly. And being able to see broadly expands that awareness.

The phone rings. The voices stop. A message is recorded on the answering machine. The voices resume.

One more soul included in the circle.

Sometimes you feel like an alien in a strange world in some kind of space suit with a life support system allowing you to live in this strange world. You feel like a stranger in a strange land, like you don't fit in. You feel insecure. You feel you are not good enough to live up to a particular set of standards laid down at some mysterious time within your being, like a voice laying down its message on the answering machine. You feel there are things you haven't accomplished proving your inability to be whole. You feel everything is so confusing you must be missing something, or fall

☆ ───

short in some area. You must have a few elements of your being that were forgotten.   If you only had them, you could then understand everything and take that piece, like a puzzle, and place it in that empty spot and suddenly everything would light up like the tree [referring to the Christmas tree in the room]. You would be instantly filled with revelation and knowledge. This is a pattern that has been set up for you within the culture that you are presently residing in.

The fire is being fed. The night is growing colder and it is exhilarating. The wind is blowing. The chanting is continuing. In this other life, in that culture, magic was such a given within the course of a day that no child would have dreamt of thinking themselves unworthy. No adult would have been raised thinking that because they did not understand the mysteries of the universe, they were less of a human being.

We use this analogy to juxtapose your present culture. In that other culture, when you were in the night, practicing magic, you dreamt of *this* culture. You dreamt of *this* night. You dreamt of gathering together in a different reality, in a different realm, in a different time. Like children who know how to play and be free, you knew then in that magical culture what your true nature was. You knew that parts of self would gather in another reality to recreate the magic you had together at that time.

In essence, as we speak tonight, we are all dreams of a different time. This culture you have been brought to has set up a particular kind of challenge to you. This is not accidental. You are not victims of circumstance. You are not simply thrust into this world to fend for yourselves. This is a very carefully constructed puzzle for you to unravel with your own interpretation. You all have the same lesson to learn but everyone's movie is different. The actors and the actresses, the plots and the sub-plots, the subterfuge and the romance...everyone's movie is playing. You're in your own one-seat movie theater, living this dramatic life in these three dimensions and these five senses. But it is the same message, and the same path. You all walk the same path.

So within this culture, as you walk together, you share the similar understanding that you have been programmed to think less of yourself. It is not anyone's fault. It is not a bad thing. It is not a mistake. It is not a trap. It is a challenge you agreed to participate in. You must give yourselves credit for choosing to undergo such a mystery.

Surely this past life would be far easier to be human in because of the room built-in not only for the natural supernaturalism that exists within the human beings, but for the rhythms and the natural flow of patterns. In that culture, when the women were having their periods they were given a chance to go away. It was simply accepted as a time of madness. A very magical time. A very special time.

This is far easier for the human spirit than to be told that because you do not fit into a behavioral pattern because of a physiological change within your body that you are less of a person and are a problem. There are all sorts of studies done on the effects of this physiological phenomenon and how to understand and change it, control it and put it back into an acceptable, non-mystery form.

In actuality, if you were allowed, this would be one of your most creative times, if you hadn't been told since you were young it was a negative thing not to talk about. That culture was much more respectful and truer to form for a woman in her magic than this one.

What we are trying to impress upon you as clearly as we can is that you need to be aware of the cultural influences on you as a soul. Again, not to say you are victims, but to understand, throughout the course of your time, that all the different realities going on have meaning. Begin to accept that you may not fit in culturally to the dictates and mores of what this society is saying. The more you do not [fit in], the more you can remove yourself from the influences and the freer you will be.

In order to understand how to free yourself from the influences, you need to know the influences and their relationship to you. You need to know, for example, how you feel when you are undergoing your menstrual period. Say that to throw back your head and howl wouldn't be appropriate. We say, from the perspective of those huddling against the cold and feeling the drums beat within them, for you to throw back your head and howl is a song of magic. If you were to then superimpose this belief within your culture, you would be deemed crazy.

Any individual on the Earth plane who has been labeled insane or in some way different, autistic, retarded, schizophrenic (and you can interchange magic for insane) is a visionary of your culture that your culture is not even aware of. If they were in a different culture that nourished and revered their being, they would not be considered crazy. They would not be going against the norm that would be then turning around and calling them crazy because they were going against the norm.

We are trying to free you. We need to pick each of you up and shake you free. This period of time on the Earth plane and this need to shake you by the scruff of the neck is an awakening. It is part of that evolutionary process.

The old habitual thought process that tells you you're not enough or too much, or any ingrained thought or belief that in any way limits you or makes you smaller, unacceptable or "different" is simply an old thought pattern superimposed upon your thinking process by the influences of the culture you are living in. This includes the messages of your family. All of you here have the same influences of your family of origin. Again, different movies playing, but the same influences saying you aren't enough. You feel there is more you should be doing, that you don't have the potential or the abilities to live up to your potential, that you are only destined to be a particular way, or that you do not have enough within you to live fully in this life.

If you are ever unsure about which are the intuitive thoughts that come from your higher power speaking to you, remember, if any thought limits or lessens you, or fills you with any kind of doubt or negative thinking, or shines an unkind light, these are all voices of your culture. We say culture inclusive both of the larger culture you're involved in and your personal culture, the personal movie playing within your own reality.

That leaves the other voices saying you have more than your fair share of abilities, talents and potential. Thoughts that say you are capable of accomplishing anything you undertake. Thoughts that say there is no limit to what you can achieve. Thoughts that help you dream at night and in the day. Thoughts that help you feel magic. These are the thoughts of your higher power. These are the thoughts of God. These are the thoughts of your guides and guardian angels.

If you can align yourself with these thoughts, a line is drawn. One side is filled with all the self doubt, lack of self respect and insecurity. The other side is filled with the unlimited potential and true magic of the universe. The more you can align yourself in that side of things, the more you will "see." There are many moments within all of your lives filled with doubt and a sense of non-accomplishment. Meanwhile, you're totally missing the awesome power of reality around you.

We would like to describe what we see when we see an individual human being. We see a flurry of energy. It's almost like a flickering of a light. The stronger the light shines, the more we are aware of the absence or the non-influence of the cultural voices that bring you down.

When you feel separated from yourself, or that you have lost the light within or are feeling depressed or like you don't fit in, there is a darkening of the light. It flickers, like hands are being held above it and the flickering is seen through the fingers. That is how it appears to us. Those particular souls are like a smoke signal to us, sending out an SOS. Being isolated, lonely or depressed flashes a sign to us that you are calling for assistance.

How many times when you thought nothing was going to happen right, "suddenly" there was a miracle (a coincidence, in your mind). Something happened that made you laugh, throw back your head and think how ironic and perplexing life can be and how out of control you really are from it. Those times of darkness and despair, even just the times of self-doubt, are like beacons to us.

We exist in a place that is also where you are, but not necessarily in your time and space. We are with you. You think it is simply yourselves. Like the voice from the other room [on the answering machine] you have brought with you all of your guides and guardian angels. As we speak it is like in your modern day hospitals when the doctor is operating. There is often times a gallery above of training physicians, great master physicians and curious bystanders overseeing. This is what is happening tonight as we speak. You have brought us together.

It is like the animals. If you look into the animals around you, you see flickerings of other intelligences. Certainly the animals have their bit of evolutionary soul. They are like beacons for us that clearly shine. They are smaller than the human energy, but clearer because they do not have a thought process telling them they are unworthy.

So when you're alone and feel you haven't done enough, think of the animals and how they do nothing and still get fed and loved. Their worth is not dependent upon how much money they make,

☆ —————————————————————————

their sparkling conversation or their flawless beauty. Their simple existence in your life is enough to merit unconditional love. You would certainly not throw your pet out if they were not affectionate. That would be counterproductive. There is often a communication with us that goes on through them. When you are hurt and flashing us a distress signal, we come to surround you. We are always there at your beck and call at any time. But when you are hurting, or in need, we come and surround you. For us, "you" are the interface between the physical being and the soul. That is where we do our work with you. When you need assistance or feel alone, don't ever think you're alone. It makes for good humor for us. We all stand around and watch you cry out about how you are so alone. Sometimes we are waving and throwing things in your path, trying to make contact past that shell you put up to deflect our signals. It is not that we are not there, it's that you are not focused on our presence.

Begin to get a concept of all the activity happening around you. Do not be fooled by walls. Do not be fooled by skin. Do not be fooled by telephones, televisions and newspapers. And do not be fooled by this culture, and a step greater, this reality you deem so permanent and makes you so separate from each other. Because again, you are gathered here in many realities.

As we speak to you tonight there is a myriad of beings with us here. They are different individuals, so to speak, different souls, different beings at different levels of their evolutionary progression. Some may speak, some may not, but all are here to share with you in trying to interface these realities.

This is not something that needs to be done at a special place or time, with particular people. It is your purpose in life every day. So forget what the newspapers say. Forget what the etiquette books say. Forget what the radio tells you. Forget the magazines and the pictures. These are all a dream of the group that sits before the fire on a cold and starry night drumming up magic. These are dreams of your soul.

Your purpose, the mission you have agreed upon and accepted with all good faith, is to be a part of the evolutionary process that is merging the realities. This is a mind boggling thought for some of you: here on this Earth, as you are in this body, your purpose is to be a part of the missing link. The years of "consciousness

☆

raising" actually pushed you into a higher level of awareness and consciousness.

The kind of communication we are doing now will someday be a given for each and every person. The concept of speaking with your guides and angels, returning to a former life to remember will be a way of life. These will not be some kookoo ideas that some charlatan had. This will be a way of being and you have all chosen to be a part of that transformation.

This means from here on in you will be pursuing a path of magical intent. All you do and say will be motivation for dealing with life as a magical creation rather than a ho-hum-drum, work-a-day nine-to-five world. The difference between the two is like the difference between a small seed and a huge acreage of blooming, ripe wheat. The difference between your life enveloped in the boredom of a limited philosophy and living this magical interface will be the difference between sitting down to stale bread and having a ten-course gourmet feast complete with alcoholic beverages.

It is the difference between the light that goes out and the light that lives on.

We have brought you here to tell you that this is your path. It may not appear what you are doing in your life on Earth is gearing toward becoming superconscious of the interface between the physical world and your higher power, but indeed you are. From this perspective, doesn't it seem more feasible, sitting in a non-magical situation, to throw your head back and howl and not be concerned about the consequences?

You are a magical being living in a magical world. You are not simply a finite body going through the motions until death. You are an eternal soul. And your awareness of how eternal you are is all coming together in this interface.

Some of you have been speaking of creating a place where you can come if you are in need of hearing the voices. From that level of evolution you can follow the light and the voices and find your way there through your own methodology, coming together in like mind.

We would like to ask you for your questions.

"When you're feeling like you can't get there, and feel so stuck, what is a method of getting closer?"

☆————————————————————————————

Very simply to change your perception. When you think you are stuck, the lens of your camera, or your eye from your soul looking into your human existence, has been closed. All you are seeing is a small part of your path. If you open to a broader perspective you see that, first of all, there is nowhere to get to. You are not going anywhere, so to speak. You have already arrived. It may not be the place where your conscious mind thinks it should be. When you find yourself in that situation, listen to your conscious mind. If what it says falls into the negative of the equation—you haven't come far enough, accomplished enough, or you are less than you should be—these voices are part of an old habitual way of thinking. It exists in your mind only because it has been there for so long. It is a bad habit.

When you feel stuck, you do not need to find more time to exercise, read more books, see more lectures and follow more instructions. Those things will come as you change your thinking process. But realize being stuck is the illusion. You have everything you need right before you. Begin to focus on those things. In order to do that, broaden your perspective so you can see more than just this pinpoint. This place you feel stuck in is not even the blink of an eye when it comes to eternity. As you broaden the picture, you begin to see, ah, the joy of your family, the beating of your heart, the sun that rises, the warmth of a love. So many things are right before your eyes. You need to only open them. That will unstick you.

Teresa: *"This place some of us have thought about creating where people can go, is that something you see really happening? Will people really go and it will mean something to them?"*

Yes. This is not merely a concept. This will be an actual physical place that will be an expansion of this particular gathering.

All of you here tonight may not continue to participate in the building and conception of this space. But the magic being drummed up tonight is essential for its conception. The idea has been planted already. The whisperings of guidance to create such a place have begun. Now it will be making the idea into a physical reality. This will actually happen. It will be a place where anyone can come in need of speaking to guides or their higher power, however you describe it, and actually sit in the way we are speaking with you tonight.

☆

This is not a revolutionary concept. In fact, this is a tremendously old concept. Throughout the many cultures that existed in the Earth plane, there were always oracles. There were prophets in the Bible. There were oracles in the Greek culture. There were seers and sages in the American Indian cultures. There were the gypsies who could foretell the future. There have always been places and people such as this who have interpreted the language of the gods into a physical reality.

Ultimately the connection will be one-to-one. You will create your connection and know it so well, your channel will be so clean and clear, you will be driven by what your intuition tells you. Your intuition is representative of your higher power, the one with the much broader picture.

This place and organization will be conceptualized and created in the next two years. The next six to nine months will be its incubation period. There is planning and ideas being drawn, people wanting to contribute, people wanting to be a part, to somehow make it a reality. You will not need to go door to door to recruit people. There will be a gathering of like minds. A bigger influence will come that will bring more people. It is not something that needs to necessarily have an instant audience. People in need will be drawn, very much like yourselves.

Think of how you were drawn to hear the voices. At a moment in your life when things were all askew and in chaos, suddenly "someone" threw a little "something" in your path. You looked down and there was a message. It brought you here to us to listen and share. This is not accidental. It is a beautiful plan you have all participated in.

So it will be with this organization you structure. See how naturally the beginnings came? See how those of like mind were drawn together? This will expand. It will be more references and word of mouth to those who are hungry, who cannot separate the voices in their head, who need to hear them reflected back. You have all experienced this process, have you not? You came before the channel confused and weak and without hope. You left clearer and stronger and more at peace and, most importantly, more in the moment.

Speaking and listening in this manner is what brought you into the moment, to the true nature of your reality. You carried that peace away with you while you thrust yourselves back into the influences of the culture and habitually closed back down. Then

☆ —————————————————————————

you sought more. You wished to come again to hear the voices tell you you're okay, you're magical and alive and well and with purpose. These voices are within you, but at this time human beings need to hear them outside themselves. It is part of the set up of the culture.

These centers or experiences are part of a magical tradition of all cultures. So you see, you are carrying on an age-old tradition that is re-emerging as more acceptable than forty years ago in your culture, or even a hundred years ago. As you progress back in your Earth history into different cultures, you find other times were far more accepting of these magical ideas.

You must always remember you are living in one of the least spiritual cultures that has existed on the Earth plane. All intentions at this time within the daily culture are not to have you become independent, free thinking, magical beings. The more you can remember this, the more you can separate yourself from its influence.

This is part of the purpose of this organization, this actual physical place you are going to create. There will be offshoots connecting different places around the country. We see you traveling to different places and training human beings to speak the voice.

The idea is not to create a congregation dependent upon you for their spiritual nurturing all their lives. The idea is to create a place within the individuals of the "congregation" to know their own voices, to transcend the need to come and hear this particular voice. To come to a place where the voices within them are so strong, the intuition so ingrained, that the old patterns, limited ways of thinking, self-doubts and anything having to do with thinking less of yourself are completely washed away. Cleaned like a slate. This side contains all of the limitless dream possibilities. That side is the old earthly way of thinking, saying there is only so much to go around. In these centers you take the cloth and wash that all away and send them on their way. So it is a stopping place, not a permanent residence. The nature of this evolutionary change is not to create a cult that will worship a set of ideals.

As you become aware of the presence of other intelligences, and laugh together and share this, even then you don't take into account we are laughing with you. The essence of what we're trying to do is to diminish that veil between the worlds that separates us so.

─── ☆

Think of it in this way: your eternal self, your "Soul Self," has long arms of power, true power. Not the kind of power that Napoleon rode off to conquer or that the boss has over you. This is true, authentic personal power, developed over the years of reincarnating, learning the lessons and making choices concerning how to use your energy. This is learning how to have personal power.

From the eternal side, these long arms of your Soul Self reach down and control a very small puppet you could consider to be you. There you are, in a job you can't stand, or involved with someone who's hurting you, or late and stuck at the stoplight. All of this evokes a sense of frustration that you have to break out, or that you're stuck. You see how silly it is from our perspective? Humoristically, you're sitting here saying, "Oh, I'm stuck, I'm stuck" and we all laugh and poke you and say, "Oh my, WHAT are you going to do NOW!?" If you view yourself in this way, you begin to see the folly of thinking you're victimized or taken advantage of. As you narrow this camera lens down to zoom in on this little life that's going on, then, yes indeed, it does look very much like you're stuck. That is not the way to gather this personal power.

Personal power is to become aware of the long arms of your soul holding you up. Becoming aware of that feels like the first split second you open your eyes in the morning. You're not sure what world you're in. Your conscious mind begins to focus back into the three dimensions and five senses. You start to feel your body and the bed, and remember what the room looks like. There you are, awakened into this consciousness. Conversely, at night, between being awake and being asleep is a very powerful place. It is like falling in the mud and proceeding through some decontamination chamber and arriving out clean again. As you fall asleep at night and leave behind the three dimensions, you're back in the eternal world.

In the wakened state your conscious mind can't completely see past the three dimensions and five senses. You can sense there's a bigger world and know you can be in touch with your higher power, but when push comes to shove you are still a human being in a human world. When you sleep at night you are free from all the distractions of definitions you have been told.

You have been told that this is a couch, and this is a wall, that's a dog, and this is a shirt. You have been told the scientific makeup

☆

of the shirt. It has been told how the chemical reactions work, the elements of the Earth and the laws of nature. You have been told all these things and you believe them. It is not necessarily not true, (it is true because you believe them) but there is something else to believe beyond that.

This goes back to what we have been saying about this limited way of thinking and doing things. You're choosing. You put yourself in a little box and wonder why you feel so closed in. In reality, you can choose to believe there is a bigger reality and a different set of rules to live by. Experiment with your own lives to see how you can make these rules work for you. That is gaining personal power.

For example, you decide to go fishing. All the way up to the lake you tell yourself you've never caught fish. Maybe you don't even like fish but you're going anyway because it's beautiful scenery and you need a break. You go out in the boat and fish and perhaps catch a few fish. Maybe you really believe you can catch a fish, but it doesn't seem to have any effect on whether you do or not. Other times you are convinced you can't and by some coincidence you catch a large fish. Then everyone pats you on the back and asks you what your technique was. You make up some story about how it was done.

You have then created the illusion from the circumstances. Whether you were fully intent on catching that fish or completely convinced you couldn't, you have created the external reality around what happened, as opposed to creating what happened around an inner reality.

You must not completely denounce the rules and regulations of your culture telling you what is possible and what is not: that it is impossible to fly without the help of a mechanical object, or to levitate or walk through walls. These things are impossible. But for us they are completely possible. In fact, there is no wall for us to walk through. It seems silly that you can only believe in one reality. We're trying to shake you loose from the shackles. Sometimes you become so invested in and intent on creating the reality from the conscious mind, from where we are, we need to give you a nudge sometimes.

Kim: *"Do we always evolve upward and are we evolving toward you?"*

There are two terms in that question that don't seem applicable. One is *always* and the other *upwards*. What you are trying to say is, is there one goal for all humans and is it to become like us? Is that a paraphrase? Then the answer is yes. It's not upwards.

You have been told upwards is a magical direction. It's quite silly because upwards is also downwards and inwards. It's all one place, and no place, at the same time. What you're talking about is personal growth. The soul is bigger than you realize just by asking that question.

You already are evolved. You already are that thing you're hoping to be. Part of you is completely conscious and frolicking here with us and can see very clearly. Using the analogy that the soul is the center and the lives encircle it, there is even a part of you that witnesses that.

What your mission is, whether or not you decide to accept it, is to expand the *view* of who you are, not expand *who* you are. If there is no time then the beginning and end exist simultaneously. Your "theoretical" quest to return to the light has already occurred and you have "evolved" back into the super-consciousness or however you can explain an indescribable concept. This is why if you were to proceed on your path as if you were already evolved, suddenly the fact that there is a woman in line with more than ten items in her cart, or your boss is delinquent in giving you help, or your husband has been a little too late one too many times becomes completely inconsequential. It becomes a blink of an eye, also, conversely and inclusively, it becomes the most important lesson you could possibly have.

We understand it's difficult for human beings to sit behind someone at the market who is very slow. Obviously you have many more important things to do with your time than to stand in the supermarket waiting. Au contraire, the lesson in the moment is as important as any celestial undertaking, any kind of metaphysical metamorphosis. Those moments, in fact, are probably more important than these moments. In these moments we gather together and *we* create the magical interface for different perceptions and levels of consciousness. It is very easy to be caught up in the magic of the moment as we create it.

But when you stand alone in the raging world you live in, filled with people who are ready to shoot you through the head as they would curse you for not moving fast enough, thrust into that "all by yourself" is like being on the front lines. This is like being back

☆ ───────────────────────────────

at the headquarters, far behind the lines where they still eat beef for dinner. Out there, in that supermarket aisle, that is the real challenge.

Get absorbed completely in the moment: What is she buying, why, what does it tell about her? What kind of pen is she using? What do her checks look like? What is she saying to the clerk? What kind of mood is she in? Where is she going after this? Does she have children? Is she still with her husband? Was she ever married? How did her parents treat her when she was young? What was her favorite toy?

If you begin to look at it that way, you look into this person who could cause you to be greatly upset. Opening the lens, you're not just looking at this one moment when she isn't moving fast enough for you, you're looking at the whole picture. Who are her guides? What are they telling her? How are they helping her at this moment? Is she even aware of them? The time you otherwise spend tapping your foot and making puffing sounds with your mouth is spent absorbed in the moment. By that time you feel you know her. Perhaps you even want to help her carry her bags to the car. This moment is the telling one. All are important. Tonight is apples compared to oranges, but the lessons are still important. You can't only eat apples and then wonder why you don't get enough vitamin C.

This is all part of evolving. Look at yourself as the globe with the soul within. Think of how small the awareness must be to go to this point on the globe, this city, this house. It's so minuscule you can barely discern it. Move into a place aligned with what we perceive. The goal is to broaden that awareness. The analogy in the supermarket illustrates one way for you to broaden that. *That* is evolution.

"Why were we taken from the magical times to this? Why couldn't we just stay that way?"

For the same reason you could not be a child all your life. That magical time was a time of childhood. There was freedom and undoubting, limitless thinking so like a child. But to simply be a child until you die is missing the whole grand performance of learning.

Learning is why you are here. To put the pieces back together. In some cultures, the training was handed down in a way that created the paradox or mystery or puzzle to solve.

You "gather" before you are born with those you are going to be involved with in this life, and make agreements and prepare your higher consciousness by setting different challenges. You are then thrust into the world.

There was a culture in the Southwest that taught from the time a child was old enough to understand language that their ancestors helped facilitate them being here. Everyone was waiting for their ancestors to return to take them back. That is the analogy of being born, living this life and dying.

The reason the culture you are in has been so devoid of supporting those magical ideas is to strengthen you. When you have to claim your power, you become more personally powerful than if you sat in your high kingdom and thought you knew the countryside. You are forced to go on some heroic, mythical journey. All cultures, all mythology, all stories passed down from word of mouth around this fire have been given for that purpose, to show the path all walk. Everyone has a different movie showing. Every journey these heroic figures go through has similar features: losing something of value, going off and finding it, being killed and then being reborn. It is for you now to claim this power, to find this power.

The Earth plane is like elementary, junior and senior high school and on through college. You go through many of the same classes with many of the same people. Some people advance, some drop out, but for the most part, there is a core group. The remembrances of the culture of the northern climes is a continuation of that.

All of you have been brought here into the masters program, which is much more difficult than learning how to count. Even for a child that learning process is generally easy. As you gain more and more knowledge, you get into the far reaches of college and the deep, complex intellectual issues they put forth to you. You are actually in college now.

"Why were we chosen to come together?"
You chose. Power chose you. You were ready. It was your birthright. It was planned.

In the northern clime, you came together and understood the nature of reality. You understood you would come back over and over again until you had evolved. You had been freely traveling to where we are now and back again. It is not a given where you live now. You are like individuals who have never been outside their hometown. You don't understand there's a whole reality here for your taking, for your integration.

There is a side of you that longs for that. Because of that you have been assembled here through mutual agreements on all our parts to participate. It is like a television show where they bring in many different experts to have a think tank analysis. Everyone talks about what they perceive and think. This is happening as we take our different turns in coming and speaking with you. Others of us are more eloquent but it is by your bidding and choosing.

"Can you tell us about our guides? Do you always have the same ones? Do they do different things at different times of your life? How do they become your guides?"

Generally speaking, your guides are souls who have been united with you for purpose and have been with you in some form or another throughout your many incarnations on the Earth plane. There is no rule for this. Everything isn't always the same, but generally it's like being in eighth grade and dating someone in twelfth grade and they graduate. We who have expanded our awareness past the lives of our Earth experiences and have then turned around to become your guides, we need this. We are like teaching assistants. We need the experience with you for our own development, for our own continued evolution.

We cannot explain much to you. Not because you are so small-minded you would not understand, there is just no language for many things we are experiencing during this part of our process. It would be like explaining to your children what it's like to hold down a full-time job and have a family. They can imagine ways in their minds, but they cannot experience it first hand. There is so much interaction going on, not only with your guides but with their guides, which is something, here again, we feel isn't explainable at this time. You have to live with the mystery. At this time you do not need to know all those other things.

The guides surrounding each of you work together with each other. When you go to an HMO with a problem in one area, a group of doctors and nurses consult, throwing around ideas and brainstorming about treatments. That's what happens with your guides and how they interact. They're also going through this grade school system all together with their own set of lessons to learn. Some of these lessons involve their influence upon you.

The greater good is your watchword, or the guiding light, in your terms, love. The lesson of the guides is how to help you see the love within you, to help you see who you are. It's frustrating for us to be in a position to exert an influence of love and then watch as you continue to put yourself into this little small box. It's not like *your* frustration. We move through it very fluidly, but it is nonetheless a sensation of time.

You don't eventually enter this world and there's no more challenge, or once you transcend the need to go to the Earth plane, you've "arrived." This is a misconception often experienced by human beings. You think someday you will arrive somewhere and then you will "be" there, and that will be that and nothing that happens hereon in will be bad or challenging.

This is such a silly misconception. If you thought you would suddenly "be" somewhere and have no more work, you'd be bored to tears. You have to be careful what you wish to achieve. If that is your wish, you will get there. You will think you have learned all you need to know and then find yourself bored. Still your higher consciousness would create another challenge for you. Not even when you transcend the Earth plane do you "arrive" somewhere. It *is* true you transcend many things that seem to grab you and hold you down and prevent you from flying. You transcend many of those things and actually learn to fly.

As you all work together so do your guides and angels. It is very much a beautiful dance of great cooperation.

As we have stated earlier, the answer for all of you is the same. You are all that you need to be at this time. You have already evolved. Part of you has already returned to the light. An eternal part of you knows all and sees all. It is your mind that prevents you from understanding, not some inherent gene preventing you from growing. It's not bad luck preventing you from seeing and keeping you under wraps except for some extraordinary time when a nugget is thrown to you and you scramble to recognize its existence. That is coming from a place of being scarce. All of you need to recognize the abundance you hold within you that is a wealth of power.

It is simply a matter of perception. You are not stuck. You are not struggling in an uphill battle like the young mythological creature who pushed the rock up the hill that always fell down. That is not your fate. It is simply a matter of perception. Instead

☆ ───────────────────────────────────

of working on trying to be more disciplined, eat better food, not watch so much TV and be more patient (and these are all advantageous), work on changing your perception. You could do this if you were a quadriplegic and could not talk, bound in a wheelchair and hospitalized, trapped in a closet, anywhere without any tool, without a book or any prior knowledge. You can change your perception. That's what we have all come together to help the world do.

What has happened here tonight is a beginning of a communion that will continue to grow. Each of you has now experienced the coming together of like mind in a way you hadn't perceived before. When you each understood in your body the superimposition of the magical time you spent together, you were reconnected. It seems odd to your conscious minds because some of you are strangers, but in essence all of you are of the same blood. This is also true of humanity as a whole.

You can begin today to come together to help broaden your perception and see from a higher plane, understand with a deeper heart and act with laughter and love rather than limitations and self-doubts. As you empower yourself in these seemingly simple ways, you can then turn to those near you and help with a hand to those who may be reaching. In this way you will truly build a sorority.

At some time there will be males introduced into the scene. They will be strong in the feminine aspect and open to the words from beyond.

With that, we thank you for the opportunity for us to have voice again. It is always a joy to speak through a channel and give our insight directly. We look forward to dreamtime with each of you and to come again. And with that you need to just watch and be amazed.

CHAPTER TWO
The Master's Program

"All cultures have birthrights,
All religions have their mythology.
Mine is in the pain of losing you
I'm gonna walk right straight back to me."

"Right Straight Back" © 1992 Barbara With

December 15, 1993

Last night was the beginning of something beyond our wildest imaginations. In fact, in some part of our minds, we're quite convinced that this is all a hoax. It isn't really happening. How *can* this be happening? What is the logical explanation? Is Barbara making up all this information as she goes along? Are we *really* going to start this center where people will come to learn to hear the voices inside them? Are we really going to lead a movement? And who are these angels anyway, that they can tell us this? Let's get real!

To top it off, last night the three of us all had the same dream! The specifics of the dreams differed, but in each of them, the other two appeared at various times, sitting on the periphery, waving and smiling.

This gives us the idea to try to consciously meet in each other's dreams. The only method we know for doing this is to, before we go to sleep, hold the image of each other in our minds and imagine being together in the dream. It requires concentrating very intensely on meeting and being totally de-invested in the dream's actualization, both at the same time.

December 17, 1993

We've come up with a name for our group. Originally we called ourselves "Psychic Sorority," but that sounds like we're excluding men. Kim came up with "Synergy Alliance" after an entire afternoon spent in a brainstorming session with Teresa and the dictionary, looking up and cross-referencing words, making copies of definitions and pasting them together. Working from a small doodle Teresa did in the margin of a notepad, Barbara has created the logo on her computer.

Synergy is a favorite word of ours. One definition means "regeneration through human will and divine grace." Another is "the action of two or more individuals to achieve an effect of which each is individually incapable." As far back as October, Kim and Teresa used the latter in their Yellow Pages ad for their kitchen design business.

December 18, 1993

Haven't had much success meeting in our dreams, but they have been telling nonetheless. Kim and Barbara had the same dream one night, about a house burning down, except in Kim's dream, three infant girls were saved from the rubble.

Teresa dreamt we were in a huge auditorium, filled to the rafters with humans and angels, and on stage was Joan Lunden and a man she could not identify. When she told a friend about the dream, she found out Joan had appeared on David Letterman that same week sharing a psychic experience she recently had.

December 20, 1993

The month has been busy with holiday preparations.

Barbara: I feel the need to forgo giving material gifts. Not only is it getting harder to concentrate on the physical world, but there's something inherently odd about shopping for socks for my brother-in-law while the mysteries of the universe are being laid at my feet.

I bring up the idea of not giving gifts this Christmas at my sister's annual birthday dinner. You would think I am suggesting assassinating the Pope! It's a good hour and a half before we reach a truce and agree that we don't have to give gifts unless we want to.

Kim: Walking up the stairs one night to get a glass of water, the thought suddenly hits me, "I can't lead a mission. I'm so ordinary." I'm awestruck and humbled.

Will this ever make sense to us? There are no reference books on how to "properly" go through an experience like this. I can't call

☆ ————————————————————————

someone and ask them if they were really scared and confused in the beginning, too. Even these questions don't make sense. After all, I'm a kitchen designer, right?

In my first personal session with the angels, they foreshadowed this. They didn't come right out and say, "You will lead a mission," but they did say something would happen that I wasn't capable of seeing at this time. They said as it unfolds for me, the changes in "latitude and longitude" might be confusing at times:

> *All is headed for a much greater outcome than what you could possibly imagine. There is a bigger purpose and plan than you are capable of understanding at this time.*

Is this mission the "bigger purpose" they were talking about last October?

Teresa: In my second personal reading in October, the angels told me I would be taking a trip in late fall or early winter. They said I would be going for a specific reason, but there would also be another purpose which they could not reveal to me at that time.

I *had* been debating about going to North Carolina for a week. My nephew was graduating from college and I wanted to spend a little time with my family before Christmas. I took that reading as my cue to book the flight!

When I arrived, I spent the first night with Dawn at her annual Christmas party. I was able to see friends I literally hadn't seen in years.

Throughout the week I shared bits of this angel stuff with family and friends. All commented on my sense of peacefulness. They'd *never* seen me this way and didn't seem to know what to do with me.

I spent much of the week trying to figure out this special reason for being there. Except for feeling brain dead, everything seemed normal.

Perhaps we are all feeling the movement in the air.

December 30, 1993

Christmas has come and gone.

Barbara: In November I ran an ad in a local musicians magazine offering my musical talents for studio work. One night a fellow named Scott called with a project for me. Because I was also thinking of recording a CD of my own, I asked if he had a piano. He only rented space in a larger complex, but the owner had one, and Scott promised to pass my name along to him.

Shocked and delighted when the owner called a few nights later, I discovered that he was a very old friend I hadn't seen for fifteen years. What a coincidence!

Back then, I often performed in Steve's studio on a live Sunday night radio show. In those days, he was consistently pleasant, always very professional but a little too detached for my taste. It seemed to me he knew something I didn't, and that made me nervous.

All these years later, walking through his studio as he tried to convince me to record there, I noticed he hadn't really changed much. He was still strikingly professional and very detached. But *I* had changed. His detachment now felt respectful of my privacy.

While we sat and talked about the project, I fretted over where to get the money for this venture. Steve's price was an excellent deal for the quality and experience I was getting, but more than I could really afford. Even though I didn't have the money, I knew I needed to do all I could to continue building my musical dreams. I silently asked for some kind of sign that this was the right situation. The angels told me to tell Steve I was a psychic and see what he said.

When I did, to my amazement he told me he was, too. Not only that, but he had levitated once, and had witnesses. Wow! He was as wacky as me! I couldn't have dreamt up a better sign. I decided to work with Steve.

From the start, the project ran beautifully. As we recorded, he often read my mind, from knowing implicitly how I wanted the lighting set while I sang, to when to fade out at the end of songs.

Today I am laying vocal tracks to an old familiar song I wrote almost ten years ago. I feel the angels present in the studio. Some are simply listening, while others want a chance to sing.

The words of a song I have sung hundreds of times suddenly have new meaning as I realize that, indeed, the angels and I wrote them together.

☆ ──

Kim: Clay and I were talking about what he calls "all this angel stuff" while driving home. His stubborn skepticism makes these amazing insights he comes up with even more exciting. I mentioned that in one of my tapes the angels refer to "death and birth." We humans talk about birth and then death, so this confused me. I was really just making conversation; I never expected that he would say, "Well, you're looking at it from your perspective. You need to look at it from their perspective in order to understand why they say it that way." I listened intently, with my mouth hanging open, I'm sure. He continued, "From their perspective, when we are born onto Earth, we leave them, which is sort of like a death. And when we die and leave Earth, we are 'born' to them."

I was stunned by the depth of his perception, especially since he is still so skeptical about this process.

We have come to realize that everyone has many "deaths and births" within each lifetime. Whatever we are going through right now certainly feels like dying. As we let go of large chunks of our old selves, new pieces are being born. This is exhilarating, albeit frightening. Even now that we're finally letting go of things we've *wanted* to change all our lives, there is still a grieving for the loss of the old parts of self. As a way of celebrating the simultaneous death and birth, we keep telling each other, "Congratulations, you're dying."

Kim: The angels and I collaborate one night on a rather poetic piece about this process of death and birth:

I am born. "She" has begun.

The woman that was has died. I mourned her in tears. In confusion. In fear. And, in an idea of a new peacefulness.

Then, in a single moment, the woman that was to be opened her eyes and stretched out the arms of her soul, and began.

I am becoming.

I now know what "present moment" means. It's where I am right now. It's what I feel right now. It is being able to focus on each precious moment as it comes, one by one. Because nothing is as important as fully living each moment as it comes.

All the moments of the past have their importance because they brought me here to this moment. All the moments in the future will be important when each of them comes.

But for now I am only here and this moment feels wonderful. So much more than wonderful. Peace. Serenity. This moment.

In a single moment I will understand how it will all happen.

In a single moment I will learn how to share what I feel.

Until those moments come, I will surround myself with the white light of all that is good. I embrace peace.

Let my soul contain and share only love.

I have already been to the light.

Let me share the light.

I am born. She has begun.

Teresa: Since my two personal sessions of talking with the angels, and our first group, I have been experiencing something I've never had before—peace of mind. Before this, if I had an unusually peaceful or happy day, the old co-dependent behavior would kick in and say, "Don't get use to it, it won't last. You'll crash and burn soon." And, of course, I always did.

This is different. This feels real. My mind, usually obsessing on my current *crisis du jour*, is simply quiet. There are no voices telling me I'm not doing it right or good enough. You know, the usual dialog.

So, here's the new me: Brain Dead. Not that I don't care, but nothing is of issue. There are no conflicts. There is only peace.

Wow! How in the world did I get here? And, more importantly, what do I do to stay here?

January 1, 1994

We decided to have a psychic sleep-over, meeting at Barbara's house in late afternoon to listen to them talk specifically about us as a trio. Because we liked the name so much, we have decided to still use "Psychic Sorority" when referring to the three of us.

The transcripts from this night outlined our direction and explained some of the new sensations we've been feeling in the weeks that have passed since our first group. None of us were really prepared for the messages they gave us. We like to play with the idea that all they say will come to pass, but none of us *really* believe it.

Only time can tell.

☆

THE ANGELS
January 1, 1994

"The Superimposition"

Dear children, you have been brought together this afternoon not by accident. Much of what we will speak of tonight is what you know well, but need verbal affirming of. We do not refer to the modern version of affirmation, to repeat a thought over and over until it becomes affirmed within you. We are speaking of a conscious connection from your five senses to your soul sense, and everything in between.

You perceive certain realities you know are absolutely true. But within you is a block that is part of human existence. It has to do with being connected to the five senses. You are close to your physical body. Your awareness is centered on this particular life, like having that lens be very small. This kind of focus on the physical world is a natural block within your psyche that does not want to accept and comprehend the "super-experiences" going on with you.

We use the word "super-experience" in the term of superimposing. You see the three of you sitting in a triangle with the candle light. We see that superimposed on a greater picture we can't describe. It is based more from the soul and intuition, telepathy, communication without words.

As you feel yourself sitting in this circle, feel this superimposition upon you. You are luminous beings. Picture your soul as this sphere we have talked about. Begin to dislodge that intense focus on your five senses. Begin to open up your perceptions to the other realities around you. This is affirming.

You have said the physical world is becoming less and less important to you. You aren't becoming indifferent to the people, love and duties in your life. As you pry your focus loose from the five senses and the three dimensions, those responsibilities and obligations become more fluid. They become less something to occupy your conscious mind about how to manipulate. Living in the moment, you become less concerned about where your children or family are, or what are your obligations tomorrow, not because you love your children any less. You just know when you are face to face with your children, you will approach them with all of the love your soul has to offer.

Don't be concerned about that. This is freeing. It is prying loose your grip on the past and the future. That is the work the three of you have in store as this new year will unfold. Your purpose is to let go of the past and the future so that all that remains is the present. When you deal with only the present, you begin to really see eternity.

The past and the future are in the moment, but in a different perspective than from the five senses, where you worry about what to do tomorrow, or where the money is going to come from, or what's going to happen three months down the line. That's different than being totally present in the moment and being able to "see" those things. When we use the word "see" we're not necessarily speaking of with eyes so much as with soul and the intent to perceive this superimposition that is a never-ending presence in your lives.

When the three of you come together you feel you can "shed your skin." You can ignore the hard objects of life and go immediately into this super-consciousness where all things are possible. This is a frightening prospect to the human ego. The human ego was designed initially to guide the soul through the Earth plane as an interpreter of the five senses and the three dimensions. It was a rule book given to human beings.

What happened in the course of the development of the human being was that the ego took control. The spiritual pursuits throughout time and civilization have been to get you out from under the control of the human ego and back into this superimposition, not just for you, but for all human beings. As you come and go to that place, the human ego becomes afraid it will "lose control" and no longer have a job, and somehow get lost in the shuffle. These are some of the voices you hear.

You are connected with your higher consciousness and are evolving. You are actually in the act of evolution. It's not something that happened when the fish crawled out of the water. It's not something that's going to happen. The process of evolution is happening now, as we speak.

☆

The ego must learn to conform, to go back to its original purpose, which is merely an interpreter of this Earth plane. The best way to shrink the ego so it won't overwhelm your perspective is either through fear or pain. You have all attested to the fact that out of your most painful times come your clearest vision. That is because the ego is frightened beyond its comprehension and has shrunk away.

Kim, your ego has shrunk so quickly it's still in a stage of rebellion. Your position in the evolutionary process has become very strong. You are in a transitional phase where, now secured in this superimposition, the ego cries like a clinging child, whining about nothing in particular. It would be different if it was actually in danger of losing its life, or terribly, seriously hurt. Your ego has been reduced. It does not like that and it rebels. Over time you will become more like Teresa, where the ego has learned to work in conjunction with the super-self. That is a powerful place to be.

This is a transitional period. You need not be concerned about it. You will quickly work together with your ego and your higher power in this state of super-consciousness. Your ego will decide it likes this arrangement because it doesn't have to be in control. It will go back to doing its original job, which is interpretation. This change is very important to your individual development and the development the three of you together are going to create.

The reason there are three of you is because there is a balance in three. If you were to take a vote, there could not be a tie. One has to be swayed to do what the other two would do. Then you are all brought into alignment. To align the thought process is easier with three than two or four.

The three of you lived in different lives together in preparation for this life, where you've come together, seemingly out of complete coincidence. The changes that have taken place have been facilitated through the affirming voices of the angels. While Kim and Teresa have known each other a long time, it has only been recently that these concepts and this super-awareness has been brought to the surface. Your time together has been a preparation.

In one life, the three of you lived in Italy. You were all brothers. You were very wild. None of you married, and were all complete womanizers. You were constantly getting into trouble by romancing a certain woman, leading her into the depths of a romance, then finding another woman without even saying good-bye.

You didn't go to church. To you, spirituality meant being completely human and delving as far into the five senses as you could without regard for consequence, circumstances or the feelings of other people. *[But still]* there was a certain sincerity about you. You lived and loved with this great passion. There was something about being involved in a relationship that triggered you to feel you were living life to the fullest.

How this carries through to this life is, when you come together, you feel you have an ally in living life to the fullest. Only now you define it as the process of evolution. The time you spend together talking and exploring, generating ideas, investigating avenues and allowing that magic to work within you is spurred on by that life that drove you to live to the fullest.

Even a life that does not appear to have been very spiritual is still part of your preparation for this life. Throwing yourself into life to be fully human is also to be very spiritual.

This is why your life in Italy was so important. You got the need to be constantly involved with the physicality of a relationship out of your systems. This is not to say you won't have relationships. But as you come together free of this need, you are much more conscious of the superimposition.

You are going to be living in a different reality. People will think you are crazy. The world will not understand. You say they would have burned you at the stake. But people will be drawn to you. You have what they want and need. You have an answer for them, but you aren't the end-all and be-all.

We have stated this will be a stopping place, not the end of the line. This is perfectly all right because you, individually and together, are not motivated from the ego place. If you were, it would be a stopping place. You would want to command and control people.

Instead, it is a stopping place where you listen. Listening will be such a large part of the teaching and healing you do. Not that you listen to their problems, but you listen to our voices. You listen to their questions and to our voices. You sit back and allow us to speak through you, but "you" are not saying a word.

There is very little actual physical knowledge you need to bone up on or learn. So much of the facilitating involves listening.

People need to learn to listen, to their higher powers and to the voices of the people around them. People question why there is so much crime and killing, and why things are so difficult in this society. Listening has become obsolete.

Now what society listens to is the voice on the television set telling you what to buy and how many were killed in other parts of the world. Or they listen to the media or read the newspapers, which is internal listening. Society is now locked into listening to the wrong voices. To teach how to listen to one's own voices and to each other will be a very powerful tool.

Teresa: *"Will there be others with us?"*
Yes, absolutely. You will start slowly with small groups within homes or other places. You will begin to get the word out. Part of your process will be to reach a number of people, whether it be through the media or word of mouth or a mailing list. You will offer this to people who you may not think would be interested, not just people who are metaphysically aware.

You will begin to invite people to regular meetings. You will build a list of names. A clientele will be brought to you. The groups will get bigger and bigger. By the summer you are going to have to find a place to fit these people, perhaps a church or some type of a rented hall. In some way you will have this gathering of minds.

People will come from other parts of the country to experience this. The organization you will create will at first be the three of you. You will all speak our voices but also serve in other roles within the organization. You may have guest psychics from other organizations from other parts of the country. You bring people in to help you run the show. It becomes a very large organization that needs official setting up.

Then the organization becomes a channel for money. You will need to decide how to use the money for the highest good. Do not think that giving yourselves money is a negative thing. You must do it in proportion to what you want to get back. In other words, if you get $100,000 and you each take 33-1/3 thousand dollars, that would not leave the channel open to receive.

If you each took $10,000 or $20,000, and sent the rest back into the world, you would keep the channel open for the flow. Do not give absolutely everything away so you cannot run the business. But if you hoard it, it's like emotions. Keep them locked away inside, and you block the flow of feeling spontaneous and in the moment. Money is the same way.

There will come a time when you must decide what to do with it. Other sources of financial prosperity will happen for you. Financial prosperity will not be an issue. When the organization gets to be such a place, then bring people aboard to help you run it. People who come to help will also be understudies or apprentices, students who will also benefit from the superimposition of the organization.

Within the next six months the three of you will be the basic core. This is necessary because of the combination of energy—the synergy of the energy—the three of you create together. You blow a hole through the five senses and three dimensional awareness. The more the three of you come together and become empowered, the more powerfully and quickly the process will move along.

People will come who you do not expect. People will not come who you do expect. Leave yourself open to any and all possibilities. You will be pleasantly surprised.

Kim: "Teresa and I are experiencing this inability to be concerned with day-to-day things. Because our focus is so much on other worldly things around us, we aren't focusing on the earthly things, like our jobs. We're completely content to do everything we can to share our spirituality, the three of us. I'm not sure how we are ever going to get our focus so we keep the earthly things going in order to then experience this spirituality that's coming."

Let us ask you this: what can you do today to further your job? Is it something you could leave this room to go do? Probably not. You could, if you were very creative and ambitious, think of something, such as blanketing the downtown with flyers concerning your business, hoping to generate some business. In that sense, yes, you could physically go do something. When the time comes to actually do something, you will.

You yourself have said at this time you don't have the money to pay the bills. What else can you do today? You could go into work and feverishly make calls to give yourself comfort that you are doing something toward generating your business. There is a good chance out of those calls you would actually generate some business.

It is not that you are ignoring your responsibilities. You are experiencing a euphoric sense of newness of this way of life. Even

☆

Teresa is experiencing this peace of mind that cannot be moved. In a lifetime span, this is still new.

You are going through this honeymoon stage of awareness. You will understand all of the work you put into whatever it is—your children, your job, the rest of your life—is not wasted time. It is not unimportant. It is not to be ignored.

We do not think you should simply go off and rent an apartment and sit for the rest of your lives in a triumvirate, being aware of the superimposition. There will come a time when you begin to realize how this mind frame is affecting how you approach your jobs.

Things for you are going to pick up greatly in the next few months. We see you sitting in your place of business, reaffirming it is almost by "magic," that you didn't apparently lift a finger to make this happen, that it was just luck. But it was fully intended by your higher powers. It does not mean to simply sit back with your legs up and never pay your bills again. Do what is humanly possible. It will work out.

If, by some chance, "working out" meant the business folded, that would also be intended. Something else would come and fill up that place. When a door closes, another one opens. If you fear you're going to be so involved in this spiritual world that you'll completely ignore the three dimensions, this will not be. This is simply a period you are going through.

Look at the timing of what you're going through and how business has been. As you needed this initiation, we shall call it, isn't it interesting how your physical world has played out? You haven't been rushed to work long hours. The holidays make it acceptable to lay back from work. This need not be a concern. All things will flow from this new mind set.

When you begin to learn how to manipulate the energy, creativity and power of coming from the eternal place, then you begin to actually make your dreams come true. You begin to work with this concept of intention. You *intend* to make the business work. You *intend* to make more dollars. And you do so without even caring if it happens. That is the paradox.

The final outcome is not what's important. For example, you begin to intend the business will boom. You intend to make more money. So you set about the process of doing this. Whatever that process would be, however you generate more business, you become so absorbed in the process it doesn't matter what the outcome is because you are doing the process.

Doing the process is where the power lies.

Not in the money that comes at the end of the process, the process itself. This is true of anything, not just art or music or spirituality. It's everything. If you absorb yourself in the process of everything, you are living in the moment, and there is all eternity.

When you get up in the morning and brush your teeth, what do you think of? You think of what you're going to have for breakfast, your day, how you slept, all these things.

But if you arose every morning and felt the floor beneath your feet and those first breaths of consciousness again, and when you got to the bathroom, you felt the grip of the toothbrush in your hand, and you brushed your teeth with the greatest of intent, and felt every bristle and every turn, and the excitement and the flavor of the toothpaste and the rinsing of the mouth, you would find your life dramatically different. Within those processes lies the power.

The day-to-day things needed to run your business sometimes seem unimportant to you. In a sense, no, they are not [important]. But they are very important.

The life you lived where you threw yourself into humanity was the same concept. You threw yourself in. You got absorbed in the process as you lived in the moment. That is what your approach to your business should be. Don't worry about making enough money or if it's what you really want to do. Look at what you have committed to and then decide if this is the business you want to be in. If it's not, then that is another process.

If you are with the business you started and the processes you have begun, then you throw yourself in and enjoy every moment you work and live. Push toward building your business. This doesn't mean you have to be happy at every moment. Life is a grand array of emotions. Be happy to be involved in whatever the process is, whether it's agonizing or joyful. Whatever the human element is within the process, live it and enjoy it. Then you are applying this spirituality.

This is how the spiritual element works within the physical reality. This sense that you are living on this other plane where you want to stay will even out in a few weeks. You will become more accustomed to living in that superimposition and understand more intrinsically how the physical world relates to that. You will be drawn to being involved in things that reinforce that spirituality as opposed to getting dragged into mundane events and relationships.

You learn to approach the mundane from this spiritual level and change what happens in the physical sense. You use that power to affect the outcome. You have experienced this already. Each of you faced angry people demanding things of you and remained in your center. People who have known you for years are astounded at your centeredness and peace of mind. Like Teresa's trip. You came away thinking you hadn't influenced anyone in any way and yet, in retrospect, just by being, you had a profound effect on more people than you realize. It may not show outwardly in some of the people you were with. You may never connect with them as you did with your sister, but it was very influential.

Part of the lesson is to live this spiritual way and look at the material world as something transient which, in a different reality, does not exist. To know that everything is important and nothing really matters, to believe without believing, to intend without intending is very powerful and teaches the people around you, too.

Teresa: "I was saying earlier that when I go to bed, I want to be more in touch with my dreams. I don't know how to start. You talk so much about dreamtime and how important it is, but I lay there and I feel a little lost."

You began simply by being aware, by wanting to, by wishing it to be so, by intending it. It may take some repetitions of falling asleep in order to get control of that place. The only way you cannot succeed is if you lose the intent. Again, to believe that you will do it without believing is the answer. Each night when you go to sleep, if you intend and believe, and it does not occur, then you are not thwarted or driven to giving up the intention, because you never believed to begin with.

In the next few months, you will gain some advancement with this. The three of you have the power to dream together. As you begin to explore this, it will be a very powerful medium. Your ego says there are limits, only so many levels you can go. To dream together is the beginning of really becoming involved in this superimposition.

☆————————————————————————

The three of you will indeed dream together. You will begin to meet each other in your dreams and become aware of what is happening. This veil between the worlds will begin to lift. You will begin to understand how one could levitate or walk through walls. The five senses and the three dimensions will become less real.

From this dreaming will come the connection that dreamtime is where eternity really lies, not the three dimensions. They are finite. You then evolve into transcending the need to die and be reborn. You merge those worlds. This is perhaps beyond your comprehension at this time but it will become clearer as you go.

This is a lifelong endeavor you are undertaking. You have had profound dreams in the past. It's going to be years of developing this art of intending to control your dreaming and becoming aware of that particular reality. If you do not let your impatience deter your intent, you will succeed.

Kim: "Do you have anything to say about what I refer to as 'the birthing process,' of what happened to me in this last 48 hours?"

You are letting go of all the preconceived notions you have about your spirituality, family, and relationship to the Earth plane. What is very important, which you cannot underestimate, is the power of listening to our voices over the last three months and watching the transformation occur. You heard the story and then set out to become a part of it, knowing the outcome, but not really believing. Again, believing without believing.

As it unfolds, it is especially awe inspiring because you were told it would happen. This is an important part of your learning process. You were driven in the beginning to hear our voices over and over. You listened with great intent and detail to everything. Whether or not you recall consciously every detail of our tapes, you have stored that information within you so as it unfolds you remember. You are remembering the future from the past. This juxtaposing of time is as important as letting go of your preconceived ideas.

You have always been the kind of person that once you make up your mind there is no stopping you. Nothing can get in your way. In this way, it's similar to other situations in the past where you decided to make a move or change. It's getting to the point where you make that decision. But once it's made, you're off and running.

☆

This is also true with your spiritual development. You will only continue to evolve from here. It's a good ritual for you to view yourself as having been just born. It's an awakening of a part of yourself that laid dormant all your life.

This isn't an accident or chance coincidence. All of the players that came into your life in the past two days are reinforcements. On the superimposition level, you were saying "I don't believe this. I need some proof." So the universe brought one person after another to prove to you that, yes indeed, the change has taken place.

You need not worry about going back or about the future. This rebirth has brought all the awareness and elements you need to continue. But your path diverges from where it apparently was going. Your path now changes and becomes a spiritual intent rather than a physical intent.

That is the start of a very exciting path. Bathe yourself in this feeling. This is another reason why the three of you have been brought together, to reinforce this feeling. Reinforce it for as long a continuum as you can. Then you will go off. On Monday morning you will find yourself feeling you are someone very different but very familiar. It isn't someone new. It's someone old you lost and then found again.

This is indeed a vision quest you have been brought together to go on. You need not go to the highest mountain or the deepest sea in order to find the vision. Coming together, you will simply generate the energy within you. When a car dies, you bring in another battery to recharge it. You bring these three "batteries" together to reinforce and push even higher.

As the weeks follow, you will feel the veil between the worlds lifting even more. It will be exciting, somewhat unsettling. This passes as you become familiar with it. You find yourselves commenting to people you trust that you "don't live in this world anymore." Of course, we all know you live here, and you know you do. But you actually will think of this Earth plane as an extended vacation. Your real home is in the ethers, in the superimposition, living with all the other realities and lives and memories that exist in that level.

And then, you simply need to watch and be amazed.

☆ ───────────────────────────────

"Shed your wings, come down,
Earthbound,
Dance with me.
Angels sing, they resound,
Earthbound,
Dance with me."

Earthbound © 1989 Barbara With

January 2, 1994

Teresa: It's my birthday today. I have this renewed sense of hope about my life, which is quite different. It's a new year. I have some new friends and this peace I've never known. And now, I have "them."

For the first time in a long time, I believe everything is going to be all right.

Listening to the tape of last night's session again, we realize the lessons in dreaming together are not only to teach us how to meet in each other's dreams but to teach us the *art of intending*. That is, to will something to happen with all of our hearts and then completely let go of whether or not it actually comes to pass, thereby nurturing the process, not focusing on the outcome. Kim's second individual session last October speaks about the paradox of simultaneous obsession and detachment. At the time, she wondered how in the world it was possible to feel both things at the same time. This group session clearly explained in detail how that is possible.

She is still confused from the crisis that originally brought her to listen to the angels. "They" told her she is grieving, and that grief works in its own time, and a new Kim is being born. She analyzes every word they speak. Teresa, on the other hand, has taken on an unusual mien of calm and peace, as if she understands everything and has nothing more to say.

January 5, 1994

Teresa: With all the crazy changes happening for Kim and I, we sometimes meet at my house, get a movie, maybe some wine, and have what we've come to call "normal" time. Tonight we watched a movie about a man who finds himself miserably entrenched in a culture full of hatred and violence. He tries to kill himself, but through a twist of fate, ends up the hero. From this new-found position of power, he's able to make a choice about his destiny.

Acquiring the power doesn't take away his pain, so he asks to be transferred to what he thinks is going to be a barren plane. Instead, he finds a peaceful race of people who welcome him into their magical community. Drawn to their gentle spirit and open hearts, he doesn't understand at first why he feels so at home in this culture, so different from the one he left behind. Even a person's name means something special and speaks of their true nature. To let go of his old identity, he is given a new name that reflects who he has now become.

The movie prompted tears and laughter. It bore a striking resemblance to what we are going through. We decided this meant we needed new names, too. Laughing hysterically, we tried to figure out what we would change our names to that would describe who we are now...especially since we have no idea who we are now.

We came up with "Obsesses Too Much" for Kim because of the way she obsesses on the details, analyzing and processing them until she comes out on the other side with some great big revelation. It's really cool the way she does that, but I still like to tease her.

I was having trouble coming up with a name to describe me, especially in the peaceful, but brain-dead state I've been in. Kim started laughing and said all she could think of was "Shit For Brains." Well, it certainly describes my state these last few weeks, but "Shit For Brains?!" I wasn't sure whether to laugh or be offended.

I laughed.

January 9, 1994

Teresa: Today is my wedding anniversary. Fifteen years! How is that even possible? Although Randy and I have been separated for over a year now, I am still struggling with letting go. How do you let go of someone you've loved for half your life? It would be easier if I could just hate him. It makes it even harder that we're still so entwined in each other's lives.

But the angels have given me a lot of "work" to do in the letting-go department and I'm grateful for that. I'm actually beginning to get a glimpse of who *I* am for a change. Not who I am as Randy's wife, or Sarah's mom, or anybody's anything, but who *I* am.

The angels keep telling me, "As long as you wait, he will not come." I might still be waiting, but at least I'm doing something good for myself while I do.

January 10, 1994

The effects of the work we are doing together are slowly coming to the surface. Well, they seem slow in coming, but since we've only been meeting for a little over three weeks, we're actually moving at warp speed. Maybe that's why we all report feeling a physical dizziness about this work. It's hard to eat when you feel like you're always spinning. We call it the "Fourth Dimensional Weight Loss Plan."

We all have this new-found inner peace, but there are other things, too: revelations about familiar situations we were previously stuck in, positive changes in difficult relationships, broader perceptions of our lives, a new interest in learning. Perhaps the most enthralling sensation is being so inspired all the time. We can hardly wait to be together and do our work. We aren't sure what it all means but we know *something* is happening.

Teresa and Kim are wondering what will become of them. They know they're supposed to be learning to speak the voices, but they aren't getting any clear or discernible messages. It's hard for them to see how far they've actually come in the weeks we've been working together.

Making transcripts of the sessions has really aided our understanding. It's very powerful to go back to the tape and listen to the messages again. It's even more powerful to go back and read the words once the tapes have been transcribed. They're becoming something of a "handbook" for this learning process, written for us, through Barbara, and by our angels. Incredible.

☆

We use the dictionary more each day. Sometimes we look up words from the sessions with the angels, other times we seek meaning for messages from our dreams that lead us to new revelations and directions of study. Some definitions are things we've never thought of. The word "influence" is one of our favorite unexpected definitions: "An ethereal fluid flowing from the stars to affect the fate of men." Who knew?

January 11, 1994

The Psychic Sorority decides to meet again for "classroom instruction." We laugh and say we're getting our PhDs.

Tonight, Barbara is feeling particularly doubt-filled. She worries Kim and Teresa will listen to the voices, follow "their" advice and bad things will happen. Will she then be responsible? And how do we really know it's angels talking, and not her ego, striving to be that wise and powerful? She is driving herself crazy with doubt.

Teresa is tense and anxious. Kim is quiet and peaceful. In other words, "Shit For Brains" is obsessing, and "Obsesses Too Much" has a calm, unruffled aura of understanding about her. It's feeding Barbara's insecurities. She hasn't known these women long enough to know who they are in "real life." Now the only familiar aspects of their natures have been juxtaposed.

Before the session, Kim asks Barbara to help interpret something she heard "them" say about her business in a previous session. Things are markedly slow with kitchen designing. There is no money coming in. "They" told her that in a few months she will be very busy, and she and Teresa will look at each other and say, "Wow, it's just like magic!" Kim wants to know if she should invest in the advertising she's been planning based on this information.

Absorbed in her own doubts, the only thing Barbara hears is, "When's the money coming in?" She stumbles around with an answer to the question she thought she heard, but not the question Kim actually asked. And the fact that Kim and Teresa have "traded places," temporarily taking on the dominant element of each others' personalities, adds to the confusion.

On nights like this it does feel like going to school. And this night feels like one of those Tuesday night classes you want to skip to go hang at the student center drinking beers and playing pinball.

Not a chance.

THE ANGELS
January 11, 1994

"Inward, Outward, Upward"

You have come together in a knot, intertwining your energies on a number of different levels. This is due to not only your evolution as partners, but the different places of your individual evolution. We will begin to decipher the different levels for you and give you a clearer understanding of what is happening.

While you are walking together, going forward as equals, different levels of awareness are being opened in each of you.

Think of it like this: Teresa, the door opening for you is inward; Kim, yours is outward; and Barbara, upward. This is not a judgment. No one is farther ahead of the other. There are simply three coherent, congruent and yet still individual paths in the process of aligning.

Teresa, going inward means to unfold the garments that have been protecting you from the cold. Unwrap yourself to reveal the healing warmth to your heart. You have questioned yourself and your directions, particularly the affairs of the heart. That is not your main concern now. The process of unraveling your heart is the most important undertaking for you at this time.

Recently you have come to uncover more than ever what has been hidden beneath you. You speak with us often and of many subjects. If a larger interval of time passed, you would be more capable of seeing the changes occurring between the times you come to speak with us. When we speak to you so often, it gives the unrealistic sensation that you are not actually changing.

You are dealing with deeper vessels lying within your heart still left to uncover. It's painful, but not hopeless with no transformational quality. You are beginning to see a light at the end of the tunnel of pain.

You must not, any of you, underestimate the importance of these events tonight. There are deeper meanings you cannot see. You must hold this in your mind and trust. Do not assign meaning

☆ ────────────────────────────────

to events in your life and how they relate to what is happening to you emotionally.

We understand this goes against psychological training. One is supposed to examine and analyze, hold and draw correlations to. By doing that, you are defining yourself in a way you must conform to. The difference between saying, "I have a broken heart because my husband left me," and "I feel a deep pain from a yet to be revealed source" is that the latter leaves you open to discover more of the mysteries. The former defines the situation and you have to live in it, limiting the potential for finding deeper things.

It is essential to your development to understand while, yes indeed, you create the events on the Earth plane, they are only shadows of bigger scenarios cast upon time and space. Do not cling to them. Embrace them. There is a difference. Do you understand? When you cling, it is out of fear. When you embrace, it is out of love. If you go inward to the heart with fear, you superimpose that fear on other things in your life, as opposed to moving through it.

Kim, you are learning to look outward. Your abilities to define and understand complex situations and ideas is very advanced. You have a natural ability to digest and inform, taking in the external world and translating it in terms of your "movie" that is your life.

The outward movement is turning your focus away from the digestion process. To take in and give out is a natural and necessary process, part of all life and energy. But your perception is focused on the digestion process as opposed to seeing the results of the process. Focusing on your own circumstances is preventing you from seeing the scenery as you go by on the highway.

We're not saying you're not doing enough. It's an infinite critique done in an intimate fashion. We are helping you to fine tune. When we say inward, outward, upward, it's not a criticism. It's another point of view advantageous to your perception. As you look outward you find inwardly you are able to let go of the details of your digestion.

You hear our voices and don't believe them. You are in a transitional phase of learning to differentiate between what are habitual desires and wants, and what are higher visions connected to you through your higher consciousness, which is then again connected to all consciousness.

☆

Barbara's transition is upward. She is awakening to what is flowing through her. To be so inspired by something that has long been a part of her is to meet an old friend after a long time and get reacquainted. The reason the view for Barbara is upward is because to her, it's a flow from bottom to top. Standing on a precipice, looking at the space within, feeling this energy flow in a place once empty and deserted, she finds a part of self that had been secreted away. With this discovery comes an entirely new kind of enthusiasm and belief of the process.

You are constantly hovered over by numbers of entities seeking "air time," influencing you in your dreams and waking state. We have heard your request for [our] names. More than names, we would like to give you our personalities as clearly as possible so you can clearly distinguish our voices. If we can help by showing you our own definition and vocal quality, you will understand better in your own head. That is the quest for you now.

You are on the verge of discovering something quite dramatic, particularly Teresa and Kim. The change will take place imminently at your place of business. It involves the separation of the voices within your head. You will find us sooner than you think. In the meantime, we will give you distinct characteristics, and perhaps you can thus name us.

Many will come to try the voices out for size on the Earth plane. You are guinea pigs. We need to understand better how to facilitate the exchange of communication between the two worlds.

You must relinquish the idea that destination is the key. You have already voiced your concerns regarding trusting of the voices. We have heard these concerns of your children and your business. Part of you is completely unbelieving. The art you are apprenticeship to requires balancing the non-belief with the absolute, unshakable faith. This is done through time. There is purpose in time. Passing through the changes and seeing how the different events line up with what was spoken in the past about the future, only to become the past again, is the learning process that is so important to you now.

When you allow the non-belief to envelop you with doubts and fears, there are a number of things to remember. One is there is an aspect of this beautiful dance you are doing called free will. This plays an integral part in the changing ebb and flow of how the energy is transmitted. When you exercise your free will you always make an effect upon the probable and possible outcomes. The question remains: How invested are you in the particular plot of the movie? It does not matter. You can exercise your free will, only to learn a different lesson.

The mystery behind all you are delving into is greater than your conscious minds can understand. It may appear this information doesn't relate to a particular set of questions, but we assure you that you must examine it from a different perspective. When doubt and fear wash over you, recall it's only a movie and "de-invest" in the events of that movie. If we were to tell you of all the realities that exist, and the possibilities and probabilities, and how you could access them all, you would be driven insane.

You have the power to travel between any of your lives. Look at them as layers of an onion surrounding your soul happening simultaneously. Your awareness is focused on a particular layer, making you cognizant of being who you are. You begin to loosen your perspective and broaden your awareness.

You will be able to travel between those lives. This isn't your classical sense of reality. And yet, in order to accomplish this, a necessary step in your evolution, our goal has been from the beginning to loosen your tie to that awareness.

This has been a source of irritation for some who want times and places. We cannot stress to you enough the importance of letting go of the movie plot, in every scenario. It leaves your mind boggled. There is nothing left to think about (you think). You are then free to experience what we would like to show you but cannot now because you are still infants.

We would like to converse, as in conversation. We would ask you to give us information to converse with you.

[The angels caught us off guard. Conversation? We're used to them asking us for questions. That's like teachers and students. But having conversation would put us all on the same level. There was a long, long pause before Teresa asked her question.]

Teresa: *"I suddenly feel like I'm not doing anything right. I don't know if it's the words you choose, but you say there's this piece we don't believe. We jokingly say we don't believe it, and yet, I believe it with all of my being. And so, is there something we aren't aware of? This is very important to us."*

☆

Yes, there are parts you do not see. The mistake is thinking when we talk to you in this way, pointing out the blind spots, it negates what *is* seen. You would not be here if you didn't believe with all your hearts. This we know. But like a very strict teacher in a challenging class, in order for you to strive to greater heights, you must feel in some way like you have not arrived.

There are blocks in the human experience deeply ingrained in all of you for your survival. It is like the habits you formed as a child due to your family circumstances. They were survival techniques that later in your adult life became obstacles. It is the nature of human existence to have this blockage. It is what makes you fit into your world. It is what defines the world. Without those, you are then transcending the Earth plane. Your physical being is not ready to do that.

When we say you are blocked, we do not mean you don't understand the principles of which we speak. We mean you cannot implement them yet. You cannot walk through walls, or even at this point in your development distinguish the voices.

Part of this transition is that you shake up your sense of what reality is. You do not have to know the way or the reasons. You can think it's because someone did this or that to you, but there are many deeper things going on you cannot see. We are trying to invite you to see them, but it requires much more detachment.

We don't say you have not come far enough. We say we are gladly walking your path with you, side by side, because all things have already transpired in your world. We see all parts of your progress. Never in our minds do we doubt, with all of your soul, you are part of the transformational and evolutionary process. What will empower you is to admit how much you don't know and how unimportant some things are.

This is a difficult quest. You are not aware, as children are not aware, of some of the difficulty in undertaking the quest. There are familiar, comforting ideas and things you will eventually let go of. This causes grief. It is terribly difficult for a human being to actually welcome and plunge into the kind of grief transitions bring. It would not benefit you to simply sit around and only revel in the awesome things that have already occurred. It would behoove you to continue with the concept that there is a great deal more you don't know than you do. This concept will free you incredibly from the human ego thought processes that strive to keep you roped. Does this help?

☆————————————————————————————

Teresa: "It does help. I sometimes think I'm not doing it right. It's like I want step-by-step instructions, but I know it's a puzzle to figure out. It's very confusing because . . ."

Yes, it is very confusing.

"It's hard to sort between what we have to do living here day-to-day and this magical thing we feel."

There is no separation.

Kim: "You say we get too involved in the details of the movie as it's going on, and yet we feel moments of revelation when we finally figure out the lesson a particular scenario has taught us. It makes us feel we've stepped ahead. It wasn't the detail that mattered, but we need to get through the details in order to get to the lesson. Are we doing it right when we do that, or is that still obsessing on the little stuff?"

It is one thing to undertake a series of events and compare them to what you have been told would unfold, drawing from within a feeling of deep understanding. You can then observe and compare and learn from deep within.

It's another thing to take what the voices have said is going to occur and try to construct a framework for their interpretation before the events take place. These are two entirely different events in your lives.

In the case of the former, you are excelling, both of you, beyond comprehension. You are learning and absorbing like sponges. You are so full of new perception and information it practically hurts. It's like going to an amusement park and riding the thrilling rides. At the end of the day you're aching, but full of vigor and new perception. From the height of the roller coaster you saw very far. You are doing that without contention.

You have learned that process. So we move on to a new process. When the voices come to you and speak of a future event, it drains important personal power to spend energy and time constructing possible futures and trying to position the present and possible farther futures around those possibilities.

What must be done is to take the moment at hand and make the choices within your realm to make. Then let go. In two months you will be able to review the events and the voices and again learn another perspective. It cannot be done the opposite.

There are other lessons going on beyond time and events on the Earth plane. Within space and time, lessons fall in a linear fashion. You must not underestimate the rules of time. It's not a trap or a meaningless system set up so you are not able to escape. These are the lessons that will evolve you into a higher plane. We are simply trying to guide you into making the most efficient choices for your personal power. Once you get to a place where you aren't engaged in constructing possible futures, your energy frees itself to live even more in the moment, where the power really lies.

When we say your mind blocks you, we aren't casting a judgment upon you. We are looking at you as you are breaking these habits. You must go through a repetitive process until you learn on a deeper level what your blocks are.

As are all things we have taught you, this, too, is a paradox. We are asking you to simultaneously take all of the lessons of being alive in the Earth plane as seriously as anything you have taken in your lives, and at the same time, to let go completely of them as transient, unimportant events. Juxtaposing these attitudes will help to free you. Make what has been important, unimportant and what hasn't been important, important.

To you, to simply not do anything about a particular event would seem as if you are not doing enough. To us perhaps it would be the only thing you should do to gain the most fluid flow of energy and use that energy in a way that will build on itself and not drain. In that way, yes, looking at what has happened and examining the words that were written and marveling in the awe builds on your energy. But to sit and project about what could possibly happen in the future drains your energy.

We do not judge you in the sense that you have not come far enough or are not doing good enough. We speak more in terms of what is physically, objectively happening to the flow of energy within you. If it's draining you, then it's not a situation you need to indulge yourself in. It is important to understand the difference between going through a transition and having your energy drained.

The grieving process (and this is for both of you) is in play here. You have a different kind of grieving going on. One is fuller and more robust while the other is a quiet, more underlying flow of energy. We see all emotions as energy flows, like electricity within you. We don't see a flow of anger from an energy perspective and think, "This is a bad thing." We simply see it as energy flowing.

☆ ————————————————————————

These judgments come from your ego voice. It is our mission not to save you from a terrible thing or make you see all the negative things about you. It is our mission to try to expand your perceptions so that you see yourselves as this pure energy because it is more empowering. The whole concept of evolution is that you will eventually evolve past the need to come back to live within the rules of this reality in order to learn your lessons.

On an intimate scale, even that large concept can apply to any specific question you have concerning the energy flow. To see others as energy, not as "bad" or judging, detaches you even more from those people. You are then in the detached place of making decisions based on what is going to increase your energy and personal power.

That is why you have challenging people in your lives. Simply step back and let them exist without letting your energy be drained into them. It is not making them any larger either. When you stand back and allow them to exist from their own energy flow, they are left all alone to look at and examine self. They may not like it, but that is part of *their* process to achieve that transformation in their own life.

Teresa: *"Both of our ten-year-old daughters seem very interested. We've shared a lot of this with them. We were wondering if there would be any advantage to having them hear the voices? Are they too young? When will we know? When will they know? Are they ready? It's something we want to share with them."*

It is advantageous. Because you are the guardian, the caretaker, you feel it is your responsibility to help guide the energy flow around them. To fully facilitate their introduction into these concepts, speak more with them before they are given an opportunity to speak face-to-face with us, which will be very soon.

You will know as you speak with them. They will show you they are taking it seriously. Their boundaries are not so tight and tied up. They haven't had the many years of ingrained trained responses. Their relationship to their egos is more malleable.

It will come out of a flow of conversation with them. You will be talking about different ideas and out of your mouth will come, "Well, how about if we just call Barbara and ask her when we could." You won't manipulate them in any way. You will whet their appetites so they will really want to speak to the voices and find the answers. It will be very intriguing for them.

It will be necessary to follow up with them on their experience after it occurs. Spend some time with them helping them digest these ideas. It will be sometime within the next month.

Kim: *"In terms of bringing together people of like mind, you told us there will be someone who will come into this who will have a larger influence on the Earth plane. We've had a few names come to us, and one name in particular keeps coming to all three of us. It makes us think that it has significance. We want to ask who this person is, or did we misunderstand and it's not a specific person who will come to this mission we're incubating right now."*

From now until perhaps September there will be a building effect that goes on. Things will slowly begin to increase. There will be some interesting trips the three of you take, two in particular, that will help to push along your evolution.

You will begin corresponding with a number of people who you will ask for help in one way or another. You may not write them directly and say, "We need your help" but that is the gist of the push to contact people. The people who you have mentioned already will indeed be a part. Oprah will be someone particularly influential, but she will be later on, outside of this gestation period. You will be in contact with her before you actually appear with her. You will have some sort of communication that isn't involved in necessarily asking her to put you on her show. It will seem at first it's not something that will happen, but later, in a different phase of this transition, it will indeed.

This is the beginning of various kinds of situations with the media. Wayne Dyer is someone who will not come into the picture until a later part of development. Your communication with him at whatever time you choose will be important to you. Don't think if you choose to communicate with him and he does not respond with you immediately you might as well not have sent the letter. That is not so, it will take its course in time.

During this period of gestation you will decide to write to a number of people. Communicate with people who you don't necessarily think will be allies. You are never sure of who will come to embrace the concepts. All must be given a chance.

We see you sitting down after you have gained momentum and verbally expressing, in a succinct form, the concepts and experiences you have been engaged in and sending it to many, many people who you think will be of aid to you. There will be two people in the summer in different parts of the country who will ask you to come. You will go perhaps to one together and the other is still unclear if either one or two of you will go. Perhaps they come to you.

There is also the process of putting this onto paper. You have been hearing our pleas, and we thank you for your prompt and courteous action. This transcription will be essential for what will follow. You will publish this and it will be a basis of the growing outreach.

If you are looking specifically for years and time, we ask you to please try to release those concepts. It could be, if you release them, you can achieve it sooner than what we say. We are only giving you a general format to gauge by.

We have told you coming together would facilitate a more rapid change. This is true. The difficulty you will have is, for this period of time, it is not something that will sustain you and your families. You must do it as a sideline and not be distracted from fulfilling your needs within your everyday life. Yet, as paradoxical as it may be, we also tell you if you chose to put all of your time and energy into this project, you would make it happen even faster. We don't foresee that being a real possibility at this time. The gestation period is fairly clear to us and after it begins to take off there are all sorts of possibilities based on your free will.

You find a publisher and get some publications, periodicals perhaps, some kind of accredited attention. You are also working on another concept of the three of you having various kinds of business. Perhaps within your business you begin to assimilate. Perhaps some kind of design work Barbara can help with the kitchens, you will help her with music. Out of all this will come the reality you envision.

You ask about your company. We said in January you would come to a revelation. Your place of business has become more a place where you come together. Out of those headquarters comes this germination of the seeds, the conception. Is it not done mostly from this place that in reality serves as a kitchen business?

Your business will continue to ebb and flow. We don't say this to encourage you to rest on your laurels and expect you won't have to lift a finger. If you stay in your daily process and do all

☆

that you can, you will surely get yourselves by the slow period and into the busier time.

Your desires will quite possibly change as you go on. Basing your decisions today on what the possible futures are, take into account the physical manifestations. You must also remember your heart's desire. This will come into play, too. It is already transforming itself. It will continue to transform itself. You will reach a point where this business is not something you actively participate in but becomes a source of income for your husband, or someone else you trust. It carries on but not necessarily with you at the helm.

Teresa: *"I've been trying to meditate, and to have quiet time to hear my own guidance. I'm not sure how close I am. Can you tell me anything that will help me?"*

You are doing it as it should be. We don't say this obliquitously, we say this literally. Instead of concentrating on the things not present in your meditative process, concentrate on the things that are, whether it be the quietude or the solemnness of your mind. Know that in the process you are deriving the benefits. They will not show up until after you are out of the meditation.

The strongest influence you need right now is for you yourself to reassure the part of your mind that doubts. This is exactly what you're supposed to do. The ideas that you aren't doing enough and that there's a better way are blocks. You are learning how to unblock them. You need to experience the learning process of how to quiet those voices, to simply know.

We don't want to take out of context the paradox between thinking you absolutely know and simultaneously knowing you don't know, but in this scenario, "I know" is a strong and positive mantra for you. In this scenario, it wipes out all the questions about doing it right or if you're deriving the benefits.

We see you sitting very ethereally repeating to yourself "I know" and having it vibrate within your being and chase away the doubts. One of the purposes of meditation is to quell the ego voice that brings you down instead of building you up.

Kim: *"Is this a prelude to our being able to speak the voices? You said that we would do that."*

☆ ————————————————————————————————

Absolutely. All of this is. You cannot discount anything you do in an investigatory way, even the times that feel like obsessing on the little details. You cannot site yourself because you are learning how to transform it. To transform it, you must get to know it intimately. You must embrace it. The way to do this is with your humor, by not taking yourselves seriously. You each are very good at accepting criticism from without. It is your own critic that does the worst damage.

If you find yourself obsessing on the little details, the best recourse when you think you've failed again is to instantly replace them with this humor. Move more quickly to recognize and let go, instead of recognizing and feeling guilty, being punished and feeling bad. That will drain all of your energy.

You recognize and then decide to let go. If you have to do this every five minutes, it will only be less and less the more and more you do it. All of this, including our continual insistence that you let go of meaning and importance of detail, are all part of tilling up the ground to watch this growth take place.

You will begin to do this at your place of business. It is happening already but you are not aware of the influence. There is a progression. We will use the channel as a comparison. This process we are involved in at this moment is a direct line of communication. The process you two are involved in is like us standing to the side of you, whispering in your ear. Then you say it, not sure if you really heard it from a higher source.

The key here for you is to trust. The more you trust, the more you will have the capabilities to deal with whatever challenges come at you. The more you trust in the higher power taking care of you, the more you trust in living one day at a time, moment to moment. That quiets your internal dialogue which is consistently ever present. The more you can quiet your internal dialogue, the more you can make room for that messenger who is standing whispering and nudging to actually come face-to-face. Then you will able to step aside and here the voices clearly.

When you align your ego voice with the voices that speak only of the highest good and unconditional love, you begin to experience freedom. It will become more integrated into your lives, the way you conduct yourselves and the choices you make. You gain more and more of this energy because you are not draining it into trying to help people who would be better off without your help, or intertwined in a yes/no, middle-of-the-road relationship that keeps you from going forward or backward.

When you align yourself with those voices, you make choices that eliminate those situations from your lives. You are not victims, as you know. You have created all of these situations. So you quiet the voices and open up the space. You are shining, beautiful lights that we are drawn to in order to communicate to this Earth plane.

Kim: *"You said we have already begun to hear the angels and will continue and we'll see this in our place of work, which has now become our place of spirituality. Is that what you alluded to when you earlier said the voices are going to begin to come to us and will help us to learn to distinguish?"*

Yes.

"It's like practice?"

Yes.

Teresa: *"I have a question about how I've been feeling in the past week. I had this wonderful peace for weeks, what we jokingly called "Nothing in my Brains." It was a wonderful place to be. Suddenly there was nothing there, but the peace was gone, too. I don't know how to interpret that: as a setback or different processes going on, or my self-doubts getting in the way?"*

Your self doubts create the sense that you have somehow failed. You are still laboring under the assumption you arrive somewhere and there you stay. Part of you knows all we say. So when we speak to you of this, you must be careful not to misinterpret what we say.

Your sense of peace and well-being was a sample, giving you a familiarity with this sense of detachment. The transition came when you experienced this level of understanding, although it was still a little different than complete detachment. It required a certain numbness. You yourself say it was like a huge shot of Novocain in your brain. That is not the ultimate goal.

Now you have chosen to undertake a new lesson of (again the paradox) finding your spirituality completely in the details of the Earth plane, and finding your humanity in the realm of the spiritual. You have made a decision to heal yourself and transform. This means going to the heart of the darkness, which means you are no longer numb, which means you are prepared to take on this challenge. Part of your conscious mind foolishly entertains the notion you simply acquire peace of mind and nothing else can bother you again.

When you have evolved past the Earth plane you can then compare the different states of mind. But here in your infant stage you still need the challenges in order to strengthen and grow. Your ego mind clings to the idea you have gone backwards or failed. This period of peace and numbness has been a rest period for you to gain a sense of personal self, to reflect on how far you have come and all you have been through. Even though your mind was numb, your soul was still very active.

You will muster the courage to investigate and make a stand on issues and emotions that you heretofore have ignored through your preoccupation with the details of life. When we say preoccupation, it is not negative. All human beings are taught to be preoccupied with the details of one's life. It's the basis of living in the "real world." What else is there? Many people support the idea that being preoccupied with the details of your life is what living is all about. Yes, paradoxically, it is applicable. But in this situation, you are now ready to do some different self-examination that may be painful. But the pain will be a transformation pain, not one that drains your energy.

Be prepared to deal with the challenges of this undertaking. Accept the challenge with courage and humility. Lose your self-importance so, if you aren't in a place with peace of mind, you can accept it and know you are striving for a greater picture and a deeper understanding.

"Does this challenge involve my husband, or does it go further and deeper, even before him?"

Further and deeper. He came in the middle of a period of a habitual way of thinking and dealing. Now you are moving away from that way of thinking and feeling. That way was grounded firmly in your family [of origin]. There are a few issues concerning your family that are part of this pain. It will empower you to make a decision about Randy, but it is only a part of process.

Kim: *"Teresa asked about meditation and dreaming and how she's working very hard. I don't feel like I'm working on anything specific to further my development here. I'm just going along. I think about it a lot. But I'm wondering if there's something I should be focusing on more to aid me in my process."*

You are doing what you're supposed to be doing. Your lesson is not Teresa's lesson in detail. Look at what you are going through from a different perspective. You are learning by not doing. The fact you are not doing means you are learning. In this period of time, allow yourself to simply be. That is the greatest lesson. From there you will be motivated and led to making decisions that will help to initiate your dreams coming into fruition.

Kim: "Do you love this as much as we do?"

With a resounding yes, as we stand around you. There is nothing but this love. Our mission is to bring you love to pass along to those around you. Picture us all saluting with our various beer mugs. With a somewhat humorous gesture we take out our bandanas and wipe our brows and say yes, this is what we've been shouting at you. Where we are there is nothing other than unconditional love. It is most amazing when it's for the self.

The doubts and struggles you go through are absolutely essential for your development. But they are not something we undertake. We move quickly and fluidly through these lines of energy. We are trying to get you to see more of life from that energy perspective. There are no lies or misconceptions where we are because everything is instantly telepathic. You can have nothing but love for being connected to the energy that creates this wondrous and miraculous landscape that is shared with different visions.

When you picture us, see us moving through you as if we were ghostlike figures. Keep the same vision, color and humor of seeing us surrounding you, but picture us becoming part of you. This sensation is how we feel amongst ourselves. There is a fluidity that brings us in an ebb and flow, in and out of each other's energy fields.

With all this information and all you have tried to accomplish tonight, look at what you have done. The revelations and transformations you made were very good work. Working hard to accomplish something, then achieving it, is the process of doing it. It's not how big or small it is. That is the feeling that should prevail with you as we depart.

☆ ───────────────────────────────

We again thank you for the opportunity to come together and look forward to our next encounter, which should hold some very interesting messages. Also note the kinds of transitions you go through between now and then. If you make one thing your goal, monitor your awareness onto the moment. At any time you can choose, when you're thinking about the past or future, to zero in precisely on the moment and what's happening within it. See how long you can sustain that perception. It will show you some interesting results.

As you go forth, hold the thought that all is precisely as it should be. The steps you take on your path are there for purpose and enhancement. Walk the path with surety and transform the doubts by embracing.

Then simply watch and be amazed.

Later that night...

When they told us to take note of the transitions between now and the next scheduled meeting, we all felt an eerie, premonitory insinuation. Our first road trip is already planned for next week, at the request of a friend in a small town sixty miles away. What new surprises are awaiting us there? Only the angels know for sure.

January 12, 1994

Barbara: Last night's session was very difficult for me. Again, I couldn't get beyond the doubt that plagued me about the process. I was convinced that no one would ever be interested in these sessions, these words, these lessons. My doubt was so oppressive, I stopped during the session and we listened to the tape halfway through. Standing in Teresa's kitchen, I perceived the voices to be talking very slowly, with much stuttering and stopping. This was more evidence that it was all a big mistake and that I should "stop this nonsense immediately."

It feels like a big hoax, except for one thing: I'd have to be the one doing the scamming. But there's nothing for me to scam out of these women. They have little money, certainly hold no important social or political positions, have apparently nothing that I want. In fact, Kim and I agree that if we hadn't been brought together for this specific study, more than likely, we wouldn't even be friends. The most I can get out of them, if that is indeed my aim, is perhaps a newly-designed kitchen.

Teresa: Last night was weird. During the reading I felt terrible. It sounded like they were saying we weren't doing anything right, that we didn't believe. I had all kinds of doubts swirling around in my head.

As I listen to the tape today, it doesn't sound like that at all! What the heck is going on around here?

Kim: I don't know where this feeling of calm is coming from, but I like it. I get so peaceful sometimes that it makes other people nervous. It hope it doesn't go away.

Barbara's mood was strange last night. Sort of edgy. It seems odd to me that she has such doubts. I expect Teresa and me to have doubts, this is all so new to us. But Barbara has been doing this for many years.

☆————————————————————————

Our doubts are not only about this process of talking with the angels and whether or not it's real or imaginary. Some of the doubts are about the transformations happening within us. It's easy to focus on the mystical side of this process and think *that* is what we doubt. *But the truth is we are plagued with doubts about our own ability to transform.*

Yes, it is unusual to talk to angels and have them talk back. But it feels just as alien to me as believing that I am a beautiful loving child of God who is filled with light. Six months ago I couldn't have made that statement any more than I could have believed that God would send angels to help us save the world.

January 14, 1994

Barbara: Two days later, listening to the tape, I hear something entirely different. The voices are talking very rapidly, and I have to pause more than usual to catch up while transcribing. And they address the idea of not letting our doubts diminish the importance of what we went through that night. What a coincidence.

☆ ☆ ☆

They've begun hounding Barbara to start writing a book. Barbara and Kim have always known they would each someday write a book. Another psychic told Teresa that, if she chose to, she would "write a book that would bring her notoriety." We thought it was a cool idea, but the project seemed too intimidating to take on.

Barbara: The book project began innocently with "them" suggesting an introduction. I entertained the idea, but didn't actually sit down at the computer. They nudged me with more sentences, but I still stayed away. They spoke louder and longer, getting further and further into the first chapter until I had no choice but to sit and write what they were telling me. Even now, as I write this, I feel them looking over my shoulder and coaching me. And when I edit, I hear them telling me what to take out and change. Some days the voices make me feel a bit claustrophobic.

January 15, 1994

Although we're supposed to note the transitions we go through between now and the next meeting, we have no idea what to look for. We fluctuate between believing with all of our hearts that something divine is happening here, and being absolutely convinced we're losing our minds. The information "they" send us *is* inspiring and quite obviously divinely influenced, and there is peace in knowing we can't all three be going insane at exactly the same time in exactly the same way. However, there's great conflict between what our conscious minds have been telling us for our entire lives and the messages the angels are telling us now. It's exhausting trying to live between the two extremes of the paradox. What are we to think?

Kim: Because I live my life in a state of perpetual motion, I have never been able to meditate successfully. I have not yet mastered sitting down for any length of time and staying calm and quiet, inside and out, with no other purpose but to explore my inner self.

I do, however, get little messages and revelations at different times throughout my day, while doing the dishes or peeling carrots, in the shower, or alone in the car, etc. The revelations seem to come when I am relaxed, my mind is settled and what I am doing does not require great powers of concentration. I have dubbed any time that fits these criteria "peeling carrots."

It makes sense that revelations come unexpectedly at these times. With a relaxed and open mind, you manifest whatever is in your heart. Let's face it, we don't plan time into our everyday schedule for the "bad" voices in our heads to tell us, "You're not doing it right again," do we? So why do we think that hearing the messages of love needs to be a big production number?

January 16, 1994

Barbara: Tonight I decide to call Kanti, a charming Australian woman who has been coming to me for about two years for private sessions. She's planning to move to Japan in the spring. I want to invite her to the next big group set for January 25 and share with her this new alliance I have made with these two women. I enjoy her always curious and open mind.

As I tell her about Kim and Teresa, she begins relating how she,

☆ ————————————————————————————————

too, is working in a group with two other women doing meditation. She, Lois and Rita have been meeting in each others' dreams and meditations.

I'm shocked! When "they" told us there were other groups of threes working around the country, I never imagined I would know any of them. How are these women being guided if not by having one of them speak the voices?

Apparently they sit silently together meditating and then afterward share with each other what they saw. Kanti says in one of these meditations, Lois met one of my guides, who told her we were coming into their circle. Oh, dear.

Kanti also has had the exact dream Teresa had of being in a huge auditorium filled with souls and humans alike. Except that instead of Joan Lunden, she saw Christ Jesus. Go figure.

January 18, 1994
Kim: It's been a tough day. If I think specifically about my kitchen business, it's been a really tough month! I'm sitting on the bathroom floor in candlelight, hiding from the world for a little while, writing in my journal, trying to get out my "mean" feelings...

It's hard to separate the anger about my failing business from my anger about David's abrupt departure. A part of me wants to believe the business is failing because he left. He was such an important part of the success we were finally achieving. It feels yucky to be thinking angry thoughts about him. I thought we had such a solid friendship, and yet I feel abandoned. But keeping those emotions bottled up makes me feel worse. To top it all off, I have my period. I cry. It helps.

With some regret we cancel our first road trip. The weather is terrible. Blowing snow and sixty below wind chill. Instead we call another meeting of the Psychic Sorority.

This week we are excited about speaking with "them." Kim is especially in need of some uplifting words after her tough day.

Most of the doubt from last week has cleared. The information from and about Kanti and her trio is one more awesome affirmation.

We can't get over the idea that there is another group of three women trying to do this same thing. There seems to be something about the power of three. "They" keep telling us there are people all over the globe being called to this mission and there is something powerful in hearing "them" speak through a human voice.

We don't want to say it out loud, but we think *maybe* we're starting to believe.

The Angels
January 18, 1994

"Step-By-Step Instructions"

We would like to begin by telling you we are undergoing a great deal of transition amongst ourselves. Because you cannot see our development with your human eyes as we can see yours, we need to explain to you what is happening to us as you proceed. We'll do this with as much Earth plane terminology as we can without over-simplifying.

We are a great rank of angels. Last time, you envisioned us superimposed on your environment toasting you and raising our beer mugs. This time see us as a fleet of angels in the neo-classic sense, with very large white feathered wings and long white robes, hovering about, our wings aflutter.

We are divided into three different groups. It is like three different classes going on. The power of the triumvirate that works for you also works for us.

We are working together with different sets of guides who are working in other parts of the Earth plane. The guides are working with each other also, just as you are. In fact, all that happens on your Earth plane is a smaller imitation of what goes on in the ethers.

We have three sub-sets within our group. Different individuals are being taught the same thing within each group. There are four or five guides in each of these three groups. They are headed by one guide who is not above everyone else, but has a different job description or is playing a different role.

Kim, you have association with the four or five guides working mostly on helping you with presentation. It conjures up the image of standing in front of a mirror and practicing a speech or addressing the public. They are specifically assigned to help reveal to you what is in your heart and surrounding it with a courage that will eventually allow you to stand up in front of many people and speak, not only your own voice but our voices. This is a

continuation of the threads we began to weave the last time we
spoke with you.

As you look outward, your part in teaching much of the lessons
and concepts we have been handing down will certainly be that of
taking the information in and digesting it outwardly as a speaker
and a deliverer. This does not mean Barbara or Teresa will not be
doing that work. It means the set of guides assigned to those tasks
are working with you at this time. This is why your ability to say
how you feel is being improved.

You asked about your expression of sorrowing and pain
[before the meeting]. It is interesting that you defined it as part
of the physiological change of the menstrual cycle. The menstrual
cycle is an integral part of a woman's creative process. If she were
not told it was negative and given an opportunity to nurture that
creativity, she would find those times around the beginning of the
menstrual cycle more electrically charged than other times of that
cycle.

As you cleanse your emotional palate—and this is what that
experience was like—a feeling came like a charge of electricity. You
took it and turned it into physical words. You may think the
content of the words you wrote were part of a negative process or
the actual words felt like they came from a place of lack or low self-
esteem. But in keeping with our teachings, it is the process, the
telling. The physical act of bringing those emotions outward was
the key, not what was written or what was felt.

This process is helping these guides to understand more about
what magic is contained when this is done. They cannot do this
because they are not involved in the Earth plane. They can
observe, they can speak like we are all collectively speaking tonight.
But they are not human. They cannot cross that line by themselves. Your playing out of the drama, expressing those feelings,
are a part of their learning experience. This is another reason not
to put a judgment upon what happens in your Earth plane.

This is for all of you. This is working this dance of cooperation.
You may think this is a broken record, or you have not "gotten it,"
or whatever effect may come from us telling you this over and
over. In any case, we cannot stress to you enough why it is
important for you not to assign meaning to the events that go on
within your movie. It is alright to experience and to then relate,
as if you were witnessing it.

☆ ─────────────────────────────────────

There are two parts of self, the part that witnesses what is happening, and the part that is actually involved in the process. You can witness and explain. But to then go on and explain, "The reason this happened was because my children were ornery, or my husband was cranky, or the car wouldn't start, etc.," these things have nothing to do with it at all. There will be a reluctance on your part to relinquish the assignment of meaning.

It is unfathomable to think you would go through a day without defining. If this is not a table, and this is not a couch and that is not a light, then what would it be? We understand you are not at a point where you are ready to relinquish the definitions of the world. But we are giving you information about further down the road in your evolutionary process where you are ready to let go of those definitions.

We are not giving you this to tell you that you should be working harder, or to scare you into feeling some strange power is going to overtake you and you won't be able to live in the world anymore. We are simply telling you this for the record, so later on, when you have evolved, the record will have been laid down.

This is important—to lay the record down to be reviewed so that the beginning and the end and all that transpires in between these lessons and this evolutionary process can be studied and learned from. This is the importance of the journaling and the transcription. You hear us telling you and urging you constantly to write and record. We will continue to do that. It will be part of the success of what you are doing.

There are many, many people around the country who are like-minded. There are many people who go through this experience. You have met now three other women who we talk to regularly. You must understand that the bringing together of all these like minds is going to be hinged upon the written material you provide. This is the thing that will be able to be shared. To be read and sent to a friend, and have it be read and sent to a friend. The word of mouth is what led you here. It was as if somehow, one way or another, we got word to each of you. You came and listened and were affected on a deeper level, more than your conscious mind at first.

Do you not all agree there was a power that seemed to bring you together without your knowledge of why? There was simply a draw or attraction. The combination of forces is going to provide for the organizational skills needed to get this information into a physical form and out across the air waves or through the mail. It is going to be an important part of the business endeavor.

This brings us to the concept of money, which is still being worked out within you. You are still not aligned about the concepts of money. But you have come great strides from where you had been. You have constantly commented on this new-found courage about the concept of money. But there are a few more blocks to be removed before you can go forward with the manifestation of that.

One of those blocks you possess is that money is a magical thing, and once you have it, it makes things come true. It is the converse of that—making things come true creates the money. You find yourself wondering about how to make this operation move faster so you can reap the rewards. What we are doing, and you have felt us doing this, is guiding you to the physical writing.

This is the second group of guides who work with Barbara. There is a process of taking the writings and bringing them together in a cohesive and "marketable" presentation. This is involved in the blockages. We are speaking more to Barbara specifically. There is within her mind doubt that to make something marketable will give it less validity, and there is something "inherently wrong" with actually approaching this project from a marketable standpoint. This is a misconception.

The concept of marketing has been polluted by people and organizations whose sole goal is to make you spend your money on their product, whether you need it or not. Your approach to the very legitimate concept of marketing is to make this information available to people who need it. The reason you need their money is so you can make it available to them.

Within this concept is the idea—again you are humans living in the Earth plane—that you work for a living and get paid for what you do. So incorporate the two ideas that you must work for a living and get paid for what you do, and that you want to market these written materials and ideas to people who are in need.

There are many people around the country who speak the voices and listen, and utilize other non-physical realms of communication, but there is a need for the writing done in this way to solidify those people. You will do it in such a way that no one has ever done it before. It would be like a periodical where people can

☆

write in questions and have them answered, somewhat in the form of an advice column but dealing more metaphysically. Within the group of the three of you, Barbara has been the one we have been motivating to physically sit down and collect the parts to be put together.

At this time *[Kim and Teresa]* do not have individual writings to put down, but this shall come soon. Then you will put them all together and create a written piece and look for publication, as we spoke of earlier. Barbara is more well-versed at this point in the organization of the writing.

The third group of guides deal with taking what you experience and interpreting it from a heart place. The group of guides helping Teresa are doing that. You have a need within you to feel emotionally safe. They are there surrounding you with a great deal of love, encouragement and support.

These three groups working with each of you will then move to the next. These guides also perform these same guiding lessons on other human beings. That these are the same lessons for all of the world is part of this concept.

You have finally come in contact with three other people who have also been working with us. They, too, have been learning. They have not had the advantage of hearing such a clear voice as you hear tonight. But they have been undergoing these lessons and meeting us in that interface between the worlds you create through your meditation.

As the originators of the recording, you are going to help them solidify. This has happened already on the smallest scale. This is what you will be doing on a much larger scale with many, many people. It is not that you are better than anyone else, or more advanced, or more evolved. It is simply that you have been chosen to be the ones to take this movement to a forefront. Again, not to say that others have not spoken of these kinds of concepts and ideas and have not worked in these realms. There are many. Your mission has been laid out. It is beginning.

This is why this past week has been very telling. It is one of the first steps in experiencing the effects of what happens when the guides and the Earthlings speak together and record with people who are virtual strangers. Recording is a very important part. We mean recording by the written word and the tape recording and any kind of history you can leave. Call it a paper trail. This will help verify your experiences as time goes on. Already you heard what was spoken in your small group and saw the events come to pass. This brings a beautiful meaning to the words that were spoken before the events transpired. This is the kind of documentation you will need to turn the heads of people who will need validation.

There are many you need not "preach" to who are already "converted." But your audience is going to consist of people who may not necessarily fall into your ranks. You must understand that those people are given the same mystery to unravel as you. Everyone is. How they choose to unravel it will determine how much personal power they will accumulate.

Keep on as much as you can with the transcribing of the tapes and making these papers available to those who are interested in them. They will be a trail leading you to the places you have agreed to go.

We do have what you have been looking for: step-by-step instructions. This particular set of instructions are for your meditation. Your ability to release the physical world while still in a conscious mind and go into the realms that lie between the physical world and the ethers will be essential for your development.

Teresa has begun this process with her meditation that led her to see the world view from the higher place. You still need to distinguish the voices of your ego self and our timbres and wavelengths. But you have begun to experience this world.

Here are the instructions:

1. Breathing is essential to remove yourself from the sensations of the three dimensions and five senses. As you breathe in, you are breathing in the source of all life. Do not take for granted that you are just breathing in air. Think about it as it enters your body. Physiologically, the molecules of oxygen are absorbed into the lining of your lungs and carried through the blood stream to the ends of your body, to the tips of your toes and into the deepest parts of all your organs. In an ethereal sense, you are breathing in the "stuff of life," energy that creates and

takes away life. Without that one breath, your existence would be altered dramatically.

As you breathe, picture all the concepts and hopes and dreams and ideals you want to actualize in the physical world beginning in the breath. As you breathe, you breathe in those dreams and hopes and ideals. They are then carried throughout your body to be a part of your cells and your physical memory system. They need to be there in order for you to call upon them to actualize them into reality.

2. Reach a point of calm. It does not have to be complete and absolute silence, but simply a stillness not shaken or disturbed by the ramblings of the ego self. Look for a meadow or clearing, some kind of physical spot overlooking a long view of foothills and a ravine going down and stretching off into the distant mountains.

   Picture this under the full moonlight. As you envision this meadow with this beautiful view, stand there and see the light of the full moon, which is far more mystical and ethereal than the full sun. See yourselves, the three of you in this meadow, holding hands and dancing and laughing, as if you have already transcended that veil, as if you have come to a point where you are living in both worlds simultaneously. This meadow with this beautiful view and the full moonlight is the magical spot where you come to meet.

3. When you assemble there together, take some time to sit down and watch who walks down your path. We will be there and you can talk to us directly. This kind of meditation can be recorded through automatic writing. Ask us questions and you will receive answers. In fact, under these conditions, you can ask specifics. It will be interesting to get the answers.

4. After you have experienced this vision, be sure to take note of the details. Notice the mood. Look for any other kind of detail that may change from meditation to meditation. Was there an apple tree in the orchard? Was there snow on the mountain? What time of year was it? Whatever detail was available to you, take note and bring it back on your memory.

5. When you have returned from your meditation, immediately write down all you have seen. Then come together and compare notes. Often times you will all meet in the same place. Through this kind of interaction you will begin to shake loose even more the bonds of the physical definition of things.

Kim: *"We wanted to ask you about the difference in tone we experienced in our last session together. It may have something to do with the transition you're talking about that you've experienced, but we all felt a little confused last week. I wondered if you could comment on that."*

What occurred last week was that your three different perspectives were shifted and shaken up. There were also a number of guides in the same predicament. While you came together with different attitudes and doubts and questioned the process of what was happening, they also did the same. They were delivering the message to you and you were delivering the message to the physical world. Their apparent confusion or unfamiliar tone was due to the fact that they, too, were undergoing their own changes.

You can't really say they were going through the same kind of self-doubt you were because it isn't really applicable. There was a lesson they were being challenged by. They were fighting to speak. Just as "I" have been speaking for all of us, they were all fighting for a chance to express their viewpoint.

If you listen to the recording, you will hear fluctuations that change quickly. When we say fighting, we do not mean beating on each other with their fists or shoving each other out of the way. It was simply a desire to take advantage of the opening that was presented.

☆

We have decided at this time to announce that there will be a change of voice. Another now will speak.

Sometimes we want to come back to the Earth plane, although it's not a real possibility or desire. It is like wanting to go back to being a child. You wouldn't really now, if you thought about it. You would think of all the difficulty and pain you had growing up. But there is a, sort of, what's the word, utopian or fantasized image of what it would be like to be young again. That is what we sometimes feel about being human.

It is so thrilling to do this. There are not a lot of people on the Earth plane that allow this to happen. Think about it. Think about all the people who would let us speak this way. Not many. So when the chance arises to express ourselves through whatever little window of opportunity there is, we try to climb through it.

Some of us are not well versed at speaking. It is like having to learn to be, what do you call them, toastmasters. Just as in your world, the process of learning to communicate is frustrating. Sometimes, it is for us that we stumble and stutter, but we enjoy to communicate with you.

In the next two weeks you will find some money. It may not be, to you, a great deal of money. We see you looking down at a bowl of money and laughing at how this is the beginning. And indeed it is. You need to examine the information you were told earlier about the resistance you have to accepting this money.

We hear your thought process even now. We are well aware that each of you would gladly accept money given to you. Do not force the issue, but keep in mind you still have blocks. In order to deal with them, the best methodology for you, when you are in your meditation or when you are "peeling carrots," is to ask for those blocks to be revealed. Then let go and forget. They will come to you in revelations.

As you stand there with this new, small first bit of money, bless it and give it away as soon as you can. Keep enough to do your next publication but then quickly give it away.

Also in the next two weeks, there will be a young man who will come to hear us who will be shaken open. He will be looking to you for guidance, which you will freely give.

————————————————————————————————— ☆

What is so beautiful about you women to us is that your hearts are so large and willing and filled with love and patience. The only time you have impatience, generally speaking, is for yourselves. This is something we don't understand—how you can have such patience for those you love but you so resist turning it for yourselves. Try to do that for yourselves in the next few weeks. Give yourself patience whenever anything becomes rough, difficult, painful, angry. The first thing you say is "I will have patience." That alone will soften all the blows.

In the next two weeks, also look for another woman to come into the group who has not been a part of the group yet, though you may know her, that will bring you interesting news about other experiences other people are having that will be very reaffirming.

Are there more questions?

Teresa: *"While I was meditating the other night, I felt very successful at it. Part of what I saw was exactly as you described, about the three of us in the meadow frolicking. But the other part was thinking of people I am close to and love and envisioning them on their paths. Can you tell me how accurate that was?"*

You saw what you saw. You saw the path while aligned to the energy of the guides. Accurate as far as what is actually happening in their lives? Only you can tell. Is it true what you saw? Does it ring true within you? Then that piece of doubt can be removed. You need to know you are far more powerful than you understand.

This is for both of you. In the next few weeks we would like to ask you to start to write our words. It will come quite naturally. It will happen at your place of business. You will be on the computer. You will find it so much fun you will have to be careful not to overdo so you won't lose sight of other things. It will be a breakthrough.

It does not necessarily begin with your vocal chords. It will start with your computer. You must take these step-by-step bits of information you are learning and experience it a little bit at a time. Do not rush into thinking you need to conduct your own sessions in the next few weeks. Be patient. Give yourself patience.

Do not, under any circumstances, underestimate the power of what you will see. A side of you will not believe it. Another side will be exhilarated by the experience. Disregard the disbelief. Allow it

☆

room to think and feel. If you must, use your disbelief in a humorous fashion, but know you are moving ahead at warp speed at understanding and will soon be able to speak the voices. All that has been said and done up until this point has been beneficial and necessary steps in your education. You are excellent students. By excelling at what you have done thus far, we, too, excel.

We are tremendously excited about watching this project take root and bloom. Ask for assistance. Always ask. The more specific you can be, the better. Communicate with us. It is not that we know everything and are going to orchestrate every detail of the undertaking. Part of the process—and again, for the hundred millionth time, the process is the magic—is your communication with us done through meditation, prayer, discussion and also through asking. You have all experienced the reality of asking and receiving. Recently it has been rather quick to occur, has it not? So do not be afraid to ask for help. Open yourself up to the idea it will happen very soon but be patient to allow it to happen in its own time.

We are so filled with love for you. We so treasure our relationship to you. You can never again feel alone surrounded by so many angels, hovering above you, in you, outside of you, surrounding you with a beautiful deep blue full moon light. You are flying with us in your own right. Come again with specific questions. We will do our very best to give you what you need.

Most of all, thank you for your openness and your cooperation. It is greatly appreciated. Working together in harmony in this way will also teach you to work together in harmony with other human beings on the Earth plane. This is the message for the masses at this time—not to dominate with a particular point of view but to walk in everyone else's shoes and then turn around and give support to each other. Your mission is very important and will be highly successful. You need simply to watch and be amazed!

☆

Later that night . . .

Kim: It's interesting how the angels are helping us re-frame the way we look at the events of our lives. We are learning that even the seemingly bad things have positive meaning when we look for the lesson in each experience.

Tonight the angels told me that I help them understand more about how we humans process feelings and work out problems. They said the content of my journal entry earlier today, which to me felt like I was being mean, isn't what is most important. What matters most is the process I went through, writing there in the quiet of the bathroom, trying to work things out.

There seems to be something significant about putting the emotions onto paper. I always knew it helped me to write my feelings down, but apparently it helps the angels, too. It seems to give them concrete information that helps them formulate guidelines on how to work with us. It always amazes me when I think the angels are evolving right along with us.

Every time they help us work through a problem with a little less turbulence than the last time, we all advance in our development.

January 19, 1994

Teresa: I try meditating again, this time using the step-by-step instructions from last night's session. I still can't believe they gave us step-by-step instructions!

Up until now, all I could do was breathe a lot, but I didn't see any visions. It's virtually impossible to find a place of total peace and quiet. Every time I sit down a dog and three cats are fighting to sit on my lap. And of course, I think I'm doing it wrong.

Tonight I just keep breathing until all the animals settle into their spots. "They" tell me to use the words "I know" as a mantra. I close my eyes and repeat the words in my head, picturing them swirling in front of my face. With each breath I breathe in those words.

I get to a peaceful place manifested in my mind as a beautiful meadow. Kim, Barbara and I are frolicking in the clearing in a circle, looking much like angels ourselves with flowing white dresses and flowers in our hair.

Then Kanti, Rita and Lois appear. Even though I haven't met these women yet, I somehow know it's them. The six of us hold hands and dance in the circle. We then sit down by the side of the path. The angels say to pay particular attention to who might walk by. The moment they say this, I become aware of being in two places at once. There's the me that's *witnessing* the meditation, and the me that's *participating* in it.

As the witness, I sense there are others there with me, waiting to "enter on cue." As the participant, I sit by the path, waiting nervously. I sense someone is about to emerge, but I have no idea who it will be.

My father, who passed away in 1989, is the first. He walks down the path. When he stops in front of me, I run up and hug him. Then my mother, who passed away in 1979, suddenly appears by his side.

My father says, "I'm sorry we had to leave you. I know how much you've needed us lately." Then my mother says, "It's so wonderful here." I feel her bliss as she speaks the words.

They stroll down the path. Next, my sister Bobbie is waiting in the wings. My conscious mind says "She's not dead. She can't be here." When I look again, she is gone and I see my grandmother, who passed away when I was in high school. She doesn't say anything. She just waves.

I come out of the meditation with an overwhelming sense of peace. I realize even though my parents are gone from me in physical life, they are never really gone from me. What a wonderful revelation.

☆ ☆ ☆

Sometimes it's difficult to assess the effects these teachings are having on our daily lives because there is no more repetitive, predictable flow to what may happen in a day. Most of our time is spent talking about these lessons and how they are affecting us. Each day we talk, Barbara in her office at home, and Kim and Teresa on the speaker phone at work, sharing our dreams and meditations. Some days it seems like five or six miracles occur, other days just one or two. It's so amazing, most of the time we are speechless.

Our definition of miracle has changed. We're not talking about visions of the Virgin Mary, saving our children from speeding cars, or a reversal of a life-threatening illness, although these certainly fall under the heading of miraculous. A lot of the miracles are simply revelations about what is happening to us. The biggest miracle of all seems to be this new perspective we are developing and the peace that is coming from it.

Another reoccurring miracle is the messages we receive when we analyze our dreams. Every morning we have graphic, colorful tales of where we were the night before. We are finding that dreams aren't simply night wanderings of the mind. They are brilliantly constructed movies, filled with lessons meant specifically for us. We apply a dream analysis method we learned on "Oprah," and we're able to extract the lessons and apply them immediately to our lives.

The analysis is based on the dreamer's personal and very specific definition of each component of the dream. The dreamer defines the component as if they are describing it to an alien from another planet who knows nothing about life on Earth. The answers to the meaning of the dream are within the actual words the dreamer chooses to define the components. In this way, we receive the personal messages and lessons contained in our dreams.

"They" say it's easy to exist in the ethereal world. It's out in the streets, in the process of living normal daily life, what they call the *front lines*, where the process becomes difficult. So we've taken to listening to the tapes of our sessions to learn even more about how to apply these lesson to our lives. As we do, we're waking up to the realization of what our conscious minds have been doing to us through the years of listening to these habitual tapes telling us we aren't good enough. Now the angels are giving us new "tapes." And we're finally listening.

It does feel like we're being shaken loose from this grip we have on three-dimensional reality. On the other hand, it's almost impossible to convince our conscious minds that this is really happening.

We all find it increasingly difficult to concentrate on the work at hand. For Kim and Teresa, it's kitchens, for Barbara it's music. We're becoming more and more detached from the things that have been the most important to each of us.

Kim and Teresa: Here we are, running a small business, no work, no money to pay bills, no prospects. We care, but we aren't worried. We're beginning to believe in the process so strongly there are times when we're unable to worry. Talk about a daily miracle!

Barbara: For as long as I can remember I've dreamt of being successful in the music business. Now, here I am, doing my first real recording project, investing my own money, and I can hardly force myself into my studio at home to do the prep work. Years of wanting to record a serious piece of work, and here I am, unable to get enthused.

What in the world is becoming of us?

We feel like we're being driven by forces outside the control of our conscious minds. It's the angels influencing us to undertake "their" mission. Not that we're complaining. After all, not only were we chosen, but we volunteered for this mission. And we love the classes, the investigation, the probing and watching as life unfolds just as they say, but we still need some kind of physical occurrence or stream of events that will allow our conscious minds to catch up with what we know in our souls without a doubt.

January 21, 1994
Kim: "I am beginning to look like myself."

This statement has double meaning for me, the first of which became clear today. When I checked out of my marriage, I weighed one hundred and eighty-one pounds, fifty pounds more than I needed to. I looked as bad as I felt. I even told Clay that I had built a fifty-pound wall between us over the last several years.

Since then I have lost forty-seven pounds and I am light years away from the person I was just twelve short months ago. I see a different person, physically and spiritually, when I look in the mirror.

The second meaning is harder to explain. All my life, when I looked in the mirror, I always thought, "That's not me. There's a different person inside of me than the one I see when I look in the mirror." I haven't told this to many people in my life, because it doesn't make much sense, unless you've felt it.

Now it doesn't matter if I am fat or thin, having a good hair day or if my shoes match my handbag. I always knew there was something missing I couldn't see when I looked at my reflection in the mirror. I knew it had nothing to do with my outward appearance, but I kept looking for it there anyway.

Now I am beginning to see it.

It's not the fact that I look so different physically. It's that I'm watching myself bloom, right before my very eyes. Now when I look in the mirror, I see my spirit, my soul. I'm beginning to actually look different on the outside because I feel so different on the inside.

January 25, 1994.

Kim: Standing in the showroom this morning, Teresa and I philosophize about the state of our kitchen design business. It feels like we've hit an all time low. We have no money and no real job prospects, which means no money is coming in. Often we can elevate our spirits by focusing on our angels and the lessons we are learning, but today we are just plain scared to death.

We nurture the process every step of the way: We follow up on sales leads; we get our drawings done on time; we make all of our calls. Still there is nothing. No matter how hard we try or how much we do it right, nothing is working. We haven't sold a job of any consequence since early December. The money is gone from the few small jobs we did since our last major project. Bills are piling up. Bill collectors are calling. We're trying to keep our spirits up, but we can't get a break. The harder we try, the worse it gets, and it's getting very, very dark.

In almost six years in this business, I've never had a dry spell like this. In the early days I was terrified of selling and did everything I could to avoid it, which meant we sometimes didn't have enough work. If we hit a dry spell in those days it was understandable.

Now, here we are, following the angels' instructions. We're working the process, staying in the moment, doing everything right, and still getting no results. It doesn't make sense...so we decide to look at it from another perspective.

Our fear is like standing on the very top of a mountain in a space so small there is only room for our two pairs of tiny feet standing next to one another. What we need is a leap of faith. All we have to do

☆ ————————————————————

is have faith our angels will not let us fall down the side of that mountain. If we can find just enough faith to take that one small step forward, into what seems to be only thin air, either the ground will rise up beneath us, or our angels will be there under our feet holding us up.

With this beautiful picture of being held up on the wings of angels, painted in our minds and with our words, we know we will not perish, all of our work in vain. After all, we're doing our best. We're doing all that we can do. The end result is not what matters most. What matters is to live in the moment and nurture the process every moment. And we're certainly doing that.

We don't know what will happen physically to our business. We have come to understand there is purpose in whatever lesson we're learning. We have faith we're doing the best job we can, and that our angels will not leave us.

With this new found faith in our hearts we're able to go on. We know the kitchen business will live on only as long as is necessary to get us through the transition into...what? We can't rightly say just now.

☆

CHAPTER THREE
The Green Shirt Day

All of us agree that the group on December 14th felt like a rehearsal. Tonight is like the real thing. Kanti is bringing Rita and Lois.

Barbara: For many years I've noticed that when I pass under streetlights, they go off or on. Lately the frequency has picked up. I shared the growing coincidence with the people at the group, and, much to my surprise, everyone has been experiencing it. And not only just streetlights, all sorts of weird electrical things are happening around us. My sister walks by her light in the living room and it flashes off and on. Steve, my psychic engineer, says his effects machines have been going on and off with no explainable cause. Kim's windshield wipers go on for no reason.

Thank heaven we have each other to verify these findings. Otherwise, we would all be headed for some serious time off in a well-padded, secure place.

Everyone feels a little giddy. Our solar plexuses are vibrating. What is this nervousness about—the angels getting stage fright?

☆ ☆ ☆

Fifteen people show up. And two men! Our first coed sorority party! There is a terrible snowstorm and miserable cold. Barbara has a nasty respiratory infection and a ferocious cough. She is concerned about being able to speak without coughing into the tape recorder. We all converse for about an hour as people congregate slowly. Perfect strangers don't feel a need to make small talk. Anticipation hangs in the air like the Christmas lights.

And so it has officially begun.

THE ANGELS
January 25, 1994

"Conflict Resolution"

Tonight we see a sparkling sky filled with the brilliant light of many stars. You have come together with a common goal in mind, though it may not have been conscious mind.

There is a mystery involved in coming together on this crossroads. There is purpose in that mystery. Having preconceived ideas of how events are going to fall limits your view of many other things within the situation.

Tonight, you have people who have never heard us speak before, some who have heard or been in the periphery, and others who are sitting in the center. This is not a reflection of ability to understand. It is a declaration of experience.

Within each of you individually, and then as a group, is a voice that speaks. It is not the particular voice speaking now, and it may not be our particular voices. It is the collection of voices raised together to form one voice. This is the evolutionary process. It seems simplistic to say it in this way and yet we know no better way to describe it.

Think of it as the individual parts forming together to make one large collective part. In this way, it is like a body. Think of each one of you as a particular part to the body. This person might serve the function of the kidneys. This person might serve the function of the heart. This person might be involved in the function of the brain. In this way, each individual has their own purpose, but are all working together for the common good of the body.

Within each of your bodies you would not have your kidney be in conflict with your heart, or your stomach in conflict with your veins. It is important for all of you to understand the necessity of looking at each other as parts of a body rather than human beings in conflict. This particular lesson can not be stressed enough for you.

☆ ────────────────────────────────

You often come in contact with people who you think cause you conflict. This seems unavoidable. Yet, you are the source of that conflict. You can look at someone else and lay claim to their actions and how they are causing a conflict within your life, but every conflict you are involved in is within your own self. The source is within your own self.

If you begin to look at life that way, you begin to see where your power actually lies in being able to resolve these conflicts. If you do not believe this is the basis of the evolutionary process, you only have to look around at how much conflict is in your world, not just in your own personal lives, but in the bigger world, the global community, the country, the state, the cities, the block, your home and your own minds.

Constantly dealing with conflicts is the road to evolutionary change. It may seem futile or counterproductive, but it is not.

It is through the resolution of the conflict that the Earth plane will evolve.

There are many on the Earth plane who are not attuned to understanding this within self. Even many of you here find this conceptually plausible, but in your heart it is easier to point at someone else and make them the source of the conflict. What you begin to understand as you embrace this idea is how to prevent yourself from fueling the fire of the conflict.

We begin with this concept because it is indeed the basis of evolution. You cannot evolve without embracing this concept. The Earth plane cannot evolve without overcoming the conflicts within its reality at this time. It is a slow process to you, but from our perspective, where there is no time, it is neither slow nor fast, it simply is.

Part of resolving conflicts has to do with the judgments you make. We cannot stress this enough for you. When you are in a group of people—your work situation, or neighborhood, or church—and look upon your fellow human beings in a judgmental way, you limit your ability to see them for who they truly are: souls involved on the Earth plane.

If you look at them as human incarnates, with all of their flaws, it will seem easy to judge them as bad or small-minded or unlike you. By judging them, you separate yourself from them. Thus you create the illusion and live under the misconception you are either different from them or better than they are, or perhaps, not as good. In some way, you draw a line that differentiates you from them.

☆

If you could see from our perspective, you would see the human race as one body. You would see a cluster of humanity that functions as the heart, one that functions as the liver. You would see altogether how humanity functions as a whole. The illness, the wars, the strife of your society is reflected in that image to us like a sickly person is reflected to you. Cancer in your society is the reflection of that inner conflict.

When you make a judgment of people and separate yourself, you contribute to the cause of the conflict. We hear voices now from your conscious minds saying how difficult it would be to not have judgments. You think it's necessary to have judgments in order to define reality. This is not so.

You can say, "That is a table." That is not a judgment, that is a definition. If you say, "That is a useless table," then you are making a judgment. When you think that is a useless table because it does not meet needs within you, you are totally disregarding the fact that other people may be putting their feet on it, or it is supporting the magazines and the candles. Your judgment of it is from a totally subjective point of view. That separates you from the table.

It is perhaps a difficult thing to conceptualize at this time, but you are not separate from the table. It appears you are because the three dimensions and the five senses draw the lines separating skin from wood, but you are one with that table. You are one with each other.

This is the continuing lesson that needs to be played for you as human beings on a regular basis. It is not because you are stupid or incapable of learning. It is simply the constructs of these five senses, these three dimensions are so severe in your eyes.

You have lived so intensely in this focus that the idea of being one with the table does not make sense on some level. Yet, on another level, you have been taught in your spiritual upbringing that you are one with each other. The teachings of Christ Jesus emphasize this to a great degree. Throughout the ages, these teachings have been interpreted and translated into a more human level, which has taken away from the impact and the power. Yet the basic teaching is that we are all one with each other.

Now we are telling you that you are also one with us. We share a common mind and a similar soul. Within each of you is a piece of your soul that intersects all other souls, including those of us who are here in what you have been calling the ethers. It is like a mathematical equation where a form has a common piece within and another form has the same common piece, until all human beings and souls are superimposed upon each other, sharing that piece of the soul common to all.

That is what you term God, or Higher Power. As we see you, you are sitting. We see you in your human form, separate, each in your own chairs, in your own places. But (and we will use these terms figuratively) up from behind you are these long arms of your soul that go back to the part of your soul that is viewing from a higher level. Within that part of your soul is that piece that is common to everything that lives and breathes, every bit of consciousness. That piece of God is in you.

Consequently, being human is your access to God and what you need to learn and develop in order to evolve. Take that piece that is within you and grow it until it fills your very being. In this way, it is much like a hand puppet. If you were the hand puppet simply lying lifeless on the table, it is the hand of God that would come and fill up your being and make you move and think. This is the set-up of being on the Earth plane and being human.

What has happened throughout the course of evolution is that a component within the thinking process, called the ego, has gotten out of control. It has taken over and influenced the development of human beings and culture. Now your "job" is to counteract that. This job has been set up for you throughout the course of the ages through spiritual teaching that has been passed down from generation to generation.

In this particular time, there is an opportunity for you to make a quantum leap. We cannot talk to you enthusiastically enough about this, because it is a magnificently exciting time for all of you. This is a magnificent opportunity for you to do the unbelievable. This goes back to taking that bit of God that is within you and expanding it and filling up self from within that peace.

What that will require of you is to find a way to diminish ego without completely obliterating it. Then you would lose the identity of who each of you are individually. Your ego defines you. It makes you into who you are in this particular life. Every life that you lived has a different ego involved, but the same soul. In order to fill up your inner self with this part of the soul, you first must

☆

recognize that piece of soul is within everyone. It is shared. It is a common quality that every single life form, human being, individual has.

When you look at someone and judge them as different, you diminish the soul part of self within you by allowing the ego to fill up more of yourself. If you fill yourself up with the part of soul that is the interface where we work with you, you begin to see where your responsibility for the conflict lies. Then you are able to diminish conflict and create peace from within. As you recognize this part of your own heart in your fellow human beings, this gets taken out and put in their heart.

Suddenly, do they not look different? Suddenly do you not see your heart beating in their body? Do you not feel more compassion? Do you not feel more understanding, as though you have enough patience to listen and to resolve whatever kind of conflict may arise? This is essential for your development. We cannot stress this enough.

Begin tomorrow experimenting with this perception. View every single human that crosses your path in this way. They are carrying around within their bodies a piece of your heart. Then you begin to find a sense of protection for them rather than constantly being in conflict with them.

This is not something that will overtake you instantaneously. This is not something you will simply be able to do at a snap of a finger. But as you begin to play with this idea and apply this to every scenario where you are experiencing conflict, you will see dramatic effects take place. It does not matter—your children, your partners, your co-workers, your parents—everyone you apply this concept to will show a dramatic change within. How human beings deal with each other is the essence of the evolutionary change.

There are so many who are lost now. You might count yourselves among them. On particular days as you drive or sit or whatever activity you are engaged in, there is a sense of confusion and loss that is prevalent at this time. We strongly feel you understand this intrinsically. It is a confusion. It is not a loss as if "all is lost." It is simply this sense that you have been working and working and where are you going? It is a frustration of wanting more instruction and intrinsic understanding you can apply to daily situations that can help you to evolve.

☆ ───

We can give you that. We can give you step-by-step instructions. We have indeed tried. Your part is to understand that the evolutionary process is not necessarily something that will come out of the sky like a lightening bolt, give you great insight and leave you complete. You must understand and again, we cannot stress this enough, you will constantly be undergoing the process of evolution. It is a constant.

There is a familiar phrase that says the only thing that does not change is that everything changes. This embodies the idea of the evolutionary process. The more you can embrace the idea as a state of mind, rather than something that occasionally may happen to you, or something that will happen and be over with, the more you can apply evolution to every event of your life, to every person that you meet. Every instance of being alive offers you an opportunity to evolve. You can embrace it and see it that way, then look for the miracles that come out of it.

Or you can resist and cause conflict. You can bury your head in the sand. Some days you may have to. You may feel a need to be resistant and let your ego self take over. Even in those times, know it is only a moment that is passing until you will emerge again to throw yourself into the events of the world and learn this evolution.

There is a very important time occurring right now in your Earth plane. It is a period that began a little before the beginning of this particular year and is going to move into the spring. It is not a long period. But it is a time of great possibility. When things are thrown up in the air, it is the time between when they are thrown and when they come down. There is this sense now that everything is all sort of helter-skelter.

But look at this as a fertile time to do psychic and spiritual development. Look in the day-to-day undertakings. Do not look necessarily in going to church once a week or a time to meditate. We are not saying you should not do these things. We are saying move your focus into the everyday events. Find a focus that will allow you to see through them with your human eyes.

Look into the human heart of the person sitting beside you in the restaurant, or your co-worker. Actually physically look in, see past the clothing, past the skin. Look in and see the heart beating. We are trying to get you to focus your attention on the day-to-day. What might be seemingly unimportant events will hold the answers to your questions.

Yes, engage yourself in meditation, go to church and worship, read books of inspiration and information, but do not overlook the other scenarios that are happening right before your eyes. These are where you will find God. These are where you will find God within you. These are where you find God that connects your God to your God to your God, thus and so on out, until you have created a beautiful body of humanity that works together. Is that not your goal? Is that not your desire?

Those who have begun this organization wish to better the world through their children. Children know nothing else but what is before them. They are absorbed in the process. Do you remember when you were children, how it seemed like time was eternity? That is because all eternity is contained in the moment. So when you leave here and go off in your world tomorrow and come in contact with other human beings, you will see a dramatic difference in how you perceive them. In these moments you will find that evolutionary change.

We need to tell you how important your humor is. Isn't it true that humor can unite? For example, when you tell a joke, everyone laughs and shares in the same emotion, providing, of course, it's a good enough joke. Humor cannot be overlooked. Finding humor in every situation lightens your load.

You must not underestimate the power of laughter. As you begin to look at your fellow human beings in the way we have suggested, throw in a little dose of humor. Gaze upon the fellow who is sitting next to you on the bus. As you gaze through his clothing and into his heart, think perhaps about what color his underwear is. Giving yourself a little chuckle is more freeing than being heavy and somber.

To take yourself so seriously is counterproductive. It counteracts the effects of trying to bring yourselves together. This humor doesn't have to be degrading or sarcastic, but the seriousness makes you feel self important. The whole idea here is for us to get you to feel less self important.

It is not that you are not important. In fact, each and every one of you is tremendously important. You each have a purpose to fulfill here, but for you to think constantly that you are so important defeats the purpose of you being important.

There is a difference between sarcasm, a self-defeating, cynical, biting humor, and satire. Satire is where nothing is reverent. You

☆ ————————————————————————————

can make fun in a lighthearted way of just about anything. Making fun of yourself in any situation is tremendously powerful. It puts you in a place of having nothing to lose. If you have nothing to lose, then there is no danger. There is no risk because you have already lost everything. That is quite an advantageous place to be. Who can then come and take from you, who can rob you, who can steal? Who can take your dignity, or self-respect, or anything when you have already freely relinquished it all?

There you sit with nothing but a mind and a heart. If you begin to laugh, you see that you actually are very rich. You have everything you need. The reason no one can take this away from you is not because you really don't have it. It is because you will not allow it. When someone comes to "make fun" of you, you can simply join in and throw your head back and agree. You see how that diminishes and illuminates conflict? Isn't it amazing!

We feel it is quite evident to you the different personalities sharing themselves with you tonight. This gathering is an invaluable platform for us. We are learning to speak to you this way. This is something that is going on all across the planet. In keeping with the theme of being a part of a body of humans, at this very moment in other parts of the country and other parts of the world, people are coming together in this very way, allowing us the time and the energy to speak.

Every personality that comes through has a purpose in the lessons they give to you, but it also helps them evolve. This has not ever been so widespread on the Earth plane as it is now. This evolutionary change happening has not occurred on the Earth plane in this civilization. That is why we are lining up to speak.

One purpose to having you come regularly is so you yourselves will be able to hear our voices. If you could all hear our voices in this way (which you can), you would have direct access to the interface within you—this place of God. Entering and speaking through a channel, and hearing the voice is the interface that is common to both us and you.

Meeting in meditation is a different kind of power. *That* is a dreamtime power, gathered in the ethers in that world. It is not unimportant or not powerful. *This* way, done in the three dimensions, in the five senses, holds far more impact on the conscious mind *because* it is done through the senses. In meditation and in dreams you are in that ethereal world, that eternal world. That reinforces that side of life.

It is *very* powerful to hear us speak with a human voice! This is why we ask you to come. The process of giving you this information with a human body is far more impacting than anything you can otherwise experience in the three dimensions. It is something you can later say was not as miraculous as it seems because you tend to forget. But as it is happening *now*, you cannot deny. You can say perhaps Barbara may not have that kind of insight into each of you individually.

We would like to give you an opportunity to each ask us questions. Feel free to have it be either a general question about the nature of this evolutionary change, or something specific to your particular life. It is not important to deal in generalities so that all will understand. What is important here tonight is that you have an opportunity to feel our voice directed into your heart, into that interface we all share, so the connection will be made even stronger. Then when you go out into the world tomorrow morning you can recall that connection. It will fade, but then come back and reinforce it. It will fade again, but not to the degree it did before. Come back and reinforce it. When we say "come back," we do not necessarily mean "come back constantly to this very room." Come back to the voices within your head, having heard them now so strongly. When you hear them within you, they will be even clearer.

"Do you, meaning you the entities, have a vision of where you think this is all heading to? Is there any kind of vision, or is this just a continuing process that keeps going on and on?"

Speaking specifically about the Earth plane? *Yes.* The vision we have is that human beings regain the use of their intuition so strongly that they begin to deal with each other from a place of soul as opposed to human beings. This will have a tremendous impact upon the Earth plane. Speaking of it in this way will affect the evolutionary process and how people deal with each other.

The goal sounds rather simplistic—world peace. Can you imagine that? It is difficult. But these are the beginnings of planting seeds of peace within each individual human being. The entire history of civilization has led up to this. These lessons, these groups, these training sessions that are going on all over the world are uniting people on that level.

☆ ——————————————————————————————

It will affect such a dramatic change that you will become a person you have not even dreamt of. The next few months are going to be very dramatic, for all of you. You are going to unearth the source of this fear within you. You have been working on this for quite some time in your lives. You will have major revelations about not only the source of the fear, but how to overcome it.

You will overcome the fear from within you. You will see this fear as part of your ego and your self-importance. As the ego shrinks, you open up space within to allow your intuition to take over and make your decisions for you, rather than falling into the analytical phases of weighing this and weighing that and should and can't and will and won't. It will be instantaneous decision-making—making and accepting a decision and knowing you will derive what you need from it. The strength and the courage that come from overcoming the fear will be phenomenal for you. This is going to greatly change the way you deal with life.

"I have a question regarding some of the choices and changes I'm personally trying to deal with right now. What insight do you have into ways for me to pursue them?"

A very large tree has fallen in your path. You have been sitting in front of this tree thinking about how you're going to get past it. You've thought of many different ideas of how to overcome this obstacle. You've surveyed the tree. You've pushed it and it's too heavy. If you had a chain saw, perhaps you could saw your way through it, but you don't have a chain saw. You wish some big machine could come and help you push it out of the way.

You've been sitting and thinking about this, but this is not really the impasse right now. You are so focused on what this obstacle is that you have forgotten you have the resources to overcome it.

You will find a resource within yourself that you didn't think you had that will allow you to overcome this obstacle. You are going to bodily climb over it or around it. Because the tree is so large and the branches extend so far, to go around one way and climb your way through the branches would be too complex and messy.

We strongly feel that you'll figure that out and decide to go around the other way where the roots are, because it's uprooted and flat and you can walk around. By going that way, by making that decision, you'll see where the roots of this conflict and these

☆

obstacles lie. You'll be able to take that information with you as you go around and come out on the other side.

"Can you tell us why we've been seeing these lights blink on and off for the last few weeks?"
This is just as you imagine. You opened up and began to see that there is a flow that is common to all. It is an electricity, just as emotions and thought patterns are electrical energy. As you become more in tune your energy gets in touch with other energies. You'll notice that eventually you'll be able to do this at will.

"I have a question regarding the kundalini energy. Is that part of the transformational and evolutionary process that is going on, as far as your whole system being re-routed by this subtle spiritual energy?"
Yes, absolutely, it is not even subtle. As the Earth evolves, the vibrations begin to quicken. Each individual's energy is being realigned. This is that feeling of being confused, but not really confused, and sad, but not really sad. The energy that flowed in a particular way within you is being realigned.
It is a realignment and it's quite dramatic. If you stick your finger in a socket, you get a jolt. It is as if you put yourself into a socket in the Earth, and get a new surge of energy. Eventually everyone will align to it, but in the beginning it causes some physical discomfort in different parts of the body. This is also why at this time many, many people on the Earth plane have been very sick. It's because this jolt has knocked everyone cockeyed and they have to come back to the middle and get used to the new flow.

"How do you start bringing this to the children?"
The children will find it with or without you, as Kim and Teresa can attest. Know that the children are close to us, as you were when you were children. When you were children there was no veil that separated the worlds. As you grew into adults, you were taught conventionalities and that these things didn't exist and that your imaginary friends were just that, your imagination.
What you can do for the children is to help them to understand the true nature of reality in their own language. That itself is an art some people are more adept at. If you don't know how to communicate these new ideas to children, there will be someone

around to help translate them into their language. Give children the idea that their angels are always with them, always surrounding them. Give them a sense of safety, because to a child, being loved and being safe are the two most important things in their lives. Convey to them the sense that their angels are constantly, forever with them, talking with them.

They will hear the angels, they will hear our voices, much more readily than adults will. Encourage them to write down what the angels say to them, because miraculous information will come from them.

Kim: "I've had a curiosity about my guides. We haven't talked about them since my first personal session. I have a little confusion in that everybody's guides are human and mine aren't. Could you explain more about the tombs, the mummies, and Mr. Wind? I don't understand what significance my guides have in my life."

Do you think that any other guides are human?

I guess not. But they were at one time.

So were mummies.

Never mind.

As you picture these entities who stand guard very devotedly and consistently, know that they themselves are going through an evolutionary change with you, as all of us, both human and celestial, are undertaking. They would like to tell you that they are opening up and unraveling with you, and so your need to feel them to be alive has been heard.

Teresa: "We have now met these other three women [Kanti, Lois and Rita]. It seems we are beginning to share things. Is there something more that the future holds for the six of us, something we will pursue together?"

Part of the importance of these three women is that they opened a door in your lessons and your mind. They brought you a miracle that was totally unexpected but completely validating in a time of great doubt. That act of connection was the power point. They travel in the same dreams and mediations.

However, you must understand that whether you are aware of it or not, everyone's higher consciousness is involved in this interplay. Your mission is to remember. This is the idea—even though you are not aware that this activity is going on in your dream state and in your eternal self, it is there. You can then join with those three and those three and these six in remembering and coming together and reaffirming that action.

"What is it that makes that happen? Why did that happen to Barbara, Kim and Teresa and not to us?"
Because they consciously sat down and studied. You came to hear the voices, but they gather at particular times with intent.

"If we want to gather with intent, should we do it in a different group or be with them?"
You can do it alone, or with the women you know. Intent is the key. Spend time before you sleep doing relaxation or meditation with intent to finding Teresa or Kanti. Intent is the key to remembering, to connecting with that higher power. You are just on the edge of breaking through what appears to be like a sheet of glass. You can see the other side. You know, you feel, you want, you desire and you attempt, but you are stopped by something invisible you can't see. Don't let that discourage you. Within the next month you are going to put a fist through it and it's going to fly open.

Your attempts to be aware will push you over the edge into a new level of understanding. You're going to leave behind some of your old philosophies and people you have been working with. You're going to find a new set of minds who are going to be more supportive of this concept you have been dealing with.

"We have been working with sending out light and love and we're continuing on with this work. In the evening when I go to bed I try to actually see myself stepping into the light, being embraced by the light. I send light from myself to the farthest reaches of the universe, blessing all that is and then gently returning the light to within. I'm also sending light and love to the planet, it needs lots of healing, and people. I try to see them as light walking down the street. I've had success with this. I'm feeling definite changes."
Add to your visualization when you envelop someone with your light, cut the chord and let them drift.

Kim: *"I hope it won't seem insignificant if I give you a special thank you for helping with Katie this morning and with me."*

Your love is felt. We are, not only to you but to all of you, in great awe and hold great thanks that we can be acknowledged. The work of angels has for so long been ignored. It was considered "coincidence" or a "lucky break." We cannot tell you enough how your acknowledgment brings to us a great joy and warmth. She was never in danger. But the understanding that came to pass was tremendously important for all of us. Thank you.

We would like to invite you to come again. There is so much more to talk about. We had attempted at one time to have conversation. It didn't quite work as well as it has here tonight.

You cast a beautiful light together. The more who come to share the more the light will grow. Then you simply need to watch and be amazed.

"Humility and grace
It's just the human race looking for perfection
Resurrection."

"Earthbound" © 1989 Barbara With

Barbara: This is as sick as I've been in years. At the beginning of the session, I began coughing uncontrollably. I was barely able to speak. But after I got into the first few paragraphs of the session, I miraculously fell into a healthier voice, without a cough for over an hour. Now that we're through, I have resumed my coughing jag.

☆   ☆   ☆

We all agree to experiencing the sensation that, while "their" words are general enough to apply to everyone, we each feel as if they were speaking specifically and directly to each individual. During the reading, distinct situations arose from most people's subconscious that had significant meaning in their own lives.

And "they" were so funny tonight. Such a distinct array of voices. Conflict Resolution, huh? Are they trying to prepare us specifically, as well as a general rule?

Before the session began, we made an appeal for donations. Lo and behold, here we sit in amazement with this small pile of money before us. We ceremoniously run our hands through it and give thanks, just as the angels said we would.

Later that night . . .
Kim: Standing in her kitchen after the session, Teresa and I continue the scenario from earlier today of the precipice and the comfort the angels gave us. We have to believe that if we do everything with love in our hearts, we cannot make a mistake. There is always purpose. And nurturing the process brings peace of mind. It may not bring the money necessary to save a failing business, but it does bring peace of mind.

Somewhere in the far reaches of our hearts, it is beginning to dawn on us that the weaving of the story of the precipice might be a group effort: the angels, Teresa and me. All together. I can hear, as if from far away, the whisperings of the angels, but I still cannot fully accept it in my conscious mind.

Teresa: Kim has gone and I am sitting in bed journaling before going to sleep. As I write thoughts and questions, I suddenly realize I'm hearing answers in my right ear.

I write another question. I hear another answer, much faster than the first. Finally, before I can fully formulate the question, the answer arrives.

I laugh and say out loud, "Okay, okay you guys!" I feel like Barbara, who says "they" follow her around all day trying to talk to her. It isn't scary. It's exhilarating!

January 26, 1994

Barbara: I don't want to leave the house. All I can do is cry. My nose is stuffed with steel wool. My head aches. I am angry at everyone and everything. Kim and Teresa call. Even they can't hold me up. They try. They put me on the speaker phone and talk to me about how I am being held in their arms, and they are being held in "their" arms.

I am so overcome I can't talk.

Is this the result of the dreaded "kundalini" energy they say is thrashing around now? If so, this must be the heart of the storm. It's not despair as much as shame and unworthiness, and unfathomable amounts of anger so deep it makes my skin crawl.

Teresa: I sit down again to journal before going to sleep. Like last night, I write questions and then "automatically" write the answers. It's funny, now that I know I can get immediate answers, it's hard to think up questions. Figure that one out!

I start to put away my journal when, from out of nowhere, a sentence comes into my head: "The angels are with me all of the time." I repeat this several times to myself. Then "something" tells me there's more.

I pick up my journal and open to a clean page. I write the sentence, having no any idea what will come next...

☆

The angels are with me all of the time
Hovering above me and all around
Surrounding me with the light of their love
I'm never alone cause my angels are there.

Three lovely ladies so delicately fly
Holding me close when I need to cry
Whispering comfort and bringing me warmth
And never allowing me any harm.

I know I'm not perfect
but they don't seem to mind
I fly along with them
through space and through time.

Tell me dear angels why you love me so
I'm nobody special or so I've been told
But you show me different - I'm really quite grand
And it's inside me, not through the eyes of a man.

I love my angels and they love me
These celestial beauties that one day I'll be
But for now they'll watch over, protect and keep safe
Until the day comes when I'm with them at last.

I know "I" didn't write that. I was only the instrument. I do know, however, it's been written to help me feel safe. Safety has always been an issue for me.

Written in a matter of seconds, I never consciously thought about what came next because it wasn't coming from me. It just flowed, from beginning to end. It's so beautiful, I almost wept when I read it.

January 27, 1994
Barbara: I go to the post office to send a package COD. After filling out all the forms, the postman tells me it will cost $12.45 to send a package COD. Excuse me, but isn't up-front payment

defeating the purpose of COD? And why didn't you tell me this before you had me fill out all these forms? I nearly tore his hair out.

January 28, 1994

Barbara: Still sick and angry. Sang at the Whitney last night. So sick I didn't sing, just played the piano. Two guys kept giving me money to play the same two songs over and over because they simply had to hear songs they recognized. They weren't capable of comprehending music they hadn't heard before. What "mirror" was this for me?

January 29, 1994

Barbara: Gary and I decide, after much indecision and at the last minute, to drive to the North Shore to cross country ski. Forget that I've been as sick as a dog for the past week. "I need to follow my intuition," I say. On the way up we listen to the tape of "Conflict Resolution."

As soon as we get to Two Harbors, it starts. I want to first order lunch and then call around for a room. But the restaurant doesn't have a phone. My stomach turns over and anger begins rising up behind my eyelids like steam heat. It takes a few minutes of deep breathing to calm down. I try my best to ride it through and not take it out on the waitress.

After lunch, we find a hotel room, make the decision not to take it, try to find another but can't, then go back to the first place. It's late afternoon by now, not much ski time. When we finally do get out to ski, we have the wrong wax, as it's much colder than expected. In my malaise, I tire quickly. Back at the stupid resort, we eat bad food in an atmosphere-free restaurant, then settle into bed with MTV and ESPN.

It's -27 degrees with a -33 degree wind chill. So much for intuition.

The next day dawns clear and cold. It's still below zero, but not too cold to ski. I notice a kind of quirky feeling in the air, a joy, or perhaps hope. It's crisp and clear and most definitely celestial.

☆

As I start down the state park trail on my old wooden Birkebieners, I can't help but greet people as they ski past. "This morning was made in heaven," I shout. This is a 180 degree turn-around from the woman I had been in the restaurant the previous afternoon. I don't know what's "making my day," but after the week I've had, I'm not about to question.

Suddenly, my ears begin to buzz, as if someone is singing at an inhumanly high pitch. I fancy it's a celestial song only angels can sing.

As soon as that thought crosses my mind, I "see" them. They're superimposed along the side of the trail, appearing to ski along side me. They're singing from the pine trees and reflecting in the rainbows bouncing off the snow from the mid-morning sun. When I get to a particularly steep or challenging part of the trail, I can feel them help me up the hills. They're singing a song of celebration.

Revelation after revelation begins flooding my mind. I can hardly keep up with all the inspiration rushing in: insights about my childhood, visions of Kim and Teresa's children talking to their own angels, how to introduce the children to writing music, messages from friends and family. And the music is indescribable, like total silence.

My sister's face appears before me. I later learned, at the moment I was experiencing my vision of her, she was in church playing the wind chimes and singing about how the rocks and stones tell the story of the angels. As she appears in my mind on that winter's morning, she's explaining that the reason I've been so angry is because for years I honestly thought I was better than everyone else. She's not making accusations, she's revealing a truth. And I know it's true, not because I review my life and can prove it through a series of chronological events. Rather it rings true like a reverberation in my body, like it's part of the song I'm hearing at that moment.

Humility sweeps through me. I don't react with the usual "Oh God, I'm so sorry about my past." Instead, I see how my impatience contributes to that impression. If someone is "slower" than me—in the car, in the food store, or learning a lesson—that must mean I am faster. And faster is better, after all. So when someone drags their feet, wasting my precious time, I assume I am better.

☆ ──

But this past week has felt like someone has turned up the anger, which is breeding its favorite partner, frustration. I rage at situation after situation with no relief. Just being alive is making me face my anger by getting to its root.

I ask what I should do now that I understand. "They" tell me not to assign meaning to the anger, to just feel it. In that way I won't waste any time getting to the real essence of the lessons.

We ski with abandon for hours. I haven't felt so good in a long time, spiritually and physically.

In the golden glow of a snowy evening, far away on a winter's hill overlooking the majesty of Lake Superior, I leave behind a great deal of my anger.

January 31, 1994

Barbara: Kim and Teresa are wondering about their progress. While spending the morning with them at the office, I encourage them to sit down at the computer and just listen and write. I think a little nudge might loosen them up. Both of them sit looking at me blankly, insisting it's something they don't really believe they will ever be able to do.

A few hours after I leave, Kim calls to say she suddenly began speaking the voices. A few minutes ago, she sat on the edge of her desk, her eyes open, answering Teresa's questions in seemingly the same voice that speaks through me. After that, they both sat at their computers, asking questions and typing the answers. Right on time (see: January 18). They say they've been laughing and writing and can hear the discernible difference between their own voices and the angels' voices.

Kim: I guess it's official. It's the first time I sat at the computer and let "their" words come through me. It feels exhilarating, confusing and scary, all at the same time. It's like reaching back into my mind thousands of years and hearing words come into my head I know *I* haven't put there. It's a tiny voice whispering to me in my left ear. I move my fingers and put the words onto paper.

It's odd to think of today as the first day I can hear them. In retrospect, I realize I have been hearing the voices for many days before this. I just didn't recognize them as such.

The best analogy I can give to describe the process of realizing you are hearing the voices is that it's like being pregnant with your first child. You *think* you are beginning to feel the baby kick. It starts out like little "bubbles" in your stomach. You don't know if it's really the baby, or if you are imagining it because you want it so much. As time goes on and the baby's kicks become stronger, you realize you're not making it up. You really are feeling those tiny awakenings of life inside you. Soon the baby is thumping so hard you think it's going to fight its way right out of your body.

Then you think back to those first little bubbles and you know with absolute certainty it was the baby you were feeling all along. It's a wonderful realization.

That's how it was when I began to hear "them." My self doubts told me I was making it all up. My conscious mind said I only thought I was hearing them because I wanted it so much.

What's funny is, up until now, I can honestly say that I never for one single moment ever believed that I would ever really hear the voices, much less write or speak them. Not for a single moment... until I realized that, in fact, I really am!

As we study the transcripts of our group sessions we realize "they" are giving us pieces of information about our spiritual development, and ways to maneuver through it. When they toss us a snippet about the future, we begin to speculate about how it will come to pass. We try to take control to make this possible future turn out to our benefit (of course). "They" then turn around and, like teachers addressing noisy students, reassure us that there is no need to use precious energy resources constructing the details of how we *think* life will unfold. Things will work out exactly as they were meant to, whether *we* think so or not.

Life is terrifying, remember?

But apparently, when we are left standing there, scared out of our minds, our egos, those little megalomaniacs that sometimes rule our lives, are crushed into tiny little pieces. Then anything becomes possible.

☆

When you're that afraid, you got nothing to lose, baby, nowhere to go.

So this entire process of studying and writing, reading and watching, has been an education in getting out of our own way by shutting up the ego, quieting the mind and letting the angels take over. And when we do it, miraculous things happen every day, like Kim and Teresa starting to hear the voices.

They tell us constantly that they are "lined up behind us, waiting to speak," wanting so much to talk to as many people as they can. It doesn't matter if the listener believes or not. All you have to do is listen. Period. The angels do the rest. Give them an inch and they always take a mile. What do we have to lose, for heaven's sake? We're down here on the earth, terrified of everything, and consequently, creating a world filled with terror. What's it going hurt to admit there might be a few angels in your life wanting to work with you?

February 1, 1994

Barbara: The day has come. Tonight, after almost five years of being together, Gary is sitting before me, with Kim and Teresa present, about to listen to the voices of the angels for the first time.

He has watched my transformation since these two strange women appeared out of nowhere to become my constant companions. We have spent many nights talking about how these concepts might work in his life. Because we are so close, I've been nervous about this inevitable day. After all, I know so many intimate details about his life. And I know his Virgo mind. My ego is afraid he'll have too many logical explanations of how I know all these things about him and explain away the power of the experience.

As it turns out, it only proves to be even more affirming. To begin with, he knows better than anyone that I'm just not *that* wise or skilled enough in extemporaneous speaking to think and talk so spontaneously. But more than that, the descriptions "they" use to paint a picture of Gary are perfect for his private movie.

Once again we're shown that, more important than trying to prove the significance of the words, the recipient must feel how those words, while they're being said, reverberate within the body.

☆

What pictures do those words paint? It goes beyond conscious thinking. It is more primitive than that. It is like being in a dream.

We notice new voices, funny accents and distinctly new personalities, just as they said would happen. We could see changes in their body language, in their definitions and humor. They're learning, too. It's fun meeting new friends like this. And we don't even have to leave the living room. The transcript from January 18th said there would be a young man who would be "shaken loose." That would be Gary, tonight.

That same session said to look for a woman, not part of the group yet, who would have "interesting news about other experiences other people are having that will be very reaffirming."

Oddly enough, I receive a phone call tonight from a student at the university named Sherry who is doing a research project on a murder that happened fifteen years ago in the area. Apparently, all those years ago, she was best friends with one of the victims. She got my name through a guitar player I frequently work with who is in her class. She asks if the three of us would be interested in trying to communicate with...who? One of the victims? Maybe see what the angels could tell about the facts of this unsolved murder?

An exceptionally intriguing idea...

February 2, 1994

Frankly, at this point, we're dumbfounded. Our motto has become (and you must pause for at least three seconds before you say it, and then say it real quiet and breathy and low), " ...Wow." Barbara says we can't say it anymore because we all say it too much.

What *is* there to say as we watch life unravel in exactly the way they say it will? When we use our free will to "get out of the way," suddenly our lives are imbued with a broader and more applicable love for everyone and each situation.

There's always a divine reason for everything, otherwise it wouldn't happen.

Yes, it's terrifying to watch people get murdered. It's heartbreaking to watch the situation in Bosnia. The reality of dying a slow, painful death from a terminal disease is agonizing. But when we "open the lens," we see from a bigger picture the necessity to experience everything from every angle in order to understand how to love fully. It's learning to walk in everyone else's shoes. That's the mysterious purpose in life everyone is always after.

What more is there? We could get richer, more renowned, give more money to those in need, but when all is said and done, without love and divinity, it isn't a life worth living. And it all begins at home, with learning to love ourselves. We will only see peace on a global level when every human being starts playing by the rules of the game: teaching love by "being" love.

But if the world isn't going to listen to the angels and the rumblings of the universe, somehow these lessons will be forced upon us, for our own good.

Barbara: I am worried about Kim overdoing it. I know from my own experiences that, in the beginning, it takes a lot out of you to be in that place with the angels. It's hard to explain. You don't feel the emotional drain until it's too late. Then you either slump into bed, exhausted but unable to sleep, or you weep uncontrollably for extended periods of time.

Kim and Teresa disagree with me. They don't think they are overdoing it. I try to explain that, when you start, even a small amount of contact with that dimension where "they" are can be a lot. It's like an exercise regime. Exercise is good, but if you aren't in shape, you're going to be sore when you start. When the body isn't properly adjusted to receive these higher frequencies, there is a chance of crash and burn in the early stages.

They don't care. They are having too much fun. Besides, they don't think they are overdoing it. This pisses me off. Why don't they listen to me? Don't they understand that I know what I am talking about?

But my lesson in this is detachment. I must understand that just because I have been assigned the role of teacher doesn't mean my students will act on what I tell them. I must ignore my conscious mind when it says, "I'm pissed off because they aren't listening to me" to avoid fanning the flames and causing more conflict.

When I arrive at Teresa's for our Wednesday night session, they rush to show me all the work they have been doing. They've been typing on the computer and asking each other questions. The words are indeed the same voices that have been coming through me in our group sessions. The same cadence, phrasing, verbiage. Even though they're actually hearing and interpreting the voices, it's hard for me to get through my anger. My attempt to be casual comes off instead as flip. I make an offhanded comment directed at Kim about how "Obsesses Too Much" is back.

Kim: I'm so excited about realizing that I'm actually hearing the voices, I can't wait to celebrate with Barbara. When she gets to Teresa's house, I expect that we will all share in the excitement. After all, this is no small thing! They've been telling us from the start we would learn to do this. Until I actually did it, I never thought, even for a moment, that it would ever really happen. This is a huge step for me and also a big step in the development of the mission. It's actually beginning to happen! I'm thrilled and awed and totally blown-away!

Barbara seems less than enthusiastic. Her reaction isn't what I expected. Instead of sharing the excitement, she makes a snide comment that I'm obsessing too much again. At the same time, the angels whisper in my ear that she is afraid. I try to curb my enthusiasm so as not to add to what I imagine are her feelings of insecurity. I assume she's feeling threatened in some way about us starting to hear the words of the angels. Maybe she feels we wouldn't need her anymore. That never occurred to Teresa and me.

I suddenly feel blown-off instead of blown-away. I don't understand her reaction and I take it very personally. The old dysfunctional tapes begin to play in my head. The "old me" needs acceptance and recognition from the outside. The "new me" is just learning to rely on my inner self for approval and support.

I vacillate between my compassion for Barbara's feelings and the disappointment I feel about her indifference. Her tone is enough to indicate to me, in my deflated sense of self, that I'm right to feel mocked and ignored. Many confusing emotions rush over me: Do I take care of Barbara's feelings or my own? Can I find the strength to congratulate myself instead of seeking support from the outside? Why do I feel like I did something wrong?

☆ ───────────────────────────────

When the angels start to speak to the group, I feel like they've taken on Barbara's cynical tone. I shut down. I don't hear any of their words. I suddenly want to be as far away from all of this as I can possibly get.

I sit through the reading and about a half hour of conversation afterward saying nothing. Finally, when I'm about to scream, I leave the room and retire to the kitchen to lick my wounds.

After a while the kitchen doesn't even seem far enough away. I go upstairs and lie down on Teresa's bed.

I know leaving the room is not socially acceptable or politically correct, but I need to take care of me. This is actually a big step. The old me would have stuffed my feelings and tried to make Barbara feel better in her moment of insecurity. The new me knows that Barbara has her own feelings to work through that really have nothing to do with me. My job is to work through my feelings. So I do.

February 3, 1994

Barbara: Kim was silent after last night's session. Then she left the room and refused our help at sorting through what was happening. I fear she felt again that they were telling her she wasn't doing it right. I also thought about that draining feeling.

I call the office this morning, as usual. Talking to them is completely uncomfortable. They want to chit-chat. I want to know what went on last night. Kim tells me she's "processing" and isn't ready to talk yet.

It's hard for me to watch her struggle. I can relate to how she feels, but it doesn't quell the anger of feeling she's shutting me out, first in ignoring my warnings, and now refusing my help.

I should be able to accept this without getting angry, but I can't. I am mad that I took a risk and revealed myself to them after the last big group when I was so sick. I showed them my most vulnerable side. They were there like angels, with words of reassurance, painting pictures of the two of them holding me up, encouraging me to let them support me. Now when the tables are turned, I get shut out. And on top of that, I bet I still get accused of not loving her enough!

☆

All I can do is allow my mind to rant. It brings up all my worst habitual thinking. What surprises me is how strong that tape plays, even after all these lessons about how it's just a bad habit ingrained in my thinking process. I thought I had changed. I thought I understood the root of my anger. Yet at the first sign of distress, here I am back again with these stale sentences running through my head. "I don't need you. I'm just going to pack up my toys and go. Why am I always left out?"

It suddenly strikes me how real this feels! It really feels as if I have been abandoned. As I apply the principles they have been teaching us, I suddenly begin to know in my heart Kim can't abandon me, not from the soul's perspective. Our souls are in that eternal place. In fact, Kim has nothing to do with the root of my anger.

This new perspective allows me to turn off the inner voices defining why it is that I'm angry, and just feel anger. Without a definition of why I am angry, I succeed in not dragging the past into it ("I always mess up like this"), and projecting the future based on the past ("It's going to be like this all the time"). I truly just feel the anger of the moment, like an electricity running through my body. All judgments are withheld, internal dialog shuts down. It's just me and my anger, living together in the present moment.

If I wasn't so deeply involved in this teaching/learning situation, I would mistakenly conclude the reason for my anger was Kim's actions. This would create an "issue" to deal with and in my mind would justify being rude and snippy to Kim. Maybe I'd even give her a stiff talking to about what a bad listener she is. Talk about fanning the flames!

Instead a third voice is rising within, part conscious mind and part angels' voices. The angels speak clearly in my left ear. My ego sits securely to my right. And in the middle comes a voice that balances the two. This third voice doesn't have quite the wisdom the angels have. Nor does it take what the ego says seriously. I know it is me, and yet is it them, too.

Is this the evolutionary voice they speak of? Was it there all the time and I am just now getting to know it? I can't wait to share this with the girls!

☆ ───────────────────────────────

By day's end, we decide to meet for lunch tomorrow and talk through a few things.

February 4, 1994

Kim: Last night I dreamt I stood in the helm of a boat, worried it would tip over. The message is clear: You can't rock the boat. It's a *really* big boat. They're trying to tell me not to worry about the outcome of this conflict.

Also in the dream, people were playing board games. I take it to mean we're about to learn how to play one of these games. Little do we know.

I go to the computer and ask the angels what is happening with us. Being that I am the conflict avoidance queen, I'm scared to death. I'm afraid our beautiful union will be destroyed, and yet it's taking a whole lot of nerve to confront the issue. This is clearly a big lesson for me. There is too much at stake for me to follow the old patterns of avoidance. I have to come right straight at this thing between Barbara and me or it will never be resolved.

"Can you help me?"

Yes. We are. You have heard us and are moving in the right direction. Remember to take responsibility for your part and to extend only love. This is what is needed here more than ever. Let your child talk to her child. Find a place that will give you both comfort. She is afraid, so she does not look at it.

We all meet at Barbara's for lunch. It starts out congenially. We try to be pleasant and light, but something is definitely looming. We have our regular Chinese takeout, "Buddha Delight" and shrimp fried rice.

Unbeknownst to us, while we're eating and trying to be polite, one by one the angels quietly fill the room. We have no idea they're assembling, like spectators at the playing field.

The moment comes when we can no longer dance around the issue.

After talking around it for several minutes, I tell Barbara, "I need to know where I stand with you." Our relationship is so different than what I know with Teresa. I wasn't prepared for Barbara's seemingly uninterested reaction the night before to my hearing the voices. I tell Barbara I *need* her. I just need her to love me—that's all.

Barbara: Here we go. I'm being told I'm not doing enough for her. I wonder what I did to elicit such an intense distrust of my loyalties and love. After all, I'm the one who is supposedly being shut out. But my newfound understanding tells me I haven't really been shut out. Still, I feel the anger lying below the surface like a coiled snake ready to strike.

Kim: I know I am suppose to be learning not to have expectations of other people. We send out love for love's sake, not for what it gets us in return. And I know I shouldn't be judgmental about the way Barbara expresses herself. But the paradox is that if she wants me to show love and give support, I need to know that I can count on her, too. Responding sarcastically, then expecting me to come to her for love and support doesn't make much sense. This is how the straight-forward, seemingly simple lessons become so difficult. It's so easy to say, "Learn to love!" Why does it become so difficult to actually *do* it?

Teresa: I watch this dance between Barbara and Kim, understanding quite clearly what Kim means when she says she needs Barbara. It's not the unhealthy "I need you." It's "I need to know you will support me, no matter what. I need to know I can count on you." The kind of relationship Kim and I have.

It seems Barbara heard, "I need you to save me." I also understood that position, and how Kim has perpetuated this. In my life, I have learned all too well you can only save yourself. And I know Barbara and Kim know it, too. I'm at a loss how to bring these two back together in the middle.

Barbara: I try to explain about the third voice rising in between my ego and the angels. I want to share with them the joy I feel discovering this voice. I try to tell them how I was almost duped into believing they had abandoned me. I still can't figure out why Kim is questioning if I will be there for her. I mean, I sat on the couch last night, waiting for her to come down to talk. Then I called in the morning and was told she was "processing." What more am I suppose to be doing? The anger is starting to surface. No one seems to be listening to me.

Teresa is sitting, obviously feeling uncomfortable, picking at her food.

We talk about issues. "Issues are only issues if you make them issues." I fumble around trying to explain this new found revelation while wrestling with the rising anger.

Kim: I tell her, "Okay then, I have an issue with you. And apparently, you must have one with me, otherwise why would you be sitting there yelling at me about how there are no issues?" I'm not sure how we're going to deal with these issues if she's convinced there are no issues, so I hold fast to what the angels said about extending only love.

Before we know it, we're screaming at each other. I want Barbara to know that I need her. Barbara keeps saying she's not responsible for my feelings. Teresa finally intervenes.

Teresa: I want to make each of them understand each other. Neither of them is really listening to what the other is saying. I restate Kim's position as I understand it. I think Barbara might listen if it comes from me.

Barbara: Teresa starts telling me about the kind of relationship they have. It sounds co-dependent to me. And now it feels like they're ganging up on me. I keep trying to explain about not having issues, but my voice is getting louder and more heated.

By now, we have a full-fledged fight on our hands. "Our last session was 'Conflict Resolution.' Let's just get the transcript and see what it says we should do." I march off to the other room to find the transcript.

Teresa: I tell Kim I just want to leave. Kim agrees. It goes without saying Barbara wants us out, too. But here we are, committed to the moment and to the process.

Barbara returns with the transcript and begins looking for anything that might shed some light on this twisted, angry knot we have become. She reads a few lines, then starts telling a story about a similar situation that occurred in her musical trio.

Barbara: I begin to read the transcript aloud:

*You can look at someone else and lay claim to their actions and how
they are causing a conflict within your life, but every conflict you
are involved in is within your own self. The source is within your
own self.*

This sounds like support for my contention that issues are only
issues if you make them so.

I bring up the subject of the singing group I started. One of the
girls, Aisha, left the group because it was time for her to branch out
on her own. I try to explain to Kim and Teresa, if only Aisha and I
had used this idea about not being the source of each other's conflict,
we could have parted amiably, acknowledging that, because the
direction of the group was not her direction, it was simply time to
part ways. Instead we fought over other unrelated details of our
lives.

Kim: I ask Barbara why Aisha's direction was no longer aligned
with her direction. She says it was because she was the leader of the
group and Aisha disliked the parameters Barbara had set. This only
further proves my point. What I am having trouble coming right out
and saying is that I am sick of being told she is the leader. Who's in
charge is not as important as knowing that our relationships are
built on solid ground, someplace we know we can count on when we
are estranged. It seems to me that because she has to be the leader,
it pushes people away. She might be the "leader" when it comes to
teaching us to hear the voices, but Teresa and I are here to teach her,
too. We are here to teach her how to love through her anger.

"Most of the time our souls are together," I say. "But for those
times when they aren't, I need to know you'll support me regardless."

Barbara: I didn't bring up the singing group to convince them
that I was the leader of *this* trio. I didn't think of myself as the leader!
In fact, I'm not really crazy about being the teacher here. This is nuts!
And how in the world can our souls *not* be together? I mean, we're
talking about our souls here, we're talking about all eternity. And
how does not having issues translate into the idea that I don't love
her?

I try to tell her it's only her perception that makes her think we
aren't together, in the same way it's only my perception that makes

me feel abandoned. She keeps insisting she needs a guarantee that, when our souls aren't together, we will somehow be able to make them return. I argue back that they ARE always together.

I reach down and pull on my green sweatshirt. "Kim, for you to stand there and beg me to be there for you is like saying, "Oh, God, Barbara, I wish you were wearing a green shirt."

"This is hardly as trivial as what you're wearing," she throws back.

"No, don't you see what I'm saying? 'Oh, God, Barbara, I WISH you were wearing a green shirt!' Look! I AM wearing a green shirt!"

She looks at me blankly. There's split second of silence. Then *SWOOSH!* Satori! A rush of angels wings fills the room. We all look at each other and immediately start to cry.

Something is happening in this very moment, in this movement of angel wings that we have never experienced before: a true revelation. More than that, it's a simultaneous recognition of instantaneous truth.

The truth is, we are all right. And the entire episode is right, because this entire episode is meant to teach us conflict resolution.

It all becomes clear in an instant. We sit and hold tight to one another. Then, amidst the tears, we each take a turn talking about our fears while the others really listen.

Kim: I need to acknowledge how the power of my doubts affects my perception. I need to widen my lens and see how I alone am creating the isolation I am feeling. My decision to withdraw at the end of the night may have been a positive step compared to previous behavior, but it still fostered the separation that I have been looking to Barbara to remedy.

Barbara: I need to be more outwardly supportive of Kim and Teresa's progress and open my own lens to see these events in the bigger picture of things. We have been working for a month together within the framework that someday they, too, would hear and speak the voices. The moment it happened, I was snide and sarcastic. Yes, we are all souls together in eternity, but if we don't treat each other with love and respect everyday, it's all just a theory. And, while I play the role of the teacher sometimes, Kim and Teresa also have many things to teach me about love that are just as important and profound as what I am teaching them. And isn't that what the voices have been talking about, learning to love ourselves and each other? I need to learn, once again, that we are equals. I am not better because I am faster.

Teresa: Barbara and Kim also need to listen—to me, to each other, to themselves, and to the angels, and come more into the middle instead of clinging to their respective extremes.

But the biggest kicker of all is, from the angels' perspective, the whole fight has been right. All along the way, the angels have been pushing us here and prodding us there to play out these roles in order to make these discoveries because it's also part of a larger plan. They need to teach us how to use "Conflict Resolution" amongst ourselves so we will be qualified to turn and teach it to others. It's a master stroke of psychology, devotion and faith on their part.

We're sure that "rush of angel wings" must have been them applauding. After all, they divinely inspired the whole thing so they could gather and watch. They probably had bets down on just how long it would take us to cycle back to their words.

We scraped and scrambled for a while, but we did it. We all felt like pawns in a chess game, just like Kim's dream. But what a beautiful chess game. Everyone wins! Clever, aren't "they?"

PART II

Who Knew?

CHAPTER FOUR
The Children

"...become as little children"

Matthew 18:3

Children believe they are the center of the Universe.
They love unconditionally.
They are honest, without judgment.
They stay in the Present Moment.
Children talk directly to God.

© Kimberly Lilith Phelps 1994

February 5, 1994
Barbara: After what we have dubbed "The Green Shirt Day," people have been reacting to me in the oddest ways. Last night at the gig, the bartender, who has not spoken more than two paragraphs to me, was suddenly my best friend. He even offered to make me a tape of some music he thought I'd like. And the waitress, always cool and aloof, set a tip jar at the end of the piano, and suddenly, there was $20 in it! People couldn't get to it fast enough to put more money in it!

Everyone looked at me differently. First they'd look, then look away, then look back until I noticed them and hold my eye for a second longer.

Very, very strange.

It feels as if these changing reactions are a direct result of the fight. I don't really understand what one has to do with the other, but it's as if the fight blew a hole through the fortress I have built around my heart. Now people can see in. Or maybe they see a deeper love shining out of that hole, even though I don't think I look different or am doing anything differently to solicit these responses.

No one in my life has ever had the desire, wherewithal or guts to get in my face the way Kimberly and Teresa did yesterday. It took all the gumption they could muster to say what they said to me. They helped me see that I have used anger all my life to keep people away, and then complain that I feel left out. I act snippy and arrogant, then feel sorry for myself because people "abandon" me. Could it possibly be that I am creating this condition for myself? Just like these positive, unsolicited responses to the opening of my heart draw people to me, do my negative actions and attitudes actually drive people away?

Since Kim and Teresa have come into my life, my entire perception of who I am is changing. I must admit, it's almost impossible to accept that I create all the turmoil of my life. Why in the world would I want to do that to myself? What is the underlying force that drives me over and over again to create situations that leave me feeling alone and isolated and left with only my anger, without anyone to play with?

These questions keep plaguing me. I can't seem to understand what it is I am doing wrong. What am I missing? Why do I feel, on some days, that all these lessons the angels are teaching us are the most miraculous thing that ever crossed my path, and on others, I feel like telling the world to go take a flying leap?

Like today. All I wanted to do was to pick up the rented laptop. At every turn something was thrown in my way to block me: traffic, flat tire, then when I got to the rental place, they amazingly had no record of my order. By the time I got back to the office, I was raging.

So what's the use of all this teaching and learning with the angels if I still get so angry over something as unimportant as traffic? In my mind, I understand everything, all the concepts about how everything begins within. But when push comes to shove and I find myself as out of control as I've always been, how do I actually make the leap to the peace instead of the anger?

Does this mean I am not working hard enough? Maybe it really is all a hoax. Maybe I will never understand how to bring peace into my life. Maybe these angels are really just teasing us with promises of a peace that can never be.

☆ ──

And yet I cannot deny the miracles, like these changing reactions to me at the hotel. That was nothing I worked to achieve, much less even knew could happen. And every week I do sessions for people who want to hear the angels speak, and I watch as, right before my very eyes, they become inspired and clear. With every one of the transformations I witness, I am more convinced about the divinity of it all.

So one moment I'm able to create total divinity, and the next becomes absolute chaos spinning out of control. What's a girl to think? What's a girl to do?

The one thing I do know is that I am spending more and more time at the office with Kim and Teresa working on understanding what we're being taught. That seems to be the one place where, even when things don't make sense, I at least feel safe being confused. We joke about how someday someone's going to cart us all off to the Funny Farm. We all agree we'll be perfectly happy, as long as we can have a tape recorder, a computer, a piano, and the same rubber room.

Good news! Gary and I officially decide to use those airline tickets he won in the United Way contest at work to go to Hawaii. It's odd, usually tickets like these can only be used within the continental United States, but for some reason, we can get to Hawaii with them. I was not excited about the idea at first, it seems like a long flight, and where would we stay? But his sister in California has a friend with a house on Kaua'i that she rents for next to nothing. That's a good enough reason for me to want to go there! So that's where we'll be headed at the end of the month! Wow!

Kim: Today I read, "As you think, so shall you be." I am learning that if my thoughts are centered on what is missing, then what's missing appears to grow. I'm beginning to see that this is what most of my relationships have been like. I have always talked about what's missing, what I don't have. I hear myself whining about how I am alone again, without love or friends. From this perspective, it could appear that so far, I have created an entire life of NOTHING!

The angels, bless their hearts, have been trying to teach me how to focus less on what's missing and more on what is really here:

every day, every hour, every moment, to keep my focus on what is in my present. Because of that changing perception, as opposed to moving away from Clay, I feel myself pulled toward something else. As I let go of the anger and perceptions of lack in our relationship, different pieces come into focus and I can see the relationship for what it really is — a *piece* of my life, but not the source of my life. In this open, receptive state of seeing what I do have, I am then able to fully recognize that God is my source. And that source is within me. I am moving toward me!

All of this is still so new in my life. It's hard to believe that four short months ago, with my focus on my failing relationship, my life seemed to be in the toilet again. For all the struggle to let go of the old ways, these changes have been tremendously liberating. I've heard stories about God finding people and turning their lives around, but I had no idea what that meant or how startling the turn around could be.

And my children: Is it possible that the miraculous transformation of my life will enable them to experience their own young lives from a higher perspective? At my age, I have to un-learn all the old stuff that screwed me up and re-learn a new way of living and looking at life. Is it possible that, if I can make these changes in my life, my children can view the world differently from the onset? If I make no other contribution to the world than to make it easier for our children to grow up feeling greater peace and love in their lives, it will be enough. What will it take to truly make a difference for ourselves and them?

Teresa: Katie and Sarah just got home from listening to the angels for the first time! Kim and I took them over to Barbara's, and we all cuddled together on her big down comforter while the angels spoke directly to our babies. Both have been asking us lots of questions. "They" said the girls would be ready soon, and boy, are they ever!

Katie and Sarah have been almost inseparable since birth. Kim and I met in Lamaze class, remember? So the girls have been together since then, too. During the times when we moved the family back and forth to North Carolina, if you asked either girl who her best friend was, she would always say the other, even when they lived 1,200 miles apart and didn't see each other but once a year. Their bond is just as strong as mine and Kim's. To bring them together and share this with them meant everything to us.

I (oh, ye of little faith) asked in a previous session how the angels would speak to these children so they would understand. Boy, did I feel dumb for asking. The girls understood exactly what was said to them. What's more, they asked the most incredible questions. There's something precious about a little ten-year-old voice asking, "So what is this fourth dimension and sixth sense and how do we get there?" Wow!

Sarah wanted to know about an incident I had told her about that happened when I was pregnant. Randy and I were driving home late one night and, for no apparent reason, Randy stopped at a green light. I turned to him and asked why he had stopped. He said he didn't know. At that moment, a car flew across the intersection, running the red light on the cross street.

Randy and I have always believed that, for a moment, the hand of God picked us up. The angels' explanation about what happened that night was proof.

The way the girls absorbed the reading was incredible. They even made an agreement with Barbara to help her write some kids music. And, of course, there's the children's book.

Today was another one of those small miracles we keep talking about.

THE ANGELS
February 5, 1994

"The Children"

There is an interesting energy in the connections between all the women here today. You children are not just children to your mothers. You have lived different lives before this one. You have been sisters, and brothers. In fact, Katie was Kim's mother in one life. The reason you lived these different lives in different relationships is to understand what it is like to walk in each other's shoes.

At the age you are now, you have a limited ability to understand what we are saying in your conscious mind. Your conscious mind is the part of you that talks to you continually. It is hard to quiet the conscious mind. Sometimes you lie in your bed at night and talk to yourself.

But a deeper part of you lives forever. You were existent before you were born, and you will live on after you leave the Earth plane. We will try and use terminology you can understand. Try and draw pictures in your mind of what we are saying.

You feel an inseparable connection between the two of you. Think about friends you were close to who moved away to a different school or weren't in your class this year. They seemed to have disappeared from your mind. It was not that you didn't like them, you just didn't think much of them. But with the two of you, it does not matter how much distance is between you. Your connection goes deep inside your hearts. Your beautiful love for each other will prove to be important in the years to come.

Your own angels are with you all the time. Each of you has one angel at this time.

Sarah, your angel is very beautiful, with flowing, blonde hair. She is lit up. She glows from within, glows in the dark. She is there in the quiet times for you. While you're involved at school or engaged in some activity, you may not sense her there, but she is.

You will be able to hear her and meet her in the very quiet times when you are alone.

You are good at holding that quietness inside you. Sometimes you think it is bad, or that you shouldn't be that way. You think you should be more like your friend. This is not so. It only appears that way.

People have a tendency to look at other people, see all the good things about them, then look at themselves and, because they can't see those things in themselves, they think they're not as good. You do this with being quiet. This is a very strong and powerful ability you have. Treasure it. Remember—and your angel will tell you this—this quiet place is very special. You will be able to see your angel when you go there. Ask her any question you want. She will tell you the answer. Do this with your eyes closed. Or draw a picture of her as you see her. She is there always watching over you.

Katie, your angel is personified as a go-go dancer. She is very "up on the times" and likes to know what's happening. She has high energy and is tall and strong. She is with you all the time and talks with you constantly.

She is the kind of angel that likes to be involved in everything you're doing. She is different from Sarah's angel, not because Sarah's angel isn't with her all the time. Sarah's angel is content to sit back and not say too much about what's happening until things are quiet and then she'll talk.

Angels are growing and learning, too. As you go to school and learn how to write and read, they're learning, too, only they're learning different lessons. They need you to help them learn.

When you don't know what to do, or you're confused, you have two different methods for asking the angels for answers.

Sarah, say you don't know how to tell someone something, or you're afraid you won't do well on a test. Go away into the quiet. Don't sit and think too hard about the question you want to ask. Drawing a picture will bring you the answer.

For example, if you are afraid about taking a test the next day, sit on the side of your bed, and ask the question: "What will happen tomorrow?" And then, forget it. Go off and do a little cleaning, or read a little. Then get some paper and just draw. See what you draw. Your mother can help you find the answer to your question from what you drew.

You will be drawing with the hands of your angel. The angel is there guiding your hand. It will seem like you're drawing. Out of you will come the answer.

Katie, for you it is writing. You like to write. You can easily learn to ask a question of your angel. The angel will use your hand and write the answer. It doesn't matter how it works. It's a very complex process that even your adult friends would not be able to understand. But if you believe, if you envision your angel and believe, it will happen for you.

It is very important for you to know that your angels are always with you. They protect and love you like you were their own children. If you feel their presence, you will know that you are never alone.

You ask us questions.

Katie: *"I could never imagine a sixth sense or a fourth dimension. It's hard to understand what could be a sixth sense or a fourth dimension, and what it would be like."*

The sixth sense is fairly simple. Your eyes see, your ears hear, your mouth tastes, your skin feels, and your nose smells. And your heart feels. That is the sixth sense. When you think of it that way, it's very simple.

People have forgotten the power of love. It will transform the world. When you look at someone, you can see them or touch them, smell them, even lick them. You could hear what they said, but when you look at them with love, it expands the whole picture. That is the sixth sense.

The fourth dimension is this: you have a box this high and this wide, and this long, and it is sitting here right now. The fourth dimension has to do with the "time" of the box. This same box somewhere else the next day is in a different dimension. It's a different time. One day this box is in your bedroom. But the next day it's in your dining room. This is difficult to explain even to adults.

Sometimes time passes like an eternity. When you're waiting to go on vacation, or when you were waiting for this day to come, it seems like it took forever to get here. And yet, other times, when you don't want to go to the doctor, or take a test, it seems like time passes so quickly. That is the fourth dimension. It is time.

☆

Time is not little minutes, all exactly the same space. You could sit and count to sixty, and then count to sixty again, and say you have created exactly one minute, and then another. But sometimes one minute is actually much longer than another minute. What makes the difference is how you feel about it. If you feel anticipation, excitement and longing from your heart, the sixth sense, then time passes much slower. If you're anxious and nervous and you don't want to do something, then time seems to pass very quickly.

Conversely, if you're finally on the vacation you waited so long for—to go to Disney World—it seems like it's over, just like that. Time is fluid. It's more like water than something hard.

You may find it interesting to know that, while there is a fifth and sixth dimension, there's also a seventh, eighth, and so on. It is the same with senses. There are many, many more senses than what we have just described. But you don't speak our language yet, so we can't describe them now.

Your parents cannot describe to you exactly what it's like to own a business or raise a family. You can play act these things in your basement, but you cannot really know what goes on. You have to be older and more experienced to understand.

That is how it is for human beings. They cannot understand all those other things yet. But they will, and you will also.

All of you, not just the children, but all human beings, are just like children to the angels.

Katie: *"I was wondering about animals. Do they live more than one life? Can they come back as different animals? If in one life they're a whale, can they come back as a cheetah or something?"*

Animals have their own souls, but they are not like human beings because they don't think. What makes you be able to think and read and do arithmetic is something called the ego. Animals don't have that. The ego is a voice that tells you what's going on in the world. It's the thing that says, "Now I'm going to math class," or "We're going to take a trip," or "We must have dinner." It's telling you what's happening in your life. Animals don't have that.

They do have souls, but they are more an expression of the angels. Angels have created them for you. For example, you love

☆

your pets. You need to have them. They don't ever talk to you. They don't go out and make money. They don't do the dishes, but they make you feel love inside you.

Don't you feel that way about all animals? You have emotion for even the most unattractive animals. That's why the animals are there. To help you feel love.

A whale wouldn't come back as a cheetah because a cheetah does not need the same kind of energy as a whale. You see whales in the movies, or perhaps you will even be lucky enough some day to go to the ocean and watch as a whale jumps through the water with joy. Your heart will be filled with love and awe. Your jaws will drop as you see this beautiful creature. But it does not reincarnate in that sense.

After the whale leaves the world its soul goes back to a big pot of souls. "Soul material," we'll call it. When the time comes, part of that material could be called upon to be a part of you.

You don't start out as an ant, and come back bigger and bigger until you've evolved all the way up to the biggest creatures and then become human. It doesn't work that way. The soul of the whale, after expressing itself in that creative way, goes back into the big collection of wonderful soul energy. You human beings have a mind that thinks. This makes you different than the whale. When you are in between your lives, you have the option of going into that big vat containing this beautiful loving animal energy and using some of it for your own.

Katie: *"Can people come back in another life as an animal, or could an animal choose to become a person?"*

It is not done in that way. Animals don't make choices. When your dog needs to eat, he does not think in his mind, "I need to eat." There is some force within him that drives him to the food bowl. He doesn't think or reason. He would feel sad if you talk angrily at him, pointed your finger and told him he was bad. You could see him becoming sad. His ears would droop. But he does not think. So, no, animals do not decide to come back.

When human beings are in between lives, they try to decide what's going to happen in the next life. They draw up a basic game plan about what they're going to do. They do not choose to come back as animals because it would not serve them.

For example, all the work you do in school and all of the things you are learning with your family are helping to make you bigger and stronger to prepare you for being a grownup. Just sitting in a room does not help you grow and learn. That is what it would be like to come back as an animal.

Let's say the whale leaves the earth and all its energy goes into this big vat. And let's also say that you are in-between lives. Your soul talks with your angels and you both decide to go to this vat and take some of the whale's soul and use it for your own. Then you would know what it's like to be a whale.

Even now, when you think about any animal, you have the ability to feel what it would be like jumping through the air like a cheetah, or swimming through the water like a whale.

Teresa: *"Sarah and I were discussing an incident that happened when I was pregnant with her. Randy, and I were driving home late one night, and he stopped at a green light. I looked at him, and I asked, 'Why are you stopping? The light is green.' And he said, 'I don't know.' About that time a car came speeding from the other direction and ran the red light. If he had not stopped, we would have collided. So we've always thought it was a guardian angel that helped us in that situation. As we've talked recently, we've wondered whose it was . . . if it even could have been hers."*

It was, indeed. When you were pregnant with Sarah, she was not right there in your stomach. The body that would house the soul of Sarah was there, but Sarah's soul was more like an angel. She was hovering around like an angel, together with the angel who is with her now.

It was very simple. Sarah's angel said to Sarah, "Tell your father to stop." Sarah leaned over into her father's ear and said, "Stop."

When you were giving birth to Sarah, as soon as her body came into the world, she took her first breath. The first breath that tiny baby took sucked in the soul and consciousness of Sarah. You went from being this angel to being in your body like you are now. It was a simple act.

It was not earth shaking news that he stopped. We did that so that now, today, you would come and ask and find out the truth. And THAT is like the fourth dimension—when the past has a direct effect upon the future.

That day when you stopped in front of that light is connected with this day here. You can feel it in your hearts, can you not?

            ☆

Know now that Sarah was in angelic form and able to still help her father. It is a beautiful dance of great cooperation you are all involved in. You all have a responsibility to dance your own dance.

As the two of you go forward in your week, you're going to feel different than you have before. You may feel things aren't right. Or you might feel different than your classmates and friends because you've had this experience. It's hard to talk about it to people who don't understand. You've already had experiences where you have told someone about your mothers and their experiences and got "pooh-poohed." You won't be thinking, "I'm so different." You'll be feeling it in different ways.

You may be more emotional next week. You might find yourself crying more, or not wanting to play with anyone. This is perfectly all right. Every tear you shed is an expression straight from you heart. You should NEVER think of that as something bad.

It is important not to judge yourselves. You might have felt that crying this morning was not a good thing to do. Remember, don't think you're doing a bad thing or a good thing. Realize that everything is like a great dance.

Tears are like a cleansing rain. You know how you feel after it's been raining and raining. You go outside and the beautiful sun is shining and you have more energy. The parents say it's because you've been cooped up in the house too long. But we know the real reason. There has been a great cleansing.

Come and speak again to us. We would be overjoyed to have you here, all four of you. A brilliant light shines within this configuration. It is so heartwarming to us. We see you very clearly as a bright light that shines, and we are drawn to that.

Feel your angels around. Try to talk to them using the methods we suggested—drawing and writing—and interesting things will happen.

Do not be afraid to speak at length with your mothers. They are trained to help you understand what's happening. And a very magnificent thing is happening. This is not like recess or a field trip. This is something of great importance and magnitude. Even now, you both take up important missions in this life. You'll be challenged in the next few weeks to help set up these magnificent things for you in the future.

☆ ───────────────────────────

Allow the tears to come if they need to and let the laughter flow. Then you simply need to watch and be amazed.

"The Spring is young and I love fun.
Oh, what a glorious day we are having today.
Oh won't you please, oh won't you please,
Oh won't you please come play with me,
Come play with me today."

"Angels Day Out" © 1994 Sarah Anderson

February 6, 1994

Barbara: I've never had many children in my life. I feel more comfortable holding a golf club than I do a baby. And I am never sure what to say to older kids. Fear creeps over me that I am going to say something stupid and they will laugh at me. What do you say to a ten-year-old? I don't want to be condescending, and yet what could we possibly have in common to talk about?

After the reading, I began to understand the complexity of children. In all of their innocence, growth is rapidly taking place. It's as if you can watch them grow right before your eyes.

This morning I call over to Teresa's house. Sarah answers the phone.

"Hi Sarah, is your mom home?"

"Guess what Barbara! I wrote a song!" She hadn't even heard me ask for Teresa.

"You did??" I was floored! "How did THAT happen?"

"I don't know, I just went to the piano and started to play! And, well, the song just … came out of me!"

"Sarah! I didn't know you played the piano??"

" ME NEITHER!"

I'm suddenly in those moments, as a child, when I instinctively know that I'm supposed to climb up onto the piano bench and just play. I never have any doubts, or think that this is something I can't do. I see my tiny fingers atop the keys. What is guiding them? Who is telling me where to put them? (Need I say it out loud?)

Now Sarah is being guided by the same musical angels who taught me. I am overcome. Before I hang up I make her promise to play me the song.

That afternoon, as Teresa and Austin and I look on, Sarah performs her first composition for us on her mom's old out-of-tune upright. Tears come to our eyes, not only because this is her very first song, but because it's so simple, yet so profound. She calls it, "Angels Day Out," and it's a child's simple request to come out and play. Does she know she's talking to all us adults? I have an idea that she's speaking to someone in particular.

I go home and record a simple arrangement of her song in my studio. When I return to Teresa's with the tape and play it for her, I see a light come to her eyes that is truly precious. The gift she has given me in writing the song, and the gift I returned in arranging and performing it are more special than anything I have ever felt. In that moment I understand that I do make a difference in a child's life, in this child's life. Another one of those precious miracles.

February 7, 1994

Teresa: Last night I had a strange dream. I dreamt of being in bed with both Randy, who I've been officially separated from for some time now, and Ryan O'Neal. Ryan O'Neal?! Where did that come from? I don't remember many of the details except that I was making love to Ryan O'Neal while Randy slept right next to us. During the whole dream I kept thinking, "I shouldn't be doing this."

This morning I shared the dream with Kim and Barbara. Barbara immediately said, "Of course! It's Luddy, my friend who lives on Maui! I've called and invited him to come over to Kauai while we're there!" She said with Luddy's strong features and tousled blonde hair, that Ryan O'Neal could absolutely have been him in the dream. Of course, she then went into how perfect the whole thing is and how she could easily see Luddy and I have a succulent affair.

Could this be a sign that I might really be going to Hawaii with Barbara and Gary? Seems like a stretch to me under my current circumstances, but with what we've experienced over the last two months, I can believe anything is possible.

A succulent affair, huh? Why does the thought of that simultaneously excite the hell out of me and scare me half to death?!

☆

Barbara: Tonight, after almost five years of partnership, one week after his first session with the angels, and on my birthday, Gary has proposed! He took me to the restaurant where we met for the first time, and sat at the very table we had that afternoon five years ago:

His picture looked so...nice. Not like the usual fare that responded to personals ads. Of course, who was I to say? I'd run the ad in the first place. When I called him that first time at his office, I was flustered and gay. He seemed surprised and excited that I called to follow up with this 5' 11" journalist. A date was made. We agreed to meet on Saturday afternoon at a trendy Italian restaurant in Uptown.

I arrived first. My stomach was tight. I wanted to either run or throw up. Before I had a chance to do either, he walked by, obviously scanning the room for me. Because he didn't know what I looked like, for a split second I had the upper hand.

As he passed, I watched him walk. He seemed ... rugged... intelligent. Not a bad physique, either.

"Gary?" I called to him. "Looking for someone?"

As he turned and our eyes met, there were no sparks! Hallelujah! I had learned through legions of bad relationships that having the earth move or getting hit by a thunderbolt at first sight didn't necessarily mean a thing. I wanted to learn how to build a relationship, not necessarily instantly have one. But first I was determined to get my own house in order and make that my source of strength, not the relationship. Ergo, I was looking for something casual, fun, uninvolved. That afternoon, sitting and laughing over ziti and designer mineral water, I had no idea what was in store ...

We laughed and talked and kept ourselves interesting and interested for four hours. As we walked around the lake after lunch, I looked up and noticed he didn't seem to be much taller than my 5' 8" frame. I confronted him point blank.

"You're 5' 11"?"

"With the wind at my back I am... "

We both laughed hysterically. How silly it was to lie about something so obvious! Now, lying about one's age, that's a different matter entirely. It'll take him weeks to figure that one out!

☆ ───────────────────────────────

As we parted ways, I asked him if he was a serial killer. He said yes. Such honesty, I thought.

The rest is history.

February 8, 1994

Kim: If it's not startling enough to be watching myself transform, I am also watching my children transform right before my eyes. It's interesting that the more I have patience for myself, the more I have patience for them. And then they find some for themselves, and consequently for each other and for me.

Katie and I had a minor conflict with Clay this afternoon. After a few minutes of quiet time to think and let the angels in, I said softly in her ear, "This is a small issue. Is it worth the friendship that you and your papa share?" She said simply, "No." I said, "Maybe you could let him know that before he leaves for work."

The old scenario might have been Katie going to apologize to her papa, then the two of them trying to make their respective points about the issue at hand until another fight broke out.

However, today was different. Katie went to him and said simply, "I'm sorry, Papa. I love you." I know that her little brain was still thinking that he was wrong and she was right, but she let herself be led by love and the conflict was dissolved.

This is one of those everyday miracles, those small successes, that cannot be overlooked.

Teresa: At Kim's tonight there are nine of us. Before the session, as we gather and chat, someone questioned why it seems that women seem to welcome these lessons more than men, at least not the men we've come in contact with. Unlike our women friends, who come as often as they can and really work the information into their lives for their betterment, there are only a handful of men that have come to the sessions, but not on a regular basis.

I think it's because men in general have been taught by culture not to go to that place of feeling and emotion. Certainly everything we've been learning in these sessions points each person directly inside to that very place. There is no other way to get there. We found that out in a hurry.

The question I have is, if men don't do the work and women do, where will that lead us? Will we come to a place where all women are evolved but the men aren't? Will that automatically force men to change? I don't know, but it's interesting to ponder the possibilities.

Barbara: The angels told me beforehand that the subject would be "Inspiration." Up until now, I honesty thought they just speak spontaneously on any given night about whatever suits their fancy. This is the first time it occurs to me they have this whole book already written.

Still, I'm a little nervous knowing ahead of time what they'll speak about. Will my knowing make it any less valid? Can my ego influence what they are going to say about inspiration? Somehow, I feel like I'm cheating.

Silly me. (When am I going to stop doubting they know exactly what they're doing?)

The Angels
February 8, 1994

"Inspiration"

What we see as we gaze upon you is like looking into the heavens on a cool clear night. Your lights are shining brighter than ever. This is due to a number of different factors within not only your individual selves, but the connections you make with each other and then out into the world.

There is a phenomenon occurring at this time much greater than the sums of its parts. This time period is ripe for the undertaking of projects, processes and personal development to really come into a full bloom and fruition. This is not to say that at other times within your lives you are not capable of making these dreams or concepts come into reality. It is to say, if you choose, you can use this time to further yourself in a faster-than-normal way.

Think of it like this. You are out sailing. There are periods when the wind gusts, and, if you are a seasoned sailor, as you sit with the rudder, you are always looking for the wind. This seems like an oxymoron or contradiction, as if you could actually see the wind over a body of water. But seasoned sailors can. They see the wind and they prepare for it. And when it comes, their sails are up and off they go.

Some sailors sit at the rudder and daydream about the sky and what has happened in the past and what they're going to do tomorrow, not looking for the wind. When the wind comes there is a great flurry of activity to get the sail up and catch it and off they go.

Either way, under the conditions prevalent now, you have an opportunity to advance yourself. If you act like a seasoned sailor and are prepared for the possibilities, you have a chance to make a greater leap. There is no mistake here. We are not saying if you're so concerned about what happened yesterday or what's going to happen tomorrow that you will completely miss it. But

☆

you have a better chance of catching that wind if you are aware of its existence.

That is why you come to hear us speak. You want to look across the water to see the wind. You want to be there, ready, for when this energy comes and hits your own personal sail. Some of you here know that you were caught with your pants down, so to speak. You felt yourselves rushing to get your sails up and yet you still found yourself gliding. It is up to you. It is in your hands.

This brings us to the topic of the conversation tonight. We hear what you ask of us. You have asked for a specific message, just as you have always come looking for a particular answer. Your minds are forming together to form one voice. That is the voice we hear.

We need to speak to you about inspiration. Inspiration is a key element in your physiological makeup that helps you to anticipate the wind. Some humans hold a definition of inspiration to be the wind, something that comes from the blue that inspires you, that moves you along from a source greater than yourself.

We would like to re-define inspiration. It becomes whether or not you are ready for the wind, or if you are going to have to scramble to put your sails up.

Inspiration, then, does not become something outside of you, it becomes a state of being. This is a very powerful state to be in. It requires a great readiness to be willing, to be looking for the wind and to create that state of willingness. What is required first and foremost is humility.

Humility has been defined in a way that says you feel smaller than the wind's presence and power. This is one side of humility. The side we refer to is a different kind of humility. It sets you up to be able to be ready for the wind. Humility doesn't make you smaller than the wind. It's makes you different from the wind. Humility is that you are human, and the wind is wind.

In other words, you are not less. You are not without. You do not rid yourselves of all your personal belongings and grovel at the feet of those who you think are greater than you, including the wind. Instead, you admit exactly who you are. There is a difference between thinking you need to be subservient to be humble, and clearly defining who you are.

☆ ───────────────────────────────

It seems simplistic to say "define who you are." We hear your conscious minds saying, "Oh yes, but what is the real path to walk? What should we really do?" "Oh yes, I know who I am. What else is there?" For you to truly believe with all of your being that you know exactly who you are will be detrimental for you to having your sails ready when the wind comes. This state of thinking "I know, I know, I know" is the state of standing there totally unprepared for when power comes to move you.

We cannot stress this enough. For you to think that you know so much prevents you from knowing what you don't know. And there is so much, children, that you do not know. There is so much to discover about self. So many misconceptions have been molded within you, by your parents, by this culture, by the people around you, by the newspapers, by the television. There is so much influence bombarding you at all times, it is surprising anyone can survive in a state of inspiration.

By knowing that you don't know all these things about yourselves, you open up a part of self you have kept closed. It is deep within you. It is a resistance to being prepared. It comes partially from this misconception that inspiration is something outside you that comes to you. By accepting that you don't know, you leave yourself open to possibilities you may not have thought of before.

For example, your friend tells you that you are in denial. You say you know you are not. You have immediately prevented an opportunity for inspiration. In defining yourself in a particular way, that you are not denying, you immediately shut the door for the possibility of getting to know yourself better.

It is somewhat contradictory and confusing. It seems like we are talking in a circle. You think you know yourself. Someone comes to reflect back to you who you are. You say "No, that is not who I am," and miss an opportunity. This does not necessarily mean what this person tells you is fact or law, or an immutable characteristic of self. It means if you shut them out by saying you know, then you miss the opportunity to bring that idea into yourself, sit with it for awhile and see how it feels within your heart and your body, to see if it reverberates to be true. And if it were to be true, if it were to be one of these so called "negative traits" you don't want to see about yourself, then what a gift has been given to you. Someone came to give you a piece of yourself back.

☆

In the process of giving, you receive. That alone is a powerful process.

When you feel someone criticizing you, or telling you something you don't want to hear, you can feel your resistance. Your body physically gets tense. It is like someone rubbing salt in a wound. That is a sign you are being prepared to receive the gift of perspective from an outside source.

Every human being who comes to you with whatever they have on their plate is, in essence, God.

So you look for inspiration. Perhaps you have been feeling stuck, or confused, or incomplete, or you don't know which direction to go. You are looking for inspiration. You are turning to the outside sources to find inspiration in someone's message, painting, words or music. It is not that they are not vehicles for the inspiration. But *you* hold the vessel that captures the inspiration. Every time you discount that within yourself, every time you think you are not worthy or that it is something apart from yourself, you miss the opportunity of the wind to come to your sails.

If you think of the word inspiration itself, it is the breathing of air and life into your body. It is not the air, it is the process of breathing.

Imagine you are stuck and cannot solve a problem, or make a decision. Say you are walking a road. On this side you see a vast source of knowledge that has been given to you throughout your life. On that side you see all your resistance and confusion. You are wondering how to get the two together. The first thing you must admit is that you do not know. It seems so simple, does it not? It seems so simple that we hear each of you thinking "Oh, I know." Yet how many of you have complete clarity in your mind? This alone is illustrative of the paradox that you face.

It is very important for each of you to see yourselves as a vessel that contains the inspiration, not to see the inspiration as something outside yourself. All of the sources of inspiration you have seen, including listening to our voice, are really from within you. This does not contradict what we have told you about conflict resolution. In fact, it reinforces the idea. All of the goodness in the world, all of the beauty, all of those times when you feel as if you are riding on the crest of a wave, are within you also. Just as conflict is, so is harmony. So is magnificence, and so is joy. And you must take responsibility for that part of your part of creation. You may think it is not important, but we are telling you "Oh yes, it is."

You must also take responsibility for all of the beauty and goodness being created in the world. Otherwise you do yourself a great disservice. Otherwise you make yourself a person who is not prepared at all for when the wind comes. It is difficult for you to do this. To take responsibility for such joy somehow brings to mind the idea that you are responsible for creating that joy in a sense that is bigger than it truly is. The way to differentiate between that and what is a wonderful, embracing, acceptance of all the joy is to understand that you are a small piece in a huge world filled with souls that are collectively creating that joy. For you to take complete responsibility would be assuming too much responsibility. For you to take no responsibility and simply await some unseen force to come from somewhere else and do good and leave on its own time doesn't fulfill your stand within the picture we are trying to paint for you, week after week, time after time.

We come to tell you that you are one body. The last time we spoke, we spoke of reflecting within yourself the conflict that is without and finding your responsibility in it. It is equally important to embrace the joy. You must all share the collective responsibility of the love you are creating. This is a profound lesson. So many human beings are isolated from this.

Do you not feel often times you are alone carrying the great burden? Perhaps a dear friend or family members understand, but often times you find yourself sitting at your desk or driving your car and feeling the burden is great. Yes, isn't it nice that people understand, but still it's such a great burden. You are then removing the instruments contained within you that allow you to be able to connect, to be able to understand.

A great microcosm has been created here. Each human being has a destiny that is important. There was a time on the Earth plane where you, as humans, dealt through much more basic communication. You weren't apes, but you were very primal. There were only a few basic instinctual messages that could be given from one to the other. You were hungry, you were tired, you wanted to have sex, and you needed to hunt. That was all there was.

Now, a massive complex of electrical energy flows between all humans on the Earth. On the lines of this energy runs information so massive and intense that your human minds block out perhaps 90% of all the information. Much of the information is too vast for your minds to understand, so it is good that you block it out.

But much of what you block out is due to the fact that you have been told that this is not how you communicate. You sit down, you write a letter, you call on the phone, you make body language. To actually think there is an electrical current that runs from human to human has been very downplayed and pooh-poohed. Those within the scientific community, up until recently, have not been able to prove this. They cannot hold it, or squeeze it, or see it. Yet those who work in the healing arts, or the musical arts, or telepathic arts know it exists there.

Part of being inspired and preparing yourselves to receive this information has to do with simply accepting its reality. It's so simple that you cannot see it has such a profound effect. This is true of so many things. The simplicity contained in these messages tends to make you want to overlook them and say you know them. But if you knew them, you would not have to say you knew them. When you receive a telepathic communication from someone, you don't have to say "I know, I know, yes I know." You simply know.

Accept the fact that there are many more lines of communication, and consequently so much more knowledge that you need. Then you will begin to receive that knowledge.

The other side of receiving this knowledge is to make your free will stand up, get off its butt and do it! This is not a metaphysical terminology. This is a classic picture of someone who sits on their couch all day long and watches TV. When the news comes on they complain about what's happening in the world. The only time they get up is to go to the refrigerator and get another alcoholic beverage. Then they come back and sit down. After a while they stop and feel uncomfortable, and perhaps they get sad. They don't know what to do, so perhaps they change the channel.

This is the lethargy that humanity has fallen into. Can you see it? It has permeated so many corners of your being that you do not understand how deep it runs. We don't tell you this because we want you to feel bad about yourselves. We tell you this so you will acknowledge it and say, "Yes, I do not know how deeply it has affected me, but I'm willing to admit I do not know so that I can learn how deeply it has affected me. I understand I am not a bad person. It is not that I cannot do it. It is simply that I've been sitting on this couch for so long I've forgotten how to stand up and turn off the television. I can walk deep into the woods and sit and close my eyes and wait for the wind. I can prepare myself with humility and grace to wait for the wind to come and fill me." And that is inspiration.

So what will it take then to get you to stand up? So many of you are in the process of standing. Do you see what just the beginning has done for you? Even those of you who still struggle, even those of you who still feel as if you are not getting anywhere. Something is happening. As you begin to stand up, a power rushes through you. We are here to tell you this is just the beginning. The more responsibility you take, the more you can bathe yourself in the sunlight of all of the goodness that you are. The more you can see how you can contribute individually, from your own heart, every single day, to making the world calmer, lighter, sweeter, kinder, the more you will stand up and soon you will arise above the Earth.

If you become confused and don't know how to get unstuck, this is what we suggest you do. Find the nearest stranger and be kind to them. "It's too simple," you say. "How will that solve all of my problems?" We challenge you to try. The next time you do not know what to do, find a stranger, look into their eyes, listen to what they say. Perhaps touch them. Give them that power of kindness. Be of service to them. We guarantee you, when you come away, you will be transformed. Perhaps not completely, but you will feel something stir inside you. It will be phenomenal.

Even if you are not stuck, we suggest you try this just for fun. See what happens. We hear some of you say you are afraid of people, it's too scary to go up to someone you don't know. What if they turn you off? What if they reject you? What if they pull a gun and shoot you? We say, it's worth the risk. More than likely, you will experience their soul next to yours. Try initiating this. Don't simply wait for someone to cross your path and decide you're going to try to be nice to them. You go off and stalk with kindness. What will be more powerful is if you can find someone who needs you and give yourself to them. It does not have to be great sums of money, or saving their life, or changing their direction. You simply need to sit down and look into their eyes and give them kindness. Give them your attention.

We challenge all of you here to do this every day once, until we speak with you again. You say it sounds so simple. Can you do it? Can you do it every day? Can you go out of your way to find someone you do not know to give them your kindness? It would seem a simple thing and yet, even as we say it, some of you feel confused or lost, or that you have blocks. You feel it in your body. "Well, why would that help me? Why would that enlighten me?"

It is one way to prepare yourself to be the vessel for inspiration. Once you are filled with inspiration, people do not need to hear lengthy explanations of all of the details of your life. People can simply sit next to you and feel the wind in your sails, and that you are prepared to accept this wind. That is inspiration.

They are fidgeting with the past or fussing with the future, but the wind comes and they quickly raise their sails as they sit beside you, because they do not want to miss this. And they think perhaps you are the inspiration. But then they overlook the great responsibility they have in making the good become part of the world. Do you see the importance of accepting the responsibility for the good? It cannot be overlooked.

Oh, dear children you cannot overlook it because your purpose here is to learn to love yourself. Learn to fill yourself up with this inspiration. There is no way you can save your world without that. There is no way to turn around and give to the world if your vessel is empty. Accept and embrace the good. Celebrate the good in yourselves, first and foremost, not as if you are better than anyone else, or have more insight, or are more important than anyone else.

It comes from a place that you don't know. You don't know how you did it. You don't know how it works. You don't know how these lines of communications, these electrical energies, were created. You don't know, but you know that they exist and you are a part of them. Celebrate your place within that grand scheme. And that is inspiration.

All of the emotions that rise up within you—the anger, the sadness, the joy, the confusion, the frustration, the awe, the wonder—all the emotions are the same. You can differentiate now between being intensely angry and being intensely inspired, but they are all the same. Because it is the process, not the outcome. Once you begin to accept all the emotions as one, you begin to see

☆ ─────────────────────────────────

them for what they truly are—electrical currents that run through you. At this point they elicit definition by your conscious mind. "Oh, I am so happy, I am getting married. Oh, I am so confused. Where should I go?" But when you take away the conscious thinking, they simply *are.* This is a bit advanced for you now, but we felt as if we could give it to you while you were in such a state of not knowing. When you begin to feel the emotions as electricity, you begin to disregard what your conscious minds tells you you are feeling and why. And that is inspiration.

"I seem to block when I visualize. Is there a reason for this blockage when I try to meditate?"

You are expecting to see with different eyes than you actually see. You have a preconceived idea of what you are supposed to see and how you are supposed to see it. That is your block. What you need to do, as opposed to the child Teresa, who needed to breathe in and say, "I know" to reassure herself, is to say that you don't know. You think you know so strongly in your mind how it should be that when it is not that way, you have convinced yourself you are not doing it. What is interesting and somewhat humorous to us is that all along you do it. It's just over here and you're looking over there. You do not know that you are looking the wrong way. As soon as you admit that you do not know, your head will turn.

Kim: *"Can you give me any kind of clarity about my blind spot?"*

So we told you you have a blind spot and you can't see it. You're blind to your blind spot.

"I'm open to knowing what it is, I just don't know what it is."

And thus, it would not be a blind spot.

We joke with you because you like us to. When we spoke with you and talked of your blind spot, we knew your receptivity was low. We also know you ask us to be brilliantly honest with you because you do not like the monkey business of covering things up to make them look pretty. This is your strength, you want just the facts. In the process you were undergoing, the magnificent awe-inspiring process of allowing our voices to come through you, we hailed you and applauded and embraced you. When it came time for us to tell you instructional material, because of your emotional place, you could not hear us clearly. This was the blind spot you were working beneath.

Understand it is an inherent human quality to have a blind spot. It is not that you are not good enough, or that you personally are missing something everyone else understands and they are standing behind you laughing and pointing because you do not see it. You cannot see the back of your head. You will never see the back of your head firsthand. You can look in the mirror, you can feel it, but you cannot see it. That is why mirrors were created. Mirrors, mirrors, mirrors [pointing to people in the group]. That is why there are three of you. That is why there are nine of you. That is why there are all of you. That is why there are angels hovering over you all of the time talking in your ear. You don't know.

You were so trying to convince us that you knew, you knew, you knew. And we were telling you, we know you know this, and we know you know that, but you do not know this, so let us help you. Let us be a mirror for you. But you could not hear us. That was okay, because now you can.

You are tremendously powerful when it is time for you to be a mirror to your friends. In fact, your experience with Barbara was so powerful that, simply through your gaze and through mirroring her blind spot, you illuminated, or, as she said, "blew a hole through the granite wall around her heart." You must learn to allow others to show you your blind spot.

You don't have the same blind spot all of your life. Once you learn, you can say, "Ah, I did not see that. Yes, thank you for giving me this gift of something I could not see." Then something else falls back behind you, to the back of your head. It is the process of learning.

"Someone brought up earlier that women are more receptive to the spiritual world. Is it true? If it is true, why?"

For years and years the male has dominated the culture and has gone off and killed each other. The male has created cities, great civilizations that have then become filled with pollution. The male has created a society based on the material.

Do not misunderstand what we say, particularly you males. It is not that you were doing wrong or trying to lead the Earth into big destruction. In fact, males moved from the places of instinct we talked of before (eating, sleeping, hunting and having sex). But by not allowing the female energy to balance, everything is off kilter. This is why your culture is so non-spiritual. It only appears as if only the women are emerging. What is actually happening is the balance is being restored. More women do what more men did then. But they do it in a woman's way. They should not try to be like men, although they can do what men can do in a woman's way. This is part of this resurgence of the women in the world.

There was a very large culture that was matriarchal, rather than patriarchal. It was not allowed to develop as long as the patriarchy has, otherwise it would suffer the same kind of imbalance in different ways.

The woman is the vessel of life. It is only natural that within her are held the great mysteries. The mysteries cannot be alive and continuing without both male and female. It is not a judgment. It is a declaration of definition. Men have what is needed to bring life, and they bring it to the woman. She puts it inside herself and mixes it up and then holds open the doorway to the other world. She has the power to lift the veil between the worlds. That is simply a fact. That is why all the mystery and receptivity in women is so prevalent. It is the nature of their being.

When men and women work together, when both are partners and equals, you have a true balance of the mystery. One cannot exist without the other. The woman can live for a long time, but if the womb is not used it will go barren. Now it is the time for women to counterbalance what has been happening.

Kim: "*I want to thank you for the beautiful words you spoke to our little girls on Saturday. I see changes in my daughter already.*"

We are always filled with such joy when we can sit and say, "You're welcome." So often we are put into a mystical, untouchable place. Your children are so beautiful. Watch them in the next two weeks and see what comes from them because of that.

Go back and read the individual questions asked tonight. Take what we have told you in the first part and read those questions with eyes that see through inspiration. In that way, you will also learn from the individual lessons that may not have anything to do with each other. You will see a deeper understanding of yourself.

We thank you for coming and listening. It is a very special thing for us to do this. We hope we have given you a little bit of jewels to take with you. If you hold them and listen to them, you will find inspiration around every corner as you go on in your life.

With that, we say we look forward to your coming again when we can simply watch and be amazed.

CHAPTER FIVE
The Murder

February 11, 1994

We are headed to a small town about sixty miles north to do a session for Sherry, the woman who called us from out of the blue last month. She is doing a research project for school on an unsolved, multiple murder that happened in the area around 1970. Barbara's friend, Paul, is taking the same class. When Sherry suggested calling in a psychic to try and glean information about what really happened, he referred her to us.

Patti, one of the children who was murdered so long ago, had been Sherry's best friend. They were twelve at the time. It kind of gave us chills to think about those kids, almost the same age as Katie and Sarah.

Barbara: I purposely do not want to talk beforehand about the murder. I don't want any preconceived ideas floating around my conscious mind about what might have happened that night almost fifteen years ago.

As we drive out of the city, I feel peculiar. Trying to describe my state to Kim, I gaze out the window into the snow, but all I can come up with was that it feels like looking at the world through a sheet of glass. We chuckle. But there's something definitely going on, as if I'm sitting high up off the seat. Everything is crystal clear but very far away.

In the van, we re-read the transcripts from January 18th, which mention we will be traveling to other parts of the country to fulfill our mission. This would be us: on our first road trip. As we read the familiar words, we take much "new" information from those pages. Allowing time to pass and lessons to be learned seems to give the transcripts new life, like reading them for the first time.

We have arranged to meet Sherry at a small Chinese restaurant on the outside of town. The three of us arrive early and order dinner.

"What in the world are we going to say to this stranger?" asks Barbara. "And how will she know who we are when she gets here?"

"She'll know who we are! How could she miss us?" Kim has ordered the special, and her appetizer has already arrived.

Halfway through dinner, a woman in her mid-twenties approaches us, introduces herself as Sherry and pulls up a chair. Although she seems somewhat detached, she is very much interested in what we have to say.

After a brief, perfunctory exchange of information, we briefly tell her the story of how we came together. She listens to our ramblings with great intent. When we're through, she says she has had a heaviness in her chest the entire day and believes it to be a premonition. She takes every word in stride, as eager as the rest of us to find out what's about to happen. With tension slowly mounting, we pay the bill and leave.

From the restaurant we drive to Sherry's apartment, where we meet Paul. All together there are five of us: Kim and Teresa sit on the love seat, covered by a blanket, holding hands; Paul and Barbara sit perpendicular to them on the sofa, Barbara closest to Kim and Teresa; Sherry sits on the floor on the other side of Paul. We form something of a backward "L."

Barbara: Because no one has told us any details of the murder or the relationship between this now grown woman and the memory of her friend's horrible demise, Kim, Teresa and I are doubly anxious to hear the story. As we settle into the sofa and prepare for the voices, we have no idea that we are about to take one step closer to the dimensions of the angels. All we know is that we're beginning another reading, anticipating something mind-blowing.

Did I say mind-blowing? I don't mean to underrate it ...

THE ANGELS
February 11, 1994

"The Murder"

You have come together with your collective energies to pose particular questions about a specific topic. This is a deviation from the usual lesson plan we have been delivering to the group.

We feel it is necessary to preface the experience by saying you have an idea of why you have been brought together. It is not the wrong idea, it is only a partial idea. What goes on here will not only be an exchange of information. Be prepared to be affected merely by the process of bringing the ethereal into the Earth plane. In other words, it does not matter what questions are asked in order to be affected by the process. We need to tell you this because you think you are looking for a specific thing. In the process of going after it, you have the opportunity to find many other things.

You have questions that you need to ask of us at this time.

"Is Patti with you?"
Yes.

"How is her spirit?"
She is a beautiful, shining light. She is prone to be drawn to sound, particularly music. She is of this condition because of her experience. She was "catapulted" to a particular level of teaching in which she excelled very quickly and soon became a teacher to a particular rank. When you pass from the Earth plane, you go into a "state" where there is no time or space. It is a condition of awareness.

Like the Earth plane, specific lessons are being taught through experiences. She became involved with those of like experience to learn very quickly. She was then able to turn around and teach others because she had experienced what she did.

You sit within your circle, connected perhaps by eyesight and voice. We sit within our circle, in our playing field, you could call

─── ☆

it. She does not sit within our circle. She is sitting on the perimeter, very much aware of all that transpires at this time.

"Is her family with her?"
It appears to us that most of her family is not, in the sense of the particular lesson she is learning. If you think of the collection of human beings with their eternal souls all touching in that soul place, in that way even *you* are not separated from her. Nor is her family. But in the way that you are separated from her, her family is involved in other lessons.

Her mother did not come out of her transition into this plane as "intact." What happened to her was a great shock to her physiological makeup involving the connection between her conscious mind of her human incarnations and her soul. In effect, the surge of emotion that was generated directly before she left the Earth plane had a different effect on her.

As Patti was a catalyst for her development and growth pattern, her mother carried into that realm in her soul, in that eternal place, a "photograph" of the experience, very much like a shadow or a negative. But Patti, because of her age and youth, transformed very quickly.

Her mother was always doting and clinging, concerned about safety, sometimes to an extreme. This did not mean she was a tough disciplinarian or if Patti stepped out of line that she was quickly rasped and taught to be afraid. It was concern for where everyone was and what was going on. There were certain rules in the house that you had to do such-and-such. Her father was more of a free spirit. He was more apt to have some leeway going back and forth.

Each in their own right has gone to the particular place that best serves their needs. For example, Alice, considering her condition because of the experience, went with others who had similar experiences and are sharing so that they could learn from each other, so that they could mirror. The same is true of everyone involved in the family.

The human leaves the Earth plane and finds that group of souls in transition. Much like you have found your new friends here, they have found each other in that place. There are guides and teachers to help them.

There comes a point in this state where a decision is made to either come back and reincarnate, or to move on. It is not a decision, such as, "Should I go to college?" That is more of a free-will decision. It is more like mandatory schooling. You knew when you got to the 12th grade you would graduate and have your options to go on. You would not choose to go back to 9th grade.

That is how it is when you are in this state and in this process of learning. When we say you have decided to come back, it is not so much that you have a choice. You have so many lessons you need to fulfill and undertake. Until you do that, you are destined to come back and reincarnate.

Patti is at a point where she has that decision to make. She has an opportunity at this time, which is unique to this particular time. What is happening on the Earth plane and in the universe is that there is a great transformation going on. Those that are capable of jumping into the waters and swimming with the flow are going to find themselves much farther down stream than those who are going to jump into the waters and try to swim against the current. They will eventually find themselves downstream. It will simply take them a longer period of time to do it.

She is in a very unique position where she can transcend at this point, depending on what happens within her development. And now you have been brought into this circle, so she can choose to come into the circle and become a teacher in this fashion. This is no coincidence, you see, that you are brought.

This is why we say you think you are looking for a particular answer and yet what you are finding is that there is a much greater force influencing the whole scenario that is beyond your conscious mind. It is a much greater mission. You have been called by power. You said you have felt this in your body today. You have been called, particularly by her, because her evolutionary development is somehow hand-in-hand with yours.

Again, this is not something so outrageously different than how you were when you were young. We see a particular place where the two of you used to go. Regardless of whether it was an actual physical place, like somewhere in the woods, behind the garage or in the barn, there was a place you used to meet. A lot of dreaming and a great deal of imagination went on there. Both of you had a very active imagination. You would fuel each other as you sat brain storming on the scenario and the stories you would create.

Of course, as children of that age you were far more open to such things. As adults, you shut down to the influence of the guides, or the angels, or the entities surrounding every human being that cannot be seen with the human eye. For her in particular, she had a great awareness and often times even had names for her imaginary friends. Even as she grew older, she began to lose that sense.

And so, you have been called here to help in this evolutionary process. We feel then, within that context, it should be for you to ask another question.

"Is there something Patti would like to say or tell us about her experience?"

We would like to say first of all, of this experience, it is lewd to speak this way. At that time, a darkness fell. It is difficult to describe the actual events because there is such a terror.

Patti cannot speak to you at this time directly. She attempted to enter the channel and was not sufficiently prepared. She "turned back," so to speak, and is allowing us to speak to you now.

Her vision is of darkness, and being taken away by two particular men who were very angry. It was not as if they seemed to be angry specifically at her, but that they were unloved as the source of their anger, over a long time of actually being hit themselves.

This is not what she knew then. This is what she knows now. She feels as if they were taken from the place where they lived. There was great commotion. The fear was indescribable. There was a sense of confusion, as if no one knew what was happening, even those who were in control. The fear was too great.

Her mother kept trying to tell them this was a big mistake. The men were not in their minds. They argued themselves. In a rage of anger, the mother was killed.

At that point, you see, everything exploded. The feeling that was generated was so intense when that happened, it was is if a terrible nightmare had happened without the option of waking. This amount of terror sends a soul into a particular state of being that combines with the energies of the chaos. It was a while until they decided everyone had seen too much.

☆ ───

Time passed, as if a day or two, but they did not leave the place they were. There was a sense of complete surrealism. Then everyone was taken very quickly.

This may not be something you can understand at this point, but it is important for her to explain this very clearly. What occurred is not something she carries in memory in Earth plane vision at this state. Her recollection of the actual events lead her back to the darkness.

She needs you to know that what occurred was a miracle. She does not mean it was a miracle to be killed. That was the darkness. That was the nightmare. She is afraid you cannot understand because there is not a chance of you experiencing this even a little bit.

After leaving the body, the souls of all involved were hurled into an entirely different consciousness, much different than if you had died simply peacefully in your bed. The amount of intense emotion was a dramatic part of her evolution in her present state. For that she must bless it because she has come to a place of great joy and development. She feels, perhaps, as you might if you were the child of someone who had abused you and came into adulthood knowing yourself better. Perhaps the abuse caused you to seek therapy, and through that process, you learned a greater process about self than you would have otherwise. The process of healing the abuse as a child could give you a much more indepth understanding of suffering. That is a blessing.

That is how she perceives it now. But, to go back and remember brings her back to that moment of terror. She says for her it does not matter. But for you, it is part of your process. For her, her dance, not only with her family, but with these two men, has been ended. It is a continuum that occurred in other particular lives. Her dance with them was the end of a karmic cycle she had been involved in. She wants you to know that this does not mean she was a bad person. She was not being punished, but that she danced a similar dance with them.

In another life, she had been in the Crusades and rode eastward from Europe. She did what you would consider pillaging and raping with no conscience. It was expected of her as a soldier, trained to do that job. She had a frequent picture in her mind of how it felt to take a woman, rape her, and then kill her. Because there was no conscience, she felt as if she was doing no wrong.

☆

Part of her ability to be where she is now came first from the crusades, and finally her own death. Having had those experiences and many, many others in the lives she has lived, she had come to a point of possible transcendence.

She says she did not know their names, but go to records of prison at that time, not precisely that time, but before by some months, and look. They were escapees. The crime was not originally so bad. But after their initial desire for robbing, they simply sank too deep into their own confusion and pain.

You could investigate. They escaped from somewhere farther west than here. It was not a big crime they were running from, but they made a larger inequity. Then they went north. She says she feels as if one has now passed on, but one still remains. She says she has, of course, forgiven, and you should too. She says you will find interesting resources into this investigation you are conducting. You will probably not be able to prove anything, but you will find enough to make you a little chilly...

"If I have the opportunity to see her brother Bobby in March, is there anything she would like me to say to him?"

He is in a place in his development where his confusion about his mother is a major blockage for him, without being part of his conscious mind. He does not awaken every day thinking about his mother. But there is an unfulfilled part of him out of his sight that effects how he feels about his life and what he does.

She needs to tell him to watch within the next six months. Some big change happens for him. It involves his own experience with death. It is not that he dies or someone close to him dies and he mourns. It is a much more detached experience. He is not so emotionally distraught or harmed in this way. Within that experience, as he reaches his confusion, he will find his mother inside him.

You have completed the function of this circle and part of her transformation and his also. He is thinking he is better now, but in the next six months, as if by some unseen force, feelings will arise that make him come face to face again with his mother.

You need to tell him that if, in the next six months, he does do this, he should know as he looks at his mother that it really is her there. First of all, he may not believe you. She can talk to him, and she will. He will say, "It was the craziest thing, but it was like she was talking to me, telling me." You can assure him that she now sits closer to the inner circle. When his time is right, because of this exchange tonight, she will be better able speak to him.

What has transpired here for you is just the beginning. A door has opened, and from now on there will be as the rushing of the wind for you. When you lie at night and you think of these things, you will feel the wind blow over you. For you, that is how power manifests itself.

We will come and speak with you again, and at that time you will be ready to receive different information about yourself. And until then, you need to simply watch and be amazed.

☆

"It's a love like your momma bears
It's a love like when you're sure that he cares
It's a love proven patient and fair
The Love that's always there."

"The Love that's Always There" © 1985 Barbara Lee With

Kim and Teresa: Here we are at Sherry's apartment, a woman we just met tonight, doing something we've become so comfortable doing, and yet it has such an ominous feeling. Nothing could have prepared us for this experience. How do you explore the murder of a mother and her children and not expect to feel terror? For several minutes while Barbara was "watching" the murder take place, the pain and terror on her face were nearly unbearable. She normally doesn't cry easily and, watching her, we could tell it took all her strength to keep from screaming and sobbing out loud.

Kim: The paradox is that the angels described the entire incident without one ounce of judgment about any of it. This diffused much of the emotion I might otherwise have felt. I have a blind faith that tells me that this work with the angels is only about love and goodness and, therefore, nothing but love and good things can come from it. I trust that the angels will lead us where we need to go. I believe this without a doubt, so I anticipated this experience openly and with faith. But the horror of this scene still has not sunk in yet. I mean, how can you *not* judge the brutal murder of four people, three of them children?

Barbara: When the angels described the part about the actual murder, my vision became filled with a muted terror. I had a vague sense of watching it from Patti's perspective, but she was telling an angel to tell me. I could barely see Alice's murder taking place, as if I were watching through a long tube. And while I was aware of the terror Patti had experienced, I was numb to the emotions, like being in shock.

At the same time, I remember clearly sitting in a circle with a number of other figures. I recognize the five of us, two others I knew to be Patti and Alice, but I can't identify the rest. It feels like being suspended in mid-air somewhere. The light is faint and gray, yet strikingly luminescent. We're looking at each other through sparkling smoke. I can't make out details, but I sense the nagging feeling of trying to remembering something from long ago or far away.

Finally, we ask Sherry to tell us the whole story. Now we're watching and being very much amazed as someone else tells us their story and gets out of the way.

Sherry: Patti moved to our town at the beginning of the fourth grade. She and I rode the bus together and were in the same class. Patti was cute, small framed, and a little shy, but she made friends easily. Her family consisted of her older sister Sally (four years older than us), her brother Will (one year older) and her brother Bobby (one year younger).

Alice, her mom, was single and worked at the local newspaper. Sally was a popular girl with lots of friends and talked a lot. Will was quiet and always very nice to people. Bobby was a little on the shy side, but he was really cute: a neat, playful kid.

Alice was a hard-working mom. I don't know if she received much support from her ex-husband, but she always made sure her children were taken care of. She had a pretty smile, just like Patti's.

The family lived in a secluded old farm house. The dirt road to the house twisted for four miles through the woods. Without knowing specifically where they lived, it would be difficult to find.

I didn't really like Patti at first, but the more I was around her, the more I got to know her. She came to my birthday party that year. We played games in the house and then made snow forts in the yard. Alice came to pick her up later in the afternoon. I remember thinking she was a plain-looking person, but very nice. Patti and I made each other's birthdays fun, as they were only ten days apart.

Patti had lots of friends. We all played together when we could. The Girlfriends had a special place over by the tall row of trees behind the school. We each had our favorite trees to sit under. It was our own private area. We would lay in the leaves, talk about how goofy boys were, and tell silly stories and just be good friends.

The Girlfriends were coming to the age where we would fight over the stupidest things: who would sit with who at lunch, who would be sleeping over at the others' house, stuff like that. Patti was always the one to mend spatting friends. I remember when I was the one The Girlfriends were mad at, she didn't take sides. She was still my friend during lunch and on the bus, quick to encourage and to laugh—she had angelic qualities that most people take for granted on a day-to-day basis. So when I think of Patti, I think of peace.

Patti also liked to sing. We'd sing to the radio on the bus and make up our own words to the songs and laugh at how silly they were. In seventh grade, our group of friends were all in chorus together. Some of The Girlfriends decided to perform "What Child is This?" for the Christmas concert. Patti and Sandy slept over one night a week before the concert. I played the piano while we practiced performing the song for my family. Man, were we primadonnas! We had to work extra hard not to laugh when we sang the part *"when the ox and ass are sleeping..."*

December 15, 1978

On Friday morning, Patti wasn't on the bus. The kids often helped Alice with the paper on Thursday nights and were sometimes late for school on Fridays. But Patti and her siblings still weren't in school by noon. They were always there by 10 a.m. on the late days.

I knew something unusual was going on. The custodian at our school was always joking around with kids during lunch; but not that day. When we asked him what was wrong, he was uneasy and said nothing. Even the teachers were in an odd mood.

As the day progressed, more people were acting strangely. Since our school had a total student body of only five hundred in grades seven through twelve, we all knew each other pretty well. When a few people started behaving oddly, it was very noticeable. At the end of the day we were all concerned that no one from the family had shown up for school. This was not typical of them.

When I got home, my mother was going out of her way to be nice. I started to get ready to do my chores when the phone rang. One of The Girlfriends called and asked me if I'd heard the news. I could tell by the tone of her voice that it wasn't good news. She said, "Didn't you hear that Patti's whole family is dead? They were all killed." I yelled at her to shut up! She must be kidding! She went on to say that someone killed the whole family the night before. I was absolutely stunned. I hung up the phone and turned to my mom to tell her what happened. She already knew, she had heard it on the news earlier that day.

I ran up to my room and cried for hours. That was a long weekend for me. I wasn't able to grieve with my other Girlfriends, or just sit with someone, hold someone, or have someone hold me. My parents didn't know how to console or comfort me, they just told me to stop crying. I was frightened and alone and still wasn't sure what had really happened.

When troubling events occur in our lives, we ask God why. As a child, this was a very profound question for me. I had a trust in God to protect me. I also had a mistrust of how *much* God was really going to protect me. If He couldn't protect a good person like Patti, how could I be sure He would protect me when I knew I wasn't always a very good girl?

The story of the murders was on the front page of the Saturday newspaper. I read the article slowly over and over again. At least now I knew that Bobby was still alive. I learned that the other members of the family had been shot. The murderer(s) had beaten Alice with the butt of the gun and then shot her twice in the stomach. She was still alive when the murderer made his way upstairs. He (they) proceeded upstairs and shot Will, Sally and Patti in the head while they were in their beds. I had to read in the paper about how my best friend had the top of her head blown off with a shot gun. Bobby was shot at, but was missed under all his blankets and somehow miraculously survived. He only remembered a silhouette of a man in his doorway. Once downstairs, the murderer(s) went back into Alice's bedroom and delivered a fatal shot gun blast to her head as well.

The police didn't have anyone in custody. None of the suspects made any sense. They couldn't find a motive. Nothing was taken from the house. Even the money on Sally's dresser we were going to use to order cheap rings from a catalog for the holidays was still there. There were no answers; nothing to make this horrible thing go away.

People used to think that Patti and I were sisters when they would see us together; we both were about the same size and had long hair. Since the police hadn't found the person that killed my friend, I thought he might try to come after me. I lived out in the country too, and no one would be able to help me either. I started sleeping with a knife under my pillow. I kept it there for a very long time.

Bobby was placed in different foster homes until his father was able to regain custody of him. We were never told where he was. December 14, 1978 was the last time I saw him.

After that weekend, it wasn't easy getting ready for school on Monday. I was looking forward to seeing my friends, but I also knew how painful it was going to be. On the bus, all the kids were very quiet. I could tell that Steve, the bus driver, was sad, too. I went to the seat that Patti and I usually shared and sat down. It was so strange to sit there alone. This was how it was going to be from now on. We rode together on the bus every day for almost three years. I just sat there with tears in my eyes all the way to school.

I walked into school that morning feeling like I wasn't really there. I saw The Girlfriends standing by the lockers, holding each other and crying. One of them came up to me and we cried together. There was such a heavy, painful feeling in my chest. I knew all The Girlfriends were feeling the same way. Somehow we made it to our first period class. The principal made an announcement over the P.A. telling the whole student body about the tragedy that our community had experienced over the weekend. It was a sterile announcement. It didn't comfort any of us. There was no counseling available to help the students deal with their grief. We just had each other.

The school allowed the student body to have a memorial service for our friends. The gymnasium was filled with students and a few community members. Some students sang songs, others read poetry. It was a surreal, slow-motion afternoon. Everyone wept.

The adults wanted to make this horrible thing go away, but not allowing students to talk and work through their emotions was a mistake. Not only was a family that was deeply cared for taken from us through a horrible tragedy beyond our imaginations, but the trust

☆ ────────────────────────────────────

in our small community was also diminished. People never used to lock their houses or their cars. No one ever thought twice about allowing their child to play in the park alone with other children. If a stranger pulled off to the side of the road with car trouble, there was never a doubt about giving that person a hand. We were a caring and trusting community. Now there was fear and mistrust. Mothers kept their children close to them. Fathers kept their shot guns loaded and ready to protect their families.

At this particular time, there was a political election for a new sheriff to take office. Certain people wanted credit for cracking the case. What was not officially reported was that the investigation had not been done according to protocol. There were too many people at the crime scene. Officers entered the yard, creating additional tracks in the snow. They entered the house in an unordered fashion, accidentally destroying would-be evidence. They started to clean the crime scene shortly after the murders, surely taking away critical evidence as well. I don't believe any of these acts were intentional. Our local officers never before had to deal with a tragedy such as this. The images of a murdered woman and her three dead children were forever burned into their memories. The training they had been given about entering a crime scene was rendered useless by their emotions and adrenaline.

I still had my close friends, but it wasn't the same. I kept an emotional safety cushion around myself. Why would it be of any benefit for me to get too close to people when they could be taken away so quickly and so horribly? There is still an insulation around me that prevents people from getting too close to me.

I tried to imagine what happened to my best friend the night she was killed. In my vision, I saw Patti laying down on her side with her hands tucked under her head, peaceful. When the papers said that she was shot in the head, I envisioned a small hole where the bullet went in. I could not allow myself to see her beautiful face obliterated. As I got older, I realized what a shotgun blast to the head could do to a person. My anger would frequently resurface as this horrifying image would appear. How could this happen to such a beautiful child?! Would I ever be able to erase this image from my mind?

Fifteen years after the death of my friend Patti, I was taking a college course that focused on how to make education interesting to our students—to investigate new ways of learning. Our class project was to re-investigate an old issue or event and come up with a new twist on how to present it. My group and I discussed several local issues and then I suggested, "How about looking into why these murders were never solved?" My group thought this was an unusual event that would be interesting to look into. Paul, the tall rock-n-roller dude, said, "Hey, I know this chic who's a psychic. That might be interesting." A psychic! Now we were really getting a new twist on our research! So we set up a session with Barbara to investigate our project.

February 11, 1994 was a cold evening with plenty of fresh snow from a recent storm. Tall Paul, Barbara, her two friends Teresa and Kim, and myself were in my small living room. We started by asking how Patti and her family were and a few questions about the place where they were currently residing. Then we moved on to the events surrounding the murders. We were given a description of how the people involved were impacted by the events that occurred that night in 1978, as well as how it impacted their evolution on the spiritual plane.

The questions of "Who did it?" and "What really happened that night?" were losing their merit as we became aware of what was going on and the number of people that were being effected by an event that happened 15 years ago. This was not about solving the murder. This process allowed Barbara to communicate with a specific soul, Patti, for the purpose of helping me heal.

I found comfort at the soul level to know that my best friend was alive and well in her spiritual evolution. I also learned that it was time to let go of the pain and forgive. I wasn't sure who to forgive, but that was no longer the issue. The powerful connection I made with Patti that night and her ability to reach down from where she was and heal my heart restored my belief that, in the end, everything will be okay.

☆   ☆   ☆

As if that weren't enough for one night, almost as soon as we were through at Sherry's, we all drove over to Rose's house, where Rose, Renee and Sandy had gathered, waiting to hear the angels talk. *What else* was in store for us?

THE ANGELS
February 11, 1994

"Commitment"

You have come together in a configuration that is randomly well-balanced and filled with the light of many different stars. "Randomly well-balanced" indicates that, although some of you are strangers, there is a connection that ran in the past and will continue in the future. If you were close to one and one was close to the other, you would also be close to the other. In this way you are creating a web of energy that is permeating the room where you are and the place where we aren't (ha ha).

There is a transition occurring at this time on your Earth plane like no other. This has to do with a realigning of the energy of the Earth. If your lives have been particularly transient in some way at this time, it is not by accident. All of your depths are being shaken loose. It is an act of liberation that has been agreed upon by all who are participating, not just in this room, but on a larger Earth plane. Know that this is not a time of coincidence and accidents. The events in your life, regardless of how confusing or angry they may appear, are part of a much greater transformation going on than you can see with your human eye.

You come together tonight sensing that you have been led here by a force beyond your own conscious control. Some feel this less than others, and yet as you look about the room, you wonder how you could have actually planned this configuration. You could not because you have amongst you someone that no one has known. This is very special for the conscious connections in your minds as you listen to these messages.

The presence of the stranger gives a light that is less expectant. In other words, the presence of the stranger gives a sense of less definition of what is to come. It is not that you look at the stranger and all of your expectations fall. It is an underlying balance of power that is put on the configuration.

☆ ————————————————————————

Tonight we want to speak to you about commitment. Now when we say commitment it is not necessarily talking about Barbara's engagement, although that falls into the category of commitment.

You have come to a place where you have agreed to participate. We can use this gathering tonight, or your work or family situation. Apply it to any set of circumstances in your life, even to the point of standing in line at the supermarket or sitting in the restaurant. It is not a definition of circumstance. It is a definition of purpose.

If you went to the restaurant you would expect the purpose was to eat and that it will unfold accordingly. You may not know exactly how purpose will unfold tonight. But the concept of commitment we want to give you tonight is a commitment to the moment. This concept is very simple, like all the concepts we give you. But it is not easy to do.

There are a number of reasons why it is not easy. One is that the conscious mind tells you over and over that you have to think about the past and future. That takes away from your commitment to the present.

Sometimes you cannot be committed to the moment because of a distraction in your body. Sometimes it's as your friend of the other night who was distracted by thoughts of his dog being locked in his house. He could not be committed to the moment.

This little element of being committed into the moment is essential for your awareness to expand. We hear your conscious mind saying, "This is an easy concept to grasp in a far off, ethereal way. Of course you need to be in the moment." But we need to reel it in and help you to learn to commit to every single moment we are here on the Earth plane.

We say "we" because we have a stake in your development here. Many of you already know this in your lessons. As each of you are evolving and growing and becoming more advanced in how you deal with all of the circumstances in your life, we are also evolving. Your particular angels may not necessarily have a chance to speak through the channel tonight, but they will. The purpose of this great evolutionary and vibrational change is so there can be much greater communication between the divine and the human, so we can work more in conjunction with each other.

We have watched for so many years as the Earth plane advances and changes, rises and falls. We try to give signs of miracles in dream states, and again in meditation, and then again in the written word. You go to books and look for ideas of how to get closer to the divine. Now is the time when we have "put our foot down" and say you need to now come and talk directly. It is time for you to hear us.

That is our commitment to you. We are with you every living, breathing moment that you exist in the Earth plane. We are with you on a soul level always, too, but now we talk about the Earth plane because that is where the work lies for you.

You know you have a soul that connects to the Higher Power. But that is not in question here. We do not have to convince anyone that you have a soul that is eternal. What we need to teach you, as some will attest, by step-by-step instructions, is how to fill your human incarnation with as much of your soul as you can in order to advance yourself, in order to evolve.

Not only because, in the future, when you will leave the Earth plane, having ingested so much of the information, but so that the quality of your life can be enhanced. This comes down to commitment.

At any moment, in any situation, if you struggle or hurt, if you feel as if you're being cheated, or wasting time, you ask, "How can I not feel this way? How can I not waste time? How can I feel more involved and less trapped?" We say the answer is commitment. At every moment you have the opportunity to make a choice as to how you're going to deal with that moment.

Sometimes you are taxed by impatience because something is not moving fast enough. Perhaps you are weighted down with the burdens of struggling for a financial footing, or you have questions about your partner. Every moment you can make a decision to be committed to that moment. What that takes is to accept the mystery within the moment.

It sounds like a broad generalization but it is not so. It is a simple process you can do. When you are faced with a difficult or painful challenge, you doubt yourself and crawl into bed and pull your covers up and wonder why these things happen to you. You wonder who you are, what you're doing and how you're going to make it through this moment. What you need to do is make the commitment to be in the moment and accept the mystery that you do not know exactly what the plan is.

☆

You are so small in your perceptions because you are humans, not because you're not good enough or missing something within you that doesn't allow you to unravel the big mystery and completely understand it. It is simply that you are human at this point. You cannot deny this.

It is like talking to children. They are not bad because they do not understand all the great mysteries of adulthood. They simply are in that place. You honor that place. It is easy to do that with children but so difficult to do that for yourself. In that moment you make the commitment to accept the mystery. Then you cannot say you are worried because you don't know what happens. You say, "I don't know what happens. I accept that mystery. I make a commitment to be fully in this moment, not knowing what the next one will bring me or why it's happening." When you remove the need to know why it's happening and where it is going, all you are left with is the moment. Then you embrace that.

If it is pain that you feel, you embrace that pain. Somewhere inside, you know through your many, many experiences on the Earth plane that from this pain always comes a birth because the pain is the death. You cannot have a birth without a death. You cannot *not* have death and birth in your Earth plane. It is the basis of your existence, you see? Everything from the master plan of death and birth, bringing the human being in and then out again, to the small daily births and deaths you go through, the "letting go of your childhood" type of death and into being reborn are a natural part of what you are involved in. But you have forgotten this.

The reason you have forgotten is because, on a soul level, you have set this stage yourself to give you an opportunity to depart on one of the most heroic journeys that you can. In this culture you live in, death and birth are taboo. You are told you need to find a middle and stay there. If you are not there, something is wrong.

We are here to tell you this is not so. The beautiful highs and the wonderful lows are all part of the flow that comes from within you and then out. To go against the grain of what you are told by the norms and mores of the world you live in takes commitment and courage. It takes the stuff of the soul coming forth into your conscious mind and into the decisions you make.

When you are distraught, confused or wrapped up in things that seem beyond your control, you do this simple step of making a commitment and embracing the mystery. It is like a ferris wheel, or a roller coaster, where you seek out that moment of going over the top and down again.

As you apply the concept of commitment to these different aspects of your life, a number of things will happen for you. Some will be disconcerting until you become familiar with that state. One of those things is that it leaves you without a definition in your conscious mind of what is happening. For if you are committed to the moment and living in the mystery, then all of the voices inside your head telling you who you are and what you are doing cease to exist. If they do not cease immediately, at least they are quelled a bit. The eventual goal is for those voices to quiet.

The disconcertion involved is to be left for a while without a sense of self, so to speak, until the transition comes. Take the difficulty that is so familiar to everyone, the pain of self-doubt. When you are in the middle of the self-doubt and not knowing, and want to hide from the world, make the commitment to be there with the mystery. Then the side of self that needs to define and demand is diminished. There is room then for the soul to enter and work. This is much like we have talked about in the power that fills your sails.

If you are so busy in your mind defining why you are sad, you miss the messages that come from deep within your subterranean that want to influence and move and shape you. You all came tonight without a plan specifically for who would be here and what time. Power ran its own course. If you were to have clung to who would be here and what time it was to begin, you would have been greatly disappointed if those people didn't arrive and it didn't start on time. Then when power really did arrive, perhaps your frame of mind would have been angry and disappointed and disoriented because you didn't stick to the plan your mind had defined. You can apply the concept of commitment to every situation.

In the depths of despair, when you are so absolutely sure it is because you have not done enough, or this person is out to get you, or you have had this bad luck all your life, and you knew it would happen, etc., etc., etc., you block the ability, when power does arrive, to heal and cleanse and transform yourself. You do not see it because it does not fit into that little definition you gave it. That is where commitment comes in. Commitment will allow you to fully embrace the moment, regardless of what it is.

Practice the art of commitment in this way and it will eventually lead you to quiet this mind of yours that runs on and on and on. You create this place you can fill up with the workings of the soul, based in mystery. Then you begin to hear the voices of the angels. They will always tell you what you need and bring you the reassurance that it is all right to not know, to embrace the mystery. It is not only necessary, it is essential to your transformation to live in the mystery and experience death and birth. The more you align yourself with these inner workings, the more you free your conscious mind that for so long was trained by your parents, siblings, school teachers, radio and TV newscasts and dictates of fashion, every conceivable corner of this very non-spiritual culture that you live in.

These voices will begin to align with the voices of your own divinity. Then it becomes second nature when you're going through a death to say, "I'm going through a death. I am committed to the mystery of this experience." Then you sit back and it's like going over the top of that roller coaster. You know eventually you will come back out the other side. If you have enough commitment, you will once again come back to the top, to that same place and go down again. What changes within this whole scenario is the moving picture that you call your life and all the definitions involved in the dramatic set-up of your life.

If you think, "This idea of commitment is so simple and you know it, but what's the *real thing* I should do to make my life more fluid and better," we say this is one very essential part you should not overlook. If you doubt that it is, begin to play with the concept and apply it to your life in any situation that you are in, even situations of joy. So often in your conscious mind, when you are faced with a great joy or great happiness, your voice kicks in to tell you that you are not worth it, you didn't "earn" it. You should not be able to sit and embrace the ecstasy and the joy of being alive. And so the joy and the ecstasy come and you slap it away. You contain it and try to define it as something less than what it is. "How could it be a miracle?" you say.

It is interesting to take the parallel of how all the lights are going on and off around you through seemingly no effect on your part. You can easily say the light burnt out. What you can follow up with is, what caused the light to burn out just at that moment? You can look at someone having a spiritual experience and say, "Oh, it is merely chemicals changing in their body causing their brain to see these things." You can look at it that way. But we say, if you want the fullness of your soul, accept that there may not be an answer for why and simply be with it. When the joy comes, do not say you are not worth it, it was simply an accident or a string of good luck that will change. Embrace it, allow it to fill you up and become you. Commit to the moment. Be there with it and accept the fact that it is a beautiful, mysterious process that you cannot explain, and that is okay.

You can also apply this to people, not necessarily just making a commitment with someone but to each individual human being who crosses your path. Sometimes you are angry at people because they seem to visit bad things upon you. You don't understand why these things are happening. But if you're committed to being with that person in that experience and come to accept that you may not know all of the lessons you are meant to learn at that very moment, you are much more receptive to receiving the knowledge and the power and the inspiration of the experience. Is that not what you all seek in life? It is hard for us to imagine why you would seek anything less than that.

Also remember, in every experience, like this gathering to-night, all parties involved agreed to participate. Each bit of power brought into the room was here by commitment to the mystery. You cannot say you were dragged here against your will. You cannot say you don't want to or weren't meant to participate, or what you heard was not meant for you. You cannot say these things because you are co-creating this reality. All of you together are making this room into a room.

If you are involved in a confrontation or struggle with some-one, then you are in agreement on a soul level. Chances are, before you came into this life, you connected with the soul of that person and asked for the lesson you are to learn. You should honor that person for bringing you this gift, as painful as it sometimes may seem. If you are committed, you will fully experience the moment, accept the mystery, and then later, as you reflect, you will see what great lessons had been brought to you at that time.

☆ ───────────────────────────────────

Do not underestimate the power you have at any given moment to make a decision to commit to being fully present in the moment. At first it may take a concerted effort to actually stand in a conflict and ask yourself, are you committed? Can you accept the mystery and go forth with that? When you say yes, then you open yourself up to all of the wonders that can be had by walking on that path at that time.

Know as you go out into your world, your own personal movie plays. You all have the ability to make a commitment to the moment that is within you and in front of you. If you have the courage and the commitment to the commitment, you will find fascinating things happening. Forget that it doesn't seem like it should have an effect. Forget that it seems that it is too simple, too grandiose, too untouchable. Try it in your life and as you do, watch and be amazed.

"And the magic in the darkness can deceive
It looks just like the devil if you don't believe
But it can keep you from harm, it can heal
It will take you down
It will make you feel ..."

"Satellite" © 1994 Barbara Lee With

Barbara: As we drive home, I realize what a surreal trip this has been! Between the subzero temperatures and battling the snow, then doing two sessions back-to-back, and the information about the murder, I'm exhausted. I feel scattered and unfocused. As we share our impressions of all that has happened, I gradually return to myself.

As always, our talk is filled with revelation and discussion. What a joy to travel around and meet these strong, spiritual women. As we immerse ourselves in the process of trying to "open our lens," once again I have that strange sensation of sitting high off the seat. This time it feels like I'm in a chariot, being escorted by my own two personal angels.

Through our discussions, we're starting to be able to navigate through this sea of new perceptions and sensations. But none of us are prepared for what is about to take place. At this moment, driving through the night after a long evening of talking with the angels, we have absolutely no idea...

February 12, 1994

We decide to meet in the afternoon to shop for dresses for Barbara's wedding. She's home editing the manuscript, loses track of time and misses her haircut. Teresa is edgy and stressed, and Kim's trying to deal with her ex-husband's approach to disciplining Katie. Suffice it to say, we're all in a hazy, almost hung-over state. We think shopping will ground us, but we have many questions to ask "them" to follow up from the experiences of the night before.

Over veggie sandwiches and French onion soup, Kim vents about her ex, trying to apply the principles we're learning to that difficult situation. She needs to get her anger and frustration out. Despite how quickly we're learning, there are still many things that hold us "earthbound."

Barbara: As almost a casual comment, I mention that I saw a circle of souls during the session at Sherry's. "It's like I actually saw the presence of entities. They were sitting in a circle, somewhat in human form, but more like ghosts. Hovering above them were their guides and our angels. Patti was sitting outside the circle, behind me and to my left. " Suddenly, Teresa begins describing what she saw from her vantage point.

Teresa: I remember the perception of sitting directly across from where Barbara had sensed Patti to be. I also saw the circle of souls.

Kim: I remember seeing things from up and behind where I was actually sitting. And while I didn't sense the circle, I saw Patti in the same place Barbara and Teresa did. We realize that configuration would put the three of us in a perfect triangle, with Patti intersecting the base.

Barbara: At one point, I remember the sensation in my body that Patti herself was about to speak through me, like the angels do. It felt like she was superimposed on me. I got something of a shock, and she quickly exited and said she wasn't quite ready. From there, she moved to my right, and to the right of her sat Alice. When Sherry asked a question about Alice, Alice answered to Patti, Patti told the angel, and the angel told me, right down the line.

Along with the realization that we were aware of our Soul Selves, it begins to occur to us how strikingly different our expectations were of what we thought we were going to hear about this murder, as opposed to what the angels actually told us. None of us really thought much about it beforehand. We were so exhilarated by the feeling of being "on assignment" and on the road, none of us ever seriously stopped to consider that, to do the session, it would feel like witnessing a murder.

Instead of giving us second-hand information about who the murderer was, the victims themselves led us through the horrifying scenes and delivered a terrifying description of what had happened that night. But perhaps the most remarkable thing of all was that the description was completely devoid of any judgment. There was never once even a reprimand for the killers. Even in the face of a truly horrific crime, there was only objective detachment.

So instead of learning that the murderer was Mr. Plum in the library with the candlestick, apparently the real reason for the session was to help Sherry face the truth about what had happened to her as a child.

"Do you realize the implications here? We aren't just talking to guides and entities and angels here. We're talking about the spirits of dead people here! People who had lived, and someone knew them when they were alive. Now they've come back to talk to those people, to help heal those people through us. We're talking to dead people!"

We can hardly get out of that restaurant fast enough! We make a beeline to Kim's house and the tape recorder to ask them what the heck is really going on here. Holy shit! These are dead people!

We sit at the center island in Kim's kitchen as Barbara closes her eyes and lets the angels speak. What follows are transcripts from what we consider to be a major turning point in our mission.

Although we have always known it on some level, now we know in our conscious minds. There *is* no turning back.

THE ANGELS
February 12, 1994

"The Triad"

There has been an increase in your vibrational frequencies. You have now begun to perceive much more clearly the true nature of all we have been saying to you. All of the lessons that came before have been preparatory for your time of arrival.

To come to the circle with your human eyes closed but your third eye open, combined with all of the knowledge you have accumulated by using the power of time to reinforce the lessons within your body, has caused you to release the blocks we spoke of earlier, ingrained in you simply because you are human.

There is a much greater transformation you will eventually experience. It is beyond your conscious minds at this time. Yet, if you were told six months ago you would see and learn all that you have at this point, you would have said, "They are crazy."

Do not limit yourselves by believing the confines of space and time. We understand. It's difficult to do this when you are engaged in the activities at hand. You will see this world constantly.

It will feel as if you are existing in two places at the same time. Except, your conscious mind will require a passage of time before it can receive the messages from the part of you eternally with us, and already an angel. In other words, you will recall an experience after it occurred and realize you have been seeing the superimposition all along.

Everything indeed has changed. You are moving at light speed. It's a great wonder to behold. You are correct when you say all of your "free time" is being created for you to put your time and energy together to create what it is you are creating. It's not that there's a time limit to finish this project by, it is that you are on a roll. You are so well-tuned. That is a miraculous unfolding.

Without thinking yourselves better than anyone else, we simply have to tell you that the phenomenon you are experiencing is very rare. While there are others on the Earth plane who are speaking and working from this level, very few have the qualifications the three of you have together. To watch you work at such a rapid pace inspires us. Just as Patti's earthly demise was a miracle, the apparent lack of business and finance are a miracle at work. Would you be quite as motivated if you did not need money? Would you be quite as capable of devoting such time to this project if you had work?

When we tell you this time period holds a special power, you have comprehended this meaning on a deep level and taken it to the Nth degree. It is an enlightening and inspirational process to watch, not just for us, but for those involved in the circle.

In the next two weeks you will make even greater strides toward the actualization of the material aspect of your mission. You must trust that all we say will come to pass. You don't have to believe in your conscious minds. In fact, there is a part of your mind that remains totally unconvinced. Do not try to change its mind. There is great power in detachment. You are driven from within. We are helping on every level we can.

New voices will be coming. Some of the more powerful, familiar voices will still be here. But some of the minor voices that have been present will be changing and moving to different groups. Other voices who have been in apprenticeship with other channels are now being sent to you because you are in The Master's Program.

You have evolved and thus you attract to you more evolved entities, angels and guides. We are optimistic you will provide a clean, clear channel that will be even more transparent as you progress. Because you have no idea where it is that you are actually going, you do not have to conceptualize it in the sense that a sailor would look far off to the horizon to know what direction to go. You need only keep the sails in good repair and continue on your mission.

We cannot begin to tell you what is going to happen to you between now and the end of the month. We smile and laugh as we say that because we hear your minds saying, "Oh, heavens, what more?!" But it is true and what you need to understand, dear children, is that this is only the beginning.

Most of the time a human being requires a certain amount of time to accept the transitory phases that he or she passes though in a transformation. Because of the unique configuration of the three of you together, each of you has to learn only a third of the lesson and then, through complete osmosis, it is transferred from one to the other. This is a very unique situation on the Earth plane.

Because of Barbara's nature, you are given a glimpse into what is happening ahead of time. This is not just because she can close her eyes and allow us to speak. The inherent makeup of her physiological system has always allowed her to live in the future. For her, this has been a great burden. She says she feels out of time. What is absolutely delightful and inspiring to all of you is that this very quality leads the whole movement. This is not to say she is the leader. It is to say the quality of living in the future and coming back to the present is essential to this movement. She has been the one who has been chosen to play that part.

What is equally as powerful and absolutely essential is the depth of love and compassion Teresa has. This is not to say no one else has that within them. But the physiological makeup of her being, the vessel that holds the compassion, is a rare and beautiful phenomenon on the Earth plane. In that sense, you are completely ahead of your time also.

What is as equally important is the sense of motivation and drive and articulation that come from Kim. This is a rare and beautiful quality on the Earth plane. It is absolutely essential for the mission.

In this way, you sit in the perfect triangle. The channel would simply be a time traveler without the compassion and articulation that comes from the two of you. Teresa would simply be a kind hearted woman without the vision and articulation. Kim would be someone simply well-spoken without the compassion and vision.

You can give yourselves strong hugs because you have made an evolutionary step. You know it in your being. You feel it in the effects of your actions and words upon the people around you. Is it not interesting to you (and this was purposely drawn to illustrate) that when you speak of the day-to-day world, as you did in speaking about [Kim's ex-husband] Tom, there is particular sensation. It was not wrong to speak in that way, it was simply used to illustrate the difference between when you speak the language of the three dimensions and when you speak the language of the universe. The air around you changes. It electrifies. Your vision becomes clearer, does it not? You open the door within and revelations come pouring through.

Don't necessarily quit talking about your lives amongst yourselves. That is not the message. In this particular time, there is a unique opportunity. The most you can make of it now will benefit you for the rest of the mission, which spans beyond your lifetime.

It is like going to a movie. You would not sit and talk about what happened yesterday. You would make the most of those few hours you sit and learn the story.

That is what we can tell you to do, but that is about all. You know. The combination of vision, compassion, and articulation allows you to instantly be aware that you do not know. If one of you does not know, this ability is put into play so quickly that the other two are there to offer the gift of knowledge about self and it is received graciously.

This was the gift you gave each other on the day of your conflict resolution. So, while that day was also very instructional and filled with what you have called Satori, there are also many other gifts exchanged that will unfold as you go. It was like your session last night when "they" said there are gifts you do not know.

You could not imagine, could you? You could not have written this story. You couldn't have planned that the next day you would meet and take an evolutionary step. That is a miracle.

We will leave you at this time to tell you to embrace this rare quality that is so special and unique to the three of you. We feel almost silly telling you to make the most of this opportunity. In fact, as the words were said, laughter arose around me, I got the famous nudge and I was told, "Just what is it you think they're doing?"

And so with that we thank you with all of our hearts and tell you we are always with you and we look forward to our next communication.

"You cannot separate
The dreamer from the dream.
Every dream you ever realize
Is another dream you need."

"Right Straight Back" © 1992 Barbara With

Staring into space, sitting at Kim's kitchen island, oddly enough in a perfect triangle, we don't say a word. Their words are too profound to comment on. Our jaws are agape and our eyes are glazed over. Slowly, we begin to consider the implications of what they are saying about the three of us.

We have known for awhile about working within a triad. The angels told us on January 1st that working this way creates balance. There can never be a tie, and our thoughts can align to each other more easily with three than with two or four. They then talked on January 11th about the three different directions we've been growing. And on January 18th, the angels told us even they work in sets of three. This new description of our positions correlates to the information from these previous sessions.

Barbara: All my life I have felt as if I was terribly out of time, either way behind or too far ahead. I was either dressed in fashions that were painfully out of style, or creating new ones no one had seen before. When I was a child, I often felt as if I could gaze into the future, but no one would believe me. That left me feeling sad and isolated, and very misunderstood.

Now the angels are telling me that these very traits are the aspects that lead this movement. As the one who sits in the seat of Vision, I am supposed to go ahead and gather information. Not that I am the leader, but Vision is the position that directs the movement of the learning and growing. It is the one that provides the insight into where the path is leading. And it makes sense. As the one brought into the triad who could already speak the words of the angels, of the three of us, I am the perfect choice for this visionary position.

Teresa: All my life I have felt inadequate because I can't seem to "think" for myself. I've always been able to see both sides of the story—no matter the scenario or conflict. In my adult years, I've often felt like a doormat. When someone hurts me, not only do I feel my pain about the situation, but I also have an innate ability to see through them and feel their pain, the very pain that is causing them to hurt me. Consequently, I cut people an awful lot of slack for what they "do to me."

I've also had difficulty making decisions. I spend a lot of time thinking about how everyone else will be affected by them. I can actually feel in my body how they will feel as a result of *my* decision. And, because I understand *their* feelings on such a deep level, I am often incapacitated from making decisions for myself. I would rather be in pain than to cause pain for someone else.

Now the angels tell me I hold the position of Compassion. Maybe all this work with Barbara as Vision and Kim as Articulation will teach me how to be compassionate without rendering me ineffective in my own life. Surely, it has to be leading somewhere magnificent and that would be a fabulous place to be!

Kim: I get it big time, when the angels say that I hold the position of Articulation. I've always been a talker and fairly comfortable speaking in front of groups.

The word they used that eludes me, though, is "motivation." I have been driven all my life to do more. It's never been about money or material things. For me, it's always been about more love, in the form of, "More attention, please." So much of my motivation has come from my need to be needed, my excessive need for love and acceptance. This cannot possibly be something the angels want me to teach other people. Why do I think I have a HUGE lesson coming here?

Perhaps what is most striking about this new information is the paradox of why we are qualified to hold these respective positions. The qualities about ourselves that have always caused us so much pain are now the very things bringing us honor.

If what they are saying is true, then without each other, we are oddly incomplete. It's as if we are actually three parts of a whole instead of three wholes. Without compassion and articulation, Barbara is just someone who can see into the future. Without vision and articulation, Teresa is just kind-hearted. And without vision and compassion, Kim is just well-spoken.

The question now becomes: If we are just mere mortals without the other two, who are we when we come together? What do the combination of these three character traits create?

And what exactly do they mean when they say, "This is a rare phenomenon?" Surely there are others working in triads. We have seen that with Kanti, Lois and Rita. But can it be true that few are taking this to the extremes that we are?

There is a sense that we finally know something. This is the stream of events we have been waiting for, the ones that will give us proof that what we're doing is not just the product of our overactive and dramatic imaginations.

From that realization comes an inability to speak, as if we have looked into the eye of God and don't have words to explain it.

☆   ☆   ☆

Barbara: Teresa and I drive back to my house while Kim picks up and delivers kids. When Kim finally arrives, we sit quiet, humbled, not knowing what to say.

Huddled in my studio, we pass the time in silence. At last Kim brings up the point that, in the big picture of the murder, it's really Bobby who's the most important here. He'd lost his father to divorce two or three years before the murder. What must that fateful night alone, witnessing his family's death, have done to his heart, his mind, his soul?

As Kim talks, images suddenly begin filling my mind. I start to remember what I'd seen during the segment of the session when Patti was dying. At first, I see and feel her cowering in fear as she watches her mother struggle with the assailant. There comes a sense that, when she sees her mother get shot, she knows instantly, on some level, that she, too, is going to die.

Teresa adds, "And you know up until that very moment when Alice was shot, those kids believed with all their hearts that their mom was going to save them."

With that, a wind begins swirling around within me, with pictures and images spinning in the flow of air. I start to shake and weep uncontrollably.   I see Patti in her bed, under the covers, enveloped in such an intense terror that it sends her right out of her body. Before the murderers even enter her bedroom to kill her, her spirit has left her body.   I watch as her bed becomes smaller and smaller, and the tunnel darkens and finally goes black.

Then all the images stop in front of me and I know what really transpired the day before.

"What if," I say between sobs, "just like people come to us for help with their lives, what if, now the angels are coming to us for help with their missions of healing? What if Patti and Alice, along with their angels, really arranged the whole thing so we would go to Sherry so they could help her finally get over this horrible pain from her past? And what if the part about Bobby having some kind of healing experience with his mother is actually the angels planning this entire scenario so that some time in the future, maybe Bobby will stand face to face with us and his mother will talk to him?"

We are silent.   Indeed, through Kim's articulation, Teresa's compassion and my vision, we have come to see the true nature of what happened the night before.   We're talking to dead people. They're trying to get us to help them heal the loved ones they left behind. We decide to listen again to the tape we did in Kim's kitchen.

This time we roar with laughter! The humor eases our nerves. We can feel the angels, and Patti and Alice in the room with us. When they get to the part about how our conscious minds must be thinking "Oh heavens," we laugh even louder. We know that they know that we're really thinking, "Holy shit!"

We're all exhausted. After Kim and Teresa go home, I climb into bed to try and sleep. I sense the somewhat distant presence of Patti and Alice, where they'd been sitting during the session. Falling into a deep sleep, I dream all night about doors and windows.

☆ ──

CHAPTER SIX
We Are God?

February 13, 1994

Barbara: I wake up feeling nauseous. Perhaps it would be best to busy myself today with something besides thinking. I decide to edit the transcripts from December fourteenth, our first group.

Further and further into the edits, I begin to realize that back in that first group session, they foretold everything that is happening to us now. I'm stunned. I don't remember anything about it at all. I've even read this transcript five or six times. Now suddenly it reads very clearly as a guide to seeing the circle of souls that we'd seen at Sherry's:

As you sit here in this Earth plane in December 1993, superimposed upon that, can you not feel the essence of that other life?

I call Teresa. "How can this be?" I ask in bewilderment.

"I'm not really sure, but I'm having the same experience transcribing the tape from January first."

You see the three of you sitting in a triangle ... we see that superimposed upon a greater picture we can't describe. It is based more from soul, intuition, telepathy, and communication without words.

As you see yourselves sitting in this circle, feel this superimposition upon you. You are luminous beings.

We're simultaneously baffled and mortified.

It appears that the more we learn about letting go of the ego voices and allowing room for the Soul Self to fill us, the more we learn from re-reading all the sessions we've done so far. That makes all this information living: It changes and grows as we do. It's an eerie feeling to go back and see things in those words that were seemingly never seen before.

This idea of the circle of souls from the first meeting was acceptable as a metaphor. We could get excited about it as poetry. But to actually experience the sense of traveling to that soul place and seeing it with human eyes, with our physical bodies, is more than our conscious minds can handle at this time. That disbelief registers as fear in my body. Teresa and I feel the same nauseous wave.

Thinking like this certainly does add to the feeling of being totally crazy.

The more we become aware of those parts of ourselves that sit in that circle and learn to be in that place, the more we will become, like they've been telling us, cognizant of being in two places at once. We will be conscious of the part of us here in physical form, but we will also be aware of being in the circle of souls, in spirit form. They say it will take a few days to remember the superimposition, but that we will be able to see it more clearly as we progress through our studies.

Later that night ...

It is late at night. We are all three in our respective beds, talking together through the miracle of conference calling. There is something inherently terrifying about the idea of being a part of this much larger plan of healing. It seems like it should be a comfort, but due to the terror of looking into the face of the murder, we are all feeling scared and unsure about our desire to continue.

At this point we begin to realize that we cannot go back. The experiences of the past two months have changed our lives forever. Teresa and Barbara seeing the circle of souls together at the reading is particularly dissettling. Like an upset stomach, this is making us all sick.

We talk about the thoughts we are all having about whether or not there is a devil and the mythology of evil souls roaming the universe looking for unsuspecting humans like ourselves who have dared to enter the untouchable realm of spirit. Have we opened our souls to some sort of ploy on the part of something trying to trap us forever? Will we be lured in only to find, after it's too late, we're doomed to wander the earth like ghosts?

A fitful night of sleep lies ahead for us all.

Kim: Barb and Teresa are pretty freaked out about this "circle of souls" thing. I didn't see it. I did sense that each of us shifted position in some way, which had to be awareness of the Soul Self, since we did not move physically. And I knew where Patti was in relation to each of us. But I didn't see a Circle of Souls, the vision the two of them shared.

An old, dysfunctional voice seems to have kicked in, persistently reminding me that I didn't see those visions because I'm not good enough to have seen them. I'm also obsessing about the assignment of positions of the triad and how disappointed I feel. I watch as my doubts and inadequacies parade before my eyes. I am ranting and raving in my head about how compassionate I have always been. Surely there has been some kind of mistake. I want to be Compassion. What I am is, once again, not good enough.

I'm the boring one. Barbara is the big-deal, get-all-the-attention visionary. Teresa has been named Love itself. But what am I? Isn't being called Articulation just a nice way of saying that I talk too much? I have always talked too much! And no matter how hard I tried, I could never be soft-spoken. I thought I had come such a long way, but when push comes to shove, I still feel, deep down inside, that I must be basically flawed.

When I was younger, my dad gave me a card that said "Be sure brain is engaged before putting mouth in gear." My family loved to say, "Kim is talking just to hear her head rattle." Am I ever going to get it?

Dear God, please make these old, negative voices stop. Please send the voices of angels. Don't let anyone know that I go on and on in my head like this. What if Barbara found out that I'm still obsessing? Ugh, it's just like when I was a child: "Don't let Dad find out!" If Dad finds out, you better hope no one else finds out because Dad will be embarrassed, then he'll be even more angry than he was when he found out in the first place. But what is it that I am so afraid of him finding out? I don't quite know what could be so horrible.

Maybe it's that I can't be perfect, no matter how hard I try. I've spent my entire life thinking that if I can't be perfect, then I must be shit. Isn't there a middle road somewhere?

I certainly function well each day. Nobody can tell from the outside how badly I feel on the inside. Surely everybody isn't walking around feeling like this. Or are they? Maybe I'm not the only person pretending to be whole.

February 14, 1994

Barbara: It's a beautiful morning to go skiing. As I glide through the dried yellow prairie grasses, the angels and I have a long conversation about the murder, about fear in general, and about how to protect ourselves.

They say as long as we fill ourselves with the light of love, in the end, nothing in the universe can hurt us. Even if we were chopped into little pieces, we would then make great fertilizer, and what would we care? We'd be dead! And our souls would live on, learning and growing with the angels, where there is only unconditional love.

I trust them completely. I know with my body that this fear we feel is partly because we are going places few humans have chosen to go to in order to understand the true nature of ourselves. I feel honored to have been chosen, to have chosen to participate in this mission.

I call Kim and Teresa, excited about how I'm going to inspire them with the angels' morning message of love and light and laughter, but they're already feeling better. It's a new, sparkling sunny day, and we have much work to do if we're going to save the world.

Kim: This morning, I feel inspired to write a thank you letter to the angels:

I knew if we asked you for comfort, you would give it. Barb just called to tell Teresa and me the wonderful experience you created for her when she went skiing. You said that you were sorry that we were so scared by what we saw the night we spoke to Patti. We understood that there were reasons for what we were feeling, but it was so helpful to get your input about it. You are always so reassuring whenever we need it.

It was comforting how you superimposed the lessons of the murder onto our lives by thought. It makes perfect sense that by experiencing Patti's terror in the way we did, without judgment, we were able to be moved by it without actually experiencing harm ourselves.

It is such a wonder to watch you work. You weave the words in such a magical way. Each person takes what they are able to understand when the messages are given, which is always amazing, but the most miraculous part is how the messages become more profound as each day passes. Thank you.

February 15, 1994

Barbara: I spend the entire day in the studio with Steve mixing my songs. We work closely with little talk. The many layers of the music become a puzzle in my mind as we mutually decide, for the most part without words, what should go where and how everything should sound. I get lost in wave after wave of vocal harmonies and rock-and-roll guitar.

After the session, I'm supposed to meet Gary for dinner and a show. We've had tickets for months to see the touring company of "Miss Saigon." My session ran late, and as I race out of the studio and get into the car, I feel peculiar. I know I am driving the car, but I'm seeing the world through a thick film that is distorting my vision. And I have the strangest sensation that I'm on the roof of the car, much like the elevated feeling coming home from Sherry's session.

Suddenly my eyelids are heavy and thick. I pick up Gary and we drive around looking for a parking spot. He tells me, "Turn right" and I turn left. When he suggests we park in our usual ramp, I can't remember how to get there. We finally find a parking space on the street and go into a restaurant.

Not only do I apparently look rather ghostly, but I can't read the menu. It's like trying to read a foreign language. I chalk it up to the stress of mixing.

☆

Over dinner, Gary and I talk about how songs are recorded. Mixing music is a complicated process. You listen to many things, first alone and then in relation to each other. For example, you listen to all the vocal lines individually. Then you listen to the lead vocal in relation to the lower harmony, then in relation to the higher harmony. Next, you listen to the lower and higher harmony together, then all three in relation to each other. You have to do this with every instrument. When you are mixing drums, you have to listen to the twelve or fifteen individual drums and cymbals, then create a balanced relationship between all of them. Then they are listened to in relation to the bass. So you are actually building a huge network of interrelated sounds that are balanced from within.

It becomes clear to me as I talk that the listening involved in mixing a song is very much like looking into infinity. The same sensation can be created holding two mirrors together so they reflect into themselves. The session this afternoon in the studio has apparently drawn me in much farther than I know or have ever experienced before.

Gary and I pass on the play, which is fine with me. If I can't read a menu, I surely can't sit in a theater for three hours and understand the plot of a musical. And Gary is tired from a long day of writing. So, with very little regret about spending $70 on theater tickets we do not use, we head home.

Kim: I'm still trying to work through my feelings about the positions of the triad and how unimportant I feel. It hasn't taken me long to work through all the issues, gripes and justifications available in a "human" argument. But then my ego and my conscious mind have to stop and look from a new direction: I cannot justify my indignant stance by saying that the assignment is wrong. Whether I like it or not, the description of Articulation fits me to a tee. I cannot say that "they" didn't know me well enough to see how compassionate I really am. If they don't know me then I better be ready to abandon my entire belief in working with the angels. Of course they know me. Of course the description is accurate. So, what is my problem?

My mind goes back to the principles of Conflict Resolution. Who am I really in conflict with? Not Teresa or Barbara. None of this is their doing. They don't even know what's going on in my tiny mind with the big ego. And I'm not in conflict with the angels, who I trust completely and who, I am sure, can hear my mind endlessly bitching and whining. I can almost hear them say, "We hate it for you."

So, is this the part where I am left with no one to be in conflict with but me? I feel the old urges to blame someone else rather than go inside and look at my own weaknesses, but I've learned enough to know that this is not about anyone else but me. And I know the point here is not to make me feel worthless. So, what is the point? What?

Teresa: I've been getting pretty good at this meditation thing lately. It's always interesting to see where I'll end up. Last night, prompted by all the discussion about whether or not I'll get to go to Hawaii, I was in for a little surprise.

I did my usual preparation, waiting for the kitties and the dog to get settled while I focused on my breathing. Once all of us were quiet, the door opened and I realized I was very high up on a cliff. The ocean was far below and a beautiful waterfall tumbled over the cliff to my right. I walked to the edge of the cliff and knew immediately I was in Hawaii. Nowhere else on the planet looks like that.

I stood there for a moment just taking it all in when suddenly I felt a nudge to leap right off the cliff and fly. I was frightened at first but then I took a leap of faith. Suddenly I was an eagle, soaring around the cliff, over the waterfall and then out over the ocean. Two beautiful whales were swimming below me. As I dove down into the water, I turned into a whale and swam along with them. I could feel the gentle rhythm of their motion and the beauty of their majesty. Beautiful beams of sunlight cascaded down through the water. For that moment, I could feel our one-ness.

Then, I pointed myself upward to breach. The moment I left the water, I was airborne again. I looked down and said goodbye to my aquatic friends then headed back to my waterfall. I landed safely on the edge of my cliff by the waterfall, once again surrounded by beautiful flowers and foliage. I turned and looked back one more time at this most breathtaking view, drinking in as much as I possibly could. I didn't want it to end and yet, at that moment, I knew it was just the beginning.

February 16, 1994

Barbara: Another beautiful day to ski. I head off to the trails in the early morning. The regional park is empty except for me and one other woman. The first time she skis past, she startles me a bit. The second time, I notice she's wearing a purple jacket. After she disappears around the corner, I hear the voice in my right ear say, *"The woman in the purple jacket has a brother who's in trouble. Tell her not to worry, that in a month he will be her ally."*

In times like these, I feel equal parts intrigued and insane. My conscious mind says, "I'm so very sure I am going to stop a perfect stranger and tell her something like that! How am I going to explain it? That I hear voices in my head? Like that's something everyone should understand!"

As I continue skiing, I debate whether to actually say something to her. I've never been afraid to shock people. I'm known for saying things that cause a stir at the least opportune moments. But I'm not sure how to explain this to someone I don't know from Adam.

I conclude that if, indeed, I've pledged to follow the instructions of the angels literally, then I have to do this, too. I decide if she is at the end of the trail when I get there I will somehow find a way to tell her what I heard.

As I conclude my run and glide to the trail head, she is nowhere in sight, but there are two other women, *both* wearing purple jackets! "They" did not say which woman specifically. They said, *"The woman in the purple jacket."* How clever of them to be so cryptic.

I approach the first woman and ask if she has a brother.

"Yes, why?"

I ask if he's in trouble.

"He was, but he's not any more. Why?"

I tell her I know she's going to think I'm a little loopy, but that I get messages. I then quote their words.

She looks perplexed, but it appears the message itself confuses her more than the messenger. She's trying to understand why they would tell her about her brother being in trouble when he's come through it already.

At that point the other woman speaks up. "How do you know it isn't my brother? Because he is in trouble. He's in trouble with me."

☆ ———————————————————————

She explains the recent discovery in her therapy of being sexually abused by her father. Her brother, normally her best friend, has turned against her. It's breaking her heart, because today is her birthday. In fact, the little ski trip is a way for her friend to try and cheer her up.

"Well, I don't think you should worry because apparently in a month he will be your ally."

"It would be an answer to my prayers."

We chat briefly, and then I leave. There is no sense of amazement on their part, no "How do you know all this?" It's a simple conversation, as if it happens every day. How can this be??

I can't get back to the office fast enough. As I drive, suddenly it becomes clear to me where I was the night before in the studio. All the while I was mixing my song, I was being given a glimpse into not only the fourth dimension, but the fifth, sixth, seventh…who knows how far into infinity the angels took me?

But what is the point of the lesson? Is the network of the relationship between all the various aspects of the music a metaphor for humanity? Are we all interrelated and connected to every stranger, just like the bass relates to the drums and so forth, so much so that we really are all part of one big song?

They told us after the murder that it would take a day to remember the superimposition, but we would become more and more aware of it's presence. As I think back to being in the studio, I distinctly recall the sensation of floating on the ceiling. I'm sure my conscious mind could not possibly understand all that I saw in those places, which is why I was deposited back on earth feeling like I had just come out of surgery.

When I get to the office, the girls immediately suggest we go eat oatmeal.

Teresa: It seems as if Barbara is truly gone. I don't know where I think she went, but she seems insane. We are fairly worried about her. Kim and I often say how thankful we are to have jobs, families and children. Somehow that seems to keep us grounded. When things get a little too "out there" for us, we can always count on a sick child or work deadline to bring us back to present moment. Barbara has Gary, but they're so independent in their relationship, I don't know if he fully understands how out-there she is getting.

Since the angels labeled us Vision, Compassion and Articulation, we are beginning to see a picture in our minds that helps during these times when things seem so crazy. We envision Barbara way out there floating around in space. There's a line from Barbara down to me. I am out there too, but not nearly as far. From me, there's another line that goes down to Kim, who was always firmly rooted on the ground. We envision her with big heavy boots on, holding the line so we don't all just float away. Kim even went out and bought two new pairs of boots a few days ago. It was very symbolic. Holding onto this picture somehow makes us feel safe because we know that none of us will let go of that line that bonds us so tightly.

Kim: The problem is, Barbara seems to be going so far out that Teresa cannot keep a hold of her and it feels like we have to pull her back to Earth with the tether line.

I'm starting to feel better about being Articulation. I guess the Angels didn't say that I was completely devoid of compassion and vision. And I suppose it's pretty important to have someone assigned to the task of grounding, especially as far out as Barbara is going.

Barbara: I may not know where I am anymore, but when I think about the angels, directing me to speak to that woman on her birthday, about her estranged brother to give her words of hope and love, I am blown away. Another daily miracle, that's all I can say…

February 17, 1994

The three of us meet to ask the angels some questions about Teresa's sister in North Carolina. What they tell us is a little unexpected. They say they've been slowing us down. Slowing us down?! If this is slower, we hate to think about what will happen when they speed us up!

☆ ───────────────────────────────────

THE ANGELS
February 17, 1994

"Circle of Souls"

There is so much we have to tell you. You have felt this as the days have past. You hear us speaking quite clearly from behind the screens in your mind, sometimes without the screens.

You are aware of the sensation of all of you being within earshot of the voices. While one may be off skiing, one driving children, one having coffee, in completely different physical locales, you hear the same message. This is a quality that has been developed by the three of you through your studies.

It is interesting to note that there are others in your circle who are also experiencing the similar voice. It is not as easy to understand who because you do not have as close contact with everyone who hears the similar voice. This is what happens when you begin to align your conscious mind with the thoughts of your eternal mind. Because the eternal mind is connected to the eternal soul, which is then again God's soul, you are in touch with all time and all people.

What is about to happen for you is that the angels are working on levels that you cannot comprehend in order to bring into reality the dreams of the angels. The angels work constantly through the human being but because of all the noise and resistance, it appears to be a "miracle" when one of their dreams actually becomes reality in the Earth plane. Because you are so well known in our field, we understand there is an instant actualization that comes about.

After your encounters with seeing the circle with your inner eyes, we felt a need to slow down somewhat. Your physical bodies are being tested at this time by these experiences. You must be careful with yourself. We don't mean you have to be meek in your movements. We mean take good care of yourself. It is like watching your children prepare for a important event in their lives. As you watch, you see them progress and learn, move simultaneously from fear to exhilaration, until the day arrives when they fully participate in the event. When it's over, you see them breathe a sigh of relief and yet with a little sorrow because all that they have worked for came into fruition and then passed.

This is what is happening for you. We are orchestrating the most wondrous of displays. You will be completely amazed. We are preparing you, body, mind and emotion, to accept the gifts that are going to be given to you. You cannot begin to comprehend exactly what these changes will be.

Within the next two months, there will be two trips. One comes completely unexpectedly and totally financed by outside sources. The other is one of your own accord in which you will meet another circle that will broaden the circle that you know now.

As we look upon you, there are several circles rotating around the three of you. Because you are our links to the physical reality, we say for us, in this set of circumstances, everything emanates from this configuration, from this circle, from this triangle. It is as if there is a boiling pot and out of the heat and the motion arise the vapors and the steam that carries into the air and through the ethers, past those who are sitting directly beside and behind you. You see a circle within a circle within a circle into eternity. These circles will become very, very large.

You are going to find money. You will feel as if you have won the lottery. It will be a time of great celebration. We condone your use of some of the funds in having a celebration.

There will be many tears of joy. What will be tremendously interesting for you is that the tears of joy are not so much that now you have money. You are complete, brilliant, shining stars with only twelve dollars. The tears of joy will be the recognition that you receive from people around you who have had major doubts. Something about the acquisition of the money is going to turn the heads of a particular group of people. They may not sit within the same circles, but within the circles there is a particular kind of skeptic that the acquisition of the money will awaken.

This is not to be judged because money is no more or less of a power than any other physicality. Water is as powerful as money. You have a glass of water, you have two dollars. You have a great raging, torrential river, you have $100,000. Do not judge the people who then come because they've seen you manifest. It does not matter the reason why they come. It does not matter that they doubt. All they need to do is hear the voices and you will provide that opportunity.

It is going to be more and more outside of your hands. You're going to feel when the wave hits, when the wind finally makes contact with the sail, you just have to make sure that you eat and sleep and have good hygiene and all else will fall into place around you. Life will become something different. The struggles you involved yourselves in in the past will seem like a dream. You will have to stretch to remember what it was like to be so caught up in the "little people's world." That will seem like your childhood. This will be as if you are teenagers. Teenagers with a mission.

Teresa: *"I have questions from Dawn. She's struggling with her Christianity and trying to put it all together with what she's feeling and learning now that makes so much sense to her but doesn't fit with her history of religion. She fears she may be jeopardizing what she calls her own salvation. Do you have any words that will help her with this?"*

The beautiful part about what she is going through is that she is learning that no one can "save" her but herself. There is a misconception that has been so long entrenched in the religions of the world: That the gods who came, came to save. This indicates that there is something from which to be saved. It is advantageous for the classical sense of the church to create the feeling of inferiority. This gives the institution a sense of power within the eyes of those who are inferior. The movement that is happening now that is not just our voices, is to embrace each individual human being with the light and the love of God.

This is not a light that comes from outside the self, that breaks through the clouds, only if you're lucky. The light and love of God come from within your own heart. You feel this with every act of kindness. You feel this with the love of friends and family. The love (the light) of God emulates from within.

So you see dear child Dawn, you have nothing to be saved from. You are already a brilliant, loving, shining child of God with all that you need to take care of the world around you.

What is happening with you is that you are questioning authority. Not just the man in the robes on Sunday but the authority that has been laid down in your own mind and taped over and over that says you are a sinner, that you are bad, and so you need this to be saved. You can still hold that image and live under that conception, if that is your choice. But do you not see how it darkens your light? Do you not see the difference of having an angel tell you you are a brilliant, shining vessel of love, inspiration for those who see you, and that you are a sinner, you are bad. You think you need this thing outside yourself to be saved. Feel the difference between those two statements. Feel how your body feels when you hear them. Does it not bring tears to your eyes to know that you are already saved? Does it not move you to think that you are the source of the light? You are filled with the power of Jesus' love rather than you are separate and always doing wrong.

The church and the transformations that are going on within it are the same transformations that are going on within your mind. As you look around you will see the same messages from different sources. That will seem coincidental.

You have to know in your heart that what you hold dear to you, what you value, what is precious to you, what you love, will not be separated from you no matter what our voices say, no matter what the man in the robes on Sunday says, no matter what anyone says. Even, dear child Dawn, what you say. You are already a brilliant light that cannot be diminished. It is only for you now, in your conscious mind, to accept all of the love you have within you in order to give it away.

You will come to some brilliant understandings very soon that will clear this from your mind. You must be prepared to go through a period of grief about leaving behind the misconceptions you have been carrying with you for a long time. The misconception is that you are a sinner. If you look up sinner [in the dictionary], it will give a clearer understanding of why you are not one. That you cannot be saved unless you go every Sunday to a specific place to do what people tell you. You can go at any time of the day or night to any place that you love that is beautiful, that is dear to you. Go at sunrise and sit by the water. You will feel God there. As you sit and watch the sun rise and struggle with the questions that come to your mind, you must understand the struggle is necessary. You, too, are on a heroic journey back to yourself. And as you watch the sun rise and clear your mind and feel God in the light of the early day, know in your heart, dear child Dawn, that this is a reflection of what is within you.

Kim: *"I understand you have some message in reference to Katie's father Tom."*

Katie's father is going to go through a miraculous transformation that will leave you quite stunned. It is going to come through her because she is going to find the strength and clarity to be able to communicate with him. His effect upon her is part of the difficulty with Tom. No one can tell him the effect that he has upon them. There are certain things he will not listen to. He will not listen to you. It's almost as if simply the sound of your voice causes him to put up his wall. You could be telling him it's a beautiful day and he's a wonderful man, but because of the nature of the sound of your voice to him, he would hear it distorted and troubled. It causes him anger.

In the next month, we see Katie being able to receive answers to her questions by herself. They will be very simple answers. This will be advantageous. She will ask a question about her father. They will answer. They will tell her her father loves her but he is in much pain. It is as if he is behind a sheet of glass and doesn't know how to touch her. They will tell her she has the power to pick up a heavy object and throw it through the glass. This will confuse her and so you can then help. In this way, she will channel you.

You will be able to guide her to know what to say when the time comes to throw the stone through the glass. It will be a simple exchange with her and Tom. It will be at the exact moment when his guard is down. He looks at his beautiful daughter with her lovely eyes telling him, "Daddy, I miss you." She will show him her pain. She will find the strength within her not to be afraid to be vulnerable with him. She will know after she is through she has a place of complete safety and unconditional love awaiting her. In that way she goes off into the front lines, a courageous young woman, changing the world in her path. It will be a beautiful sight to behold. Aside from what happens with your former husband, you will be amazed at what it does for your daughter.

"Should I share this with her, or should I wait and let you tell her and then she'll come to me?"

Allow her to find the answer and then give her everything you have.

Teresa: *"Can you share with me a little of what Sarah is feeling? She seems to be okay with everything she's learned, but it's hard to tell sometimes."*

Sarah is a very funny child. She has constructed this Safety Child; call her Safety Girl. She feels she needs to put on Safety Girl's dress in the morning, her pajamas at night. She needs to be safe. What is happening within her at this time is she's beginning to wonder what all the fuss about being safe is about. It's as if she gets up and her first thought is, "I need to be safe," and her second thought is, "Safe from what? Nothing can hurt you."

Bit by bit she begins to step out very quietly. She is so quiet, quiet like a little mouse, until one day you turn around and she's written you a beautiful song and she smiles very quietly, but to herself she feels the power. She does not have words for it. She is very quiet, but it begins to build. Very much like a very deep lake. She does not crash and fall on the rocks and attract attention. She accumulates power and keeps it safe. That is part of the advantage of being the safety girl. She guards herself well, stores her bits and pieces of power, accumulating slowly. One day you will turn around and she will have done something else quite miraculous, and you will say, "Where in the world did that come from?" And she will smile and say, "From my power." You need not worry.

"Will she have an effect on her father?"

She *has* an effect on her father. It is very quiet. Quiet like a mouse. Until one day he will turn around and she will have her power. It will not be through words, it will be through music. In that way, he will be opened. Do not underestimate what is happening with her and him at this time. You will look around soon and see them standing together. Your heart will leap for joy and you will understand what it is that made you separate in the first place. Because then you will understand what has brought you back together.

We need to leave you with the idea that all is in transition. There is not much more we can say. We have said quite a bit so far. You will come again just the three of you to prepare for your meeting [of February 26]. It will be quite a test for all three of you, who will all speak in one way or another. It is important to tell these people your story. Prepare each segment. Tape the entire thing. Your human story will be part of your publication also.

☆ ─────────────────────────────

People will be intrigued. You have what they want. You will give it to them. And nothing will be as it ever was again.

It's the time that passed,
it's the times to come,
It's absolutely everyone.
It's the seasons,
It's the elements,
It's Tribes."

"Tribes" © 1993 Barbara Lee With

February 21, 1994

Barbara: The morning dawns clear and cold, a perfect day for some laps in the pool. Things have been so intense lately, every day is filled with this buzzing energy. Swimming seems to help calm me down.

The club is practically empty. It's not unusual to be the only one in the pool this time of the morning. I take my usual warm-up laps and begin thinking about the state of my singing trio. (It seems the angels led me to work in a triad even before meeting Kim and Teresa.)

Aisha has quit the trio. I know it's time for her to establish herself and her own music, but I'm still angry that she blames me for her decision to go. I feel very wronged, hurt, and, perhaps most of all, incredibly inconvenienced. Every time I think about the work it's going to take to find someone to replace her, I dive even deeper into my anger.

I continue to turn this over in my mind as I swim. The water is cool and soothing and helps to ease some of the discomfort about this topic.

Suddenly, without warning, Aisha's face appears in front of me, not like a memory, more three dimensional, like a hologram. We are so close I can almost feel our noses touching. Then her face quickly turns into Deb's face, then Teresa, Kim, Rose, and a series of women that I've known in my life, some of whom I haven't see for a long time. Each face that appears before me is saying, "Don't you get it? It's us!" I don't really understand what they mean. What's us?

☆ ───────────────────────────

Without warning, I am no longer in the pool. I'm not aware of my body at all and can hold neither the thought or the feeling that I'm swimming. Instead, I'm sitting in a circle with these women, in the same circle we were in during the murder session. The light is fluorescent and hazy, except this time I can clearly make out who's who and where they are sitting. They're all excitedly talking at once about how, "It's us!" Each of them is trying to tell me that we are the ones controlling everything. "It's us, Barbara, don't you get it?"

I'm still confused as to what they mean. Then I see that each of them has a little hand puppet on the end of their arms. Each puppet is made in their own image. I look down and see, I, too, have a puppet that looks just like me. We're playing with them in a smaller circle, like children might with dolls. Aisha puts her puppet up into my face and says, "We create the situations 'down there.' There isn't anyone else making us do things. It's us."

This is still confusing me. I understand the concept but where is everyone else then? I mean, the angels and the guides, and, well, God?

"We are God! The synergistic effect of our energies all together creates that vast and eternal power that everyone calls God. There is no one else out here but us! But us together is what creates that force."

I'm stunned. I don't know who is actually telling me this, or if anyone in particular is speaking these words at all. I hear them inside my head, and yet all of the women in this circle with their little hand puppets are laughing and playing and nodding in agreement.

The implications are truly maddening. If indeed we're in that much control, then, truly there are no victims. If these eternal parts of ourselves are hanging around in the ethers pulling the strings of our lives, coordinating all that happens with the higher selves of everyone else, then it's true: I am in complete agreement with what happens, no matter how much I feel wronged or used or taken for granted. So, Aisha and I are really in cahoots together, and we made all those details of our breakup happen as they did for an agreed-upon purpose.

Are these the long arms of the soul they refer to in "Conflict Resolution?" Are these those "hand puppets" they reference, too?

Frankly, I'm both cynical and stupefied. Here I am, sitting in the circle of souls, learning that I am part of God, and that I have total control, not only of my own life, but I am working in cooperation with everyone else. What I don't understand is why then do we make things happen that cause so much pain and conflict? Why aren't we just making great things happen to us instead of all this muck and mire we have to wade through?

As soon as I think this, everyone stops playing with their puppets and silently looks at me. There is no answer returned to that question.

I look back at them. Theoretically, I tell them, I should now be able to, from the circle, position my little hand puppet to materialize in physical form somewhere, and then send my Soul Self in to experience what she is feeling and seeing. It would mean that, in physical form, I would be in three places at once: swimming in the pool, in the circle of souls, and wherever else I decide to materialize.

But how would I do that? I mean, is this a dream, or is some part of these women really present in this experience? Will any of these women, in their conscious minds, remember this talk? Perhaps it will show up in their dreams. Will it be like a distant memory for them or is this totally and completely of my own making?

I turn my awareness once again to the group. Everyone is still silent. They're looking at me, as if they've been reading my mind and are waiting for me to take the lead.

"Okay, then, if We are God, then I should be able to materialize in physical form in the office and see what the real Kim and Teresa are doing, exactly right at this moment! Right?"

"Yes, do that! See what they're up to! See what they're doing" Suddenly everyone is speaking at once. Everyone agrees to this experiment I'm about to undertake.

With that, the scene instantly changes. It seems between the force of all of us coming into agreement, and my intention to materialize, I'm suddenly standing in Kim's office. The air is thick, like that sheet of glass I have been looking through lately. It feels as if I'm underwater, but I can breathe. Seated at the counter are Kim and Teresa, looking at a book and talking among themselves. They're the only part of the image that's in focus. The rest of the room is spinning, like they are inside a tornado. Everything is moving very quickly around them, but they are still.

I look at them. Can they see me? I ask them, "What are you doing right now?"

Kim looks up and smiles and says, *"We're on the telephone talking about a man in trouble."*

They look at me. I look at them. Suddenly I'm swimming in the pool again.

Racing up the stairs of the club, I can hardly believe what has happened. Not only is the shock of completely being removed from the pool still ringing in my body, but the realization of the meaning of what these women were trying to tell me hits me in the face like a locker door. We are God?! I mean, I've heard this theory before, but also heard it dismissed as New Age hokum. Shirley MacLaine stood on the beach in her made-for-TV movie and shouted it to the world. I thought it was wonderful then. So why is this personal vision of the same message freaking me out so badly?

I fumble with my locker and dig out a quarter. Standing nude and dripping wet on the pay phone in the locker room, I call the office. Kim answers.

I'm out of breath and still in shock. "What are you doing right now?"

"Right now? Oh, Teresa and I are reading 'Conflict Resolution' and trying to use it to work through this stuff with Tom. What are you doing?"

I can't speak. I know Kim and her ex-husband have been fighting since before they divorced. They said in the vision, *"We're on the telephone talking about a man in trouble,"* and yet they were also reading a book. We often refer to talking to the angels as calling them on the phone. And Tom certainly is in trouble.

"I'm coming over," and I hang up.

Racing over in the car, there is no place in my mind that can make sense of what is happening in my body. Not just because of the idea that we are synergistically creating God, and that there might not be anyone else "out there" but "Us." But the sensation of leaving the pool and traveling to the office has jumbled all of my nerve endings. Was I really, in some form, in the office, the circle of souls *and* the pool at the same time? I certainly don't remember swimming. And the image of the office swirling around in the middle of a vortex was completely disconcerting. What was that? And they were sitting at the counter reading a book. And then, in "real life" they're actually reading "Conflict Resolution." How can this be?

I'm a mess. I desperately need someone to explain this to me.

As I walk through the door, they look up like nothing's happened. I half expect them to tell me they saw my ghost hovering around the office earlier.

I sit down across from them, breathing hard, as if I've run from the club. I grab the edge of the counter with my hands to steady myself.

"Hi! What's up?" Kim asks casually.

"Well, I just had another vision in the pool. Only this time it was more than a vision. I think I actually traveled here and talked to you guys."

I proceed to explain what happened. I try my best to convey the bodily feelings, but nothing like this has ever happened to me, and I'm at a loss as to what to say. I try my best to explain about leaving the pool and coming to the office. I tell them what they said to me.

"Oh, cool! We're just trying to work through all this stuff with Tom that I've been going through." Kim turns back to the transcript and continues to talk about what happened with Tom the day before.

I can't believe they're so casual!! Can't they see I'm distressed here? There doesn't seem to be a way to draw their attention to the fact that I'm completely disoriented. I bang my head on the counter. Kim stops talking and looks up.

"Guys, there was another part to the vision. It was all of us, all the women I've ever known in my life. We were sitting in a circle and we had these hand puppets. Someone was telling me that, didn't I get it, we are God. There is no one else 'out there.' It's just us. All of us together, all our energy together is creating the power that everyone calls God."

They stare at me blankly. I stare back. There's a long silence.

"What do you mean, 'We are God?'"

☆ ────────────────────────

"I mean that, just like our name, synergy, the whole is much greater than the sum of the parts, and that all our parts join together synergistically to create what everyone thinks is God. But there is no God. I mean, not like a Being that is out there, apart from us. It's all us. WE ARE GOD!!"

By now I'm frantic. The effect of leaving the pool has still not worn off. The inability of my conscious mind to understand what has happened to my body is causing me to panic. And they certainly aren't understanding what I'm trying to say. So I sit there, raving on about how we are God with Kim and Teresa looking at me like I'm speaking Chinese.

We decide to go eat oatmeal.

Barbara: We sit in a back booth at the restaurant. Kim and Teresa stared at me blankly while I blather on, trying to explain about being in three places at once. But perhaps what's most upsetting is trying to understand this synergistic vision of who or what God is. It makes perfect sense to me, since the angels have been professing all along that we are all one body, that together, the parts make up a sum that is infinitely greater than our puny little individual physical selves. But every time I pose a point, Kim comes back with the idea that we can't possibly assume that much responsibility for what happens to us, that, yes indeed there is a piece of God in all of us, but that we are still separate from God. Kim and I go head-to-head over our oatmeal while Teresa sits silently, looking as if she wants to flee.

Kim: Okay, now she's gone too far. I thought she was doing better with her ego, but this is too much. It makes me mad and sad all at the same time. We had dreams of going on Oprah someday and talking about God and angels and all of humanity coming together to save our beautiful Earth. I was beginning to have hope that the world would survive for our children and their children. I thought we were going to do something to make a difference. Now her ego is back in the picture. I am *not* going on Oprah with her if she's going to say "We are God!"

Teresa: Barbara's trying to explain more about what she saw. Suddenly, Kim and I realize she's trying to tell us WE ARE GOD. That's a bit too much. She has really gone off the deep end this time. We sit trying to eat our oatmeal and sound casual. It's not working. I can feel the discussion heating up between Barbara and Kim, and that familiar dread creeping over me when those two start going at it with each other. The more Barbara explains, somehow, what she's saying does seem possible, I guess. But my Baptist upbringing kicks in big time and I don't know exactly what to do. Kim seems quite upset and is having none of it.

Kim: I need more time to process this information and Barb seems to want some kind of instant acceptance, which, for me, is utterly impossible. First of all, I have never been exposed to such an idea in all my life...we are God?! Who's ever heard of such a thing? Barb says that she's heard of this notion before and still she's freaked out. How does she expect me to react to this? I need time.

And even if this is ordinary, everyday information, which it isn't, I'm just beginning to figure out why God would even love me. It's going to take a lot to go from feeling so unworthy to thinking that we are God. No wonder she feels crazy.

Barbara: I desperately need someone to tell me what's going on. There's no safe place in my mind for what I've experienced. If indeed we have that much power, then it's absolutely imperative that we learn to use it responsibly and with pure compassion or else we will surely destroy ourselves and maybe half the universe by underestimating ourselves. And, in fact, is that exactly what the human race is doing now? Is that why the angels have come to us with all these lessons?

Why is it so hard for Kim and Teresa to understand? What I need the most perhaps at this moment is for them to agree, to understand, to open themselves to the possibility that what I'm saying might have merit. I wouldn't lie about this vision, and I wouldn't make this up just to get attention. Why are they so adverse to even giving me a modicum of understanding?

Surely, surely, surely I am going insane ...

February 23, 1994

Tonight five of us meet for our next scheduled session, which the angels say is going to be about Honor and Articulation. At this point, we're feeling pretty disjointed. Huge questions are looming, within ourselves and with each other. We don't know who we are anymore. We turn to the angels.

THE ANGELS
February 23, 1994

"Honor & Articulation"

We tell you all greetings and thank you for coming together and asking us to speak.

A major shift in consciousness has taken place in the past few days. It is a continuation of the realigning of earth energy. All of you should take care in the next few weeks to make sure you do not overdo. There will be a heightened ability to lack sleep and sufficient nutrition.

Take care of yourselves and stay in contact with each other. The connections you have to each other are extremely important. Without a familiar voice of reassurance from outside yourself, there is a tendency to feel quite alone. As you awaken, you become aware of your connections to all of the humans you live with in your world. Working paradoxically then, you also feel equally as alone. This is a misconception and yet, there is some truth to it. You all know within your world that when push comes to shove, you and only you are responsible for your lives.

Human beings have a tendency to push off their responsibility onto others or to blame circumstances. If this thing had only occurred, then I would have been able to do that thing." This misconception is part of the transformation happening all around the world at this time. More and more it will be essential for all of you individually and society as a whole to take on more responsibility for your lives and for each other. This does not mean that you will completely eliminate complaining, but this whining that you do will be done with much more humor, as you resign yourself to tackle the tasks at hand.

We tell you this to make sure the words have been said. When you are feeling in need, or confused and alone, do not let your pride or fear or a judgment you make about yourself stop you from calling someone who is close to you who has a language you can understand. It may be just one person at this time you feel can understand and speak words that reassure you, but that person or those few people will begin to grow in your lives.

Each of you will find your lives turning and changing from the places you have been. This change has to do with coming face-to-face with your fear because, when all is said and done, for each of you, it is fear that stops you from releasing the blocks that keep you from moving forward.

Coming face-to-face with fear is very frightening and yet, if you view it from a certain perspective, you can lighten the fear of fear. The reason you will come face-to-face with your fear is to embrace it and to love it as a part of you. By loving your fear, you can then diminish it.

If you need to, personify your fear. The personification might be a thief or burglar coming into your house and trying to do you harm. But when you think of that thief making his way into your home, ominous and dark, imagine you turn on all of the lights and fill your house up with love. Put on a pot of tea and invite him to sit and talk about why he has come to visit you. Find out what it is you actually fear so you can then begin to transform that fear into love.

This process may take a great deal of effort on your part, but it is the purpose in your being here on this earth plane. As you have often said, you wonder what your purpose is. We tell you, your purpose is to be here, to feel, to love, to transform, to save the world. You cannot save the world until you yourselves empty the vessel within you of the fear and replace it with the brilliant, shining, unconditional love that is your birthright.

Tonight we speak with you about Honor and Articulation. These two elements, when working in conjunction with each other, are a very powerful medium not only to overcome your fear, but to then turn to the world and pass along all of the great goodness contained within those vessels that are your hearts. This is so essential to your personal development and, consequently, the transformation of your world.

As you look around in your world today, there is much danger. It is a frightening place to be, is it not? Yet we tell you, the world is not dangerous in the sense you think. You are not afraid because the world is a dangerous place; the world is a dangerous place because you are so afraid.

This can be a difficult concept to digest if you expect to simply think it and no longer feel fear. Thinking is the first step to change your perspective. By thinking in this way, you are no longer a victim. You become the one who can change the world by removing your fear.

If you include the element of honor, you begin to set up a situation where you bring yourself the gifts you need. Do not wait for others or situations or timing to bring you verification that you are a beautiful child of a brilliant light. Honor yourself.

When we say honor, we refer to the same sense as if you were at an awards ceremony especially designed to pay tribute to a particular person for a particular deed. You can feel how it feels to be in the audience. You listen to the stories from all the friends who have surrounded this honored person talking about the great gifts and mighty deeds this person has done. At the right moment, the honored one ascends to the podium and speaks with reverence and humility and great thanks.

When you envision this, see it is you who everyone is talking about. See it is you who needs to climb the stairs to the podium. Then see yourself looking out on this room full of people who are your friends and family who love you so dearly. Feel the humility that sweeps over you when you honor yourself, when you hold yourself in your mind's eye surrounded by the highest good, knowing the intrinsic value of your being. You cannot honor anyone else until you honor yourself.

Another definition of honor is a recognition of all the heroic steps that have been taken on the journey thus far. If you need to actually write all the powerful events you have participated in and what you learned from them, then do so. It could just be a feeling you have of knowing you have come so far; that you have learned and grown and given to people all along your path. You must never lose sight of this within yourself, about yourself.

We hear your conscious minds saying, "Oh, but I do not feel worthy of this; I do not think I am good enough to be held in such honor," we need to tell all of you, from our perspective, we see your soul clear and clean as a shining, beautiful light. Not only are you deserving of such honor, but you have been deprived of it for too long.

Now is the time for you to allow us, your angels, to come and surround you and bathe you in this unconditional love. You can lay your head in our laps and cry your tears of sorrow which will then turn to tears of joy when you realize how greatly honored we are to be honoring you.

Working hand in hand with honor comes articulation. When we speak of articulation, we talk of knowing yourself and the true nature of yourself so intimately that you can turn to those around you and express, through your words, your facial expressions, your hand gestures and your open heart, who it is that you truly are. To be human in the world means simply by that nature there is separation. You are apparently separate from each other and the table and from all of the objects in the room. And yet, from a metaphysical standpoint, from where we sit, we see it all as one.

We are not here to describe our perspective in detail. Instead, we are here to tell you that because this separation exists in your world, it is all the more important to articulate yourselves to people. Where we are, communication works telepathically. Where we are, we cannot hide. We cannot lie. We cannot pretend we are unworthy. It would be as if all of you were naked and some were trying to claim that they were other than what they were. You would all laugh and point and say, "Look at that. You have a birthmark in that place!" You could not hide it. Where we are, there is no need for articulation. It is essential for you.

There is a need within all of you to connect to the world around you so that you do not feel this separation, this sense of aloneness and isolation. These are misconceptions built into the system that you live. You look and you see your skin and you think that is where you stop. And maybe if you are lucky, you find yourself involved in a sexual experience with someone where you feel as if you are joining the physical and even then you feel you are still separate. But this is not so; you are all connected by the same soul. You all have common mind and open hearts that go from one to the other to the other. As you judge people to be bad, different or not as good as you, you accentuate that separation.

So to articulate who you are to the people around you means to know yourself so well that you do not need to put up a wall when you are sad that says you are not sad. You do not need to, when you are afraid, pretend that you are not afraid. If you can articulate who you are, you get inside yourself and become so close to yourself that you know what you are feeling while you are feeling it and you are able then to express it.

———————————————————————— ☆

The reason that honor is so important is because there is a difference between being afraid, and lashing out at those around you. That is not done with honor. If you honor yourself and feel yourself worthy and are able to turn to the people around you and give them honor, it would be impossible for you to lash out and hurt someone while you honor them. Could you imagine this very large awards banquet and having someone stand up and talk about the recipient of this great honor as if they were a small-minded nothing? That person would be escorted out.

This is what you must do for yourselves because no one else will do it for you. People can come from miles around to tell you what a great person you are, but if you do not hear it from your inner voice then you do not hear it at all. To be able to articulate your unworthiness, to be able to go inside and sit down with that fear over a cup of tea and say, "What is it that you bring to me, fear; what is the root of this fear," and to then turn to someone close to you and articulate that feeling so you have a witness to it, this is a beginning.

This is the beginning of the process of opening your hearts to all who are around you. It is the beginning of being able to open your heart to yourself and allow all of the goodness to come into it.

Even as you fight, if there's just a corner of your mind that is willing to take on whatever it comes across in order to find that beautiful box of jewels that is every human being's birthright, then you will begin to know true power. You will begin to let go of the misconceptions. Your lives become as if you have never known them before, and you begin to achieve those things that you wish and long for. And conversely, the things that you thought you wanted begin to change as you find it is more important to help those around you than to constantly be in demand for people to help you.

In this way you begin to change that piece of fear within you that is helping to contribute to the terror in your society now. Because when you honor yourself and you can articulate, then you become a beacon for others around you who are in the same boat. They will be moved by your courage to express who you really are. They will learn from your own path that you have walked first in darkness and then in honor and then articulated to share.

In many cultures, there are specific members of society who are given only the job of storytelling. To tell the story is to plant

☆ ————————————————————

in the memory the seeds that then grow into a path that has already been walked. And in that way, you are not alone.

There is a very transparent energy tonight, as if there is a sheet of glass you feel, each of you, that separates you from each other. A crystalline energy that surrounds each of you. There will come a day when all of you will break that glass. The difference between who you are eternally from your Soul Self and who you are as a human being will diminish. You will begin to operate your lives from a much higher perspective. This is not something you have to be worthy of, you already are. This is not something that if you don't do it right, you will be left behind. You all must know this because these changes are going to occur whether or not you are aware of them.

You have not been brought here tonight by accident, none of you. You made this appointment and you kept it for purpose. It was to come to hear the sound of our voice. It was to come to hear us tell you that it will be much more beneficial for you if you look at this change that is upon you and open your mind to the idea that you are filled with worth. You need to then pass your story on because all of you together will facilitate changing the world.

It is not for us at this time to talk to you of the future in the sense of what will become of this great mission you are on. Suffice it to say at this time that simply hearing the sound of our voice will cut through your conscious mind and make a connection into your heart of hearts, deep into your soul.

As you move through the days ahead and you struggle, be very gentle on yourselves. What is happening is that your conscious minds, with all of their anger and resistance and fear, are beginning to align to the sound of our voices. Our voices bring unconditional love and total acceptance, inspiration, resolutions for your conflicts, detachment from your culture, compassion, and yes, vision.

Your conscious mind will fight, fight day and night trying not to align itself. Even watch this happen. Take your conscious mind and allow it to go on and on and on. Do not judge it; do not say because your conscious mind is fighting that you are unworthy. Do not say that if your conscious mind is fighting, you should not be honored and articulate. Much to the contrary; articulate to those around you what is happening in your conscious mind and

---

☆

in that way you will honor yourself by taking yourself seriously, by giving yourself time, and by sharing with each other.

Absolutely stay in contact with each other. There is a greater mission here than you even can begin to understand. The three angels who sit here with you tonight are here to take care of you in the same sense that your guardian angels take care of you in your soul plane. Do not be afraid to make contact with them and articulate what is happening with you. You will find a great comfort in their words; you will find that you are not alone.

We ask you now for your questions.

Teresa: "Can you help us understand what's happening with the three of us that confuses us so?"

Yes, indeed; it's the workings of your three-tiered physiology, so to speak. We have spoken with you before. Each of you have a role in bringing this mission to the earth plane.

Barbara's role, as you know, is to go ahead and to see and to bring back information. What she saw was quite a shock to her physical body, which includes her mind.

Kim took the information and began to process it in order to articulate it. It is a great deal of data and so there will be a great deal of processing required.

Teresa, you took the information and felt it with all of your heart. As you did, you sensed the last pieces of dying of the old selves and looked out to your friends and felt for them also.

This is the process that is important. What you saw will be made clear as time passes. Your physical bodies are not ready to accept these concepts. This is why you are sick and feel heavy of heart, why you feel as if you are going insane: because your conscious minds cannot comprehend what you saw.

In this way, all of you must be very gentle with yourselves. If there is one thing you can do for yourselves, it would be to allow your conscious mind to rant and rave in all of its insanity. When you feel sad because you do not know who you are anymore, the one thing you need to do, all of you, is to close your eyes and fill yourself up with the light and the love and the greatest good, and feel yourself bathed in that light. Know that there is a master plan in operation and that your parts are very essential.

We have spoken with you often of your responsibilities within this mission. You are going, in essence, where very few have gone before.   And what is miraculous is that because of Teresa's compassion, combined with Kim's articulation, there is going to be a message brought to the earth plane that is going to reach many, many people. You intrinsically understand this, but it is hard for you to see because, as we have told you often, you do not need to know where you are going.

You need to stay with your heads down, keep writing, keep talking, keep bringing these beautiful people to sit before us to speak. And before you know it, you're going to turn around and everything will have changed and then your focus will go outward to the world.

Often times in culture and religion, before a great spiritual event, the priests or the shamans or the holy ones go through a period of great confusion and isolation before they bring the message of the divine to the world. This is what is happening with you. It is a ripple effect that goes out from you to all people who are involved with you at this time. Know this is a time of preparation.

You have an appointment with power that you must keep. You are only preparing. Do not be frightened; there is nothing to be frightened of. There is nothing to harm you. You are not surrounded by evil spirits who are trying to trap your souls in some strange place for all of eternity. You are not going to die. Well, yes, you will die. You are not going to die [from this]. You are simply going to go ahead of everyone else to see this change, and then with your compassion you are going to articulate it in such a way that everyone will understand. In this way your mission will begin. And it will last all of your life. You will bring all of these people with you and it will be a wondrous sight to behold.

"Speaking of articulation from earlier today, whenever I think about this stuff, tears well up in my eyes. I don't know if it's sadness or happiness. It's something I can't articulate. I can articulate the way I feel, but I don't understand where it's coming from. Can you help me with this?"

Yes, and this is true of all of you. This movement of feeling that you feel within yourselves, it swells up and you find yourself sitting and crying and crying and crying. Part of this, as you have discussed, is that this is the end of a great era on the Earth. The way that you thought, so scientifically, so grounded in three dimensions and five senses, and always having to have proof, and

☆

always having to be safe, all of this is changing. You mourn the death of that because anything that is familiar to you that dies requires mourning. It is part of letting go.

But also what happens, and for some of you this is premonitory, is that you are being filled with the divine light that makes you realize how small you really are. We do not mean small as unworthy or not being honored. We mean small as being humbled to the awesome power of the universe. As you begin to catch glimpses of your Soul Self, who you really are and what you really deserve, you weep with tears of joy and disbelief because you are caught in this time of grieving. You want so much to let go of the old and believe in the new, but you are not past the grieving yet.

So you well up with tears and you cry and cry, and you think, "I'm not really that sad," then you think, "But it isn't really tears of joy." That brings you confusion. As you weep, do not judge. Do not think you are weeping for a particular reason, even if it seems so apparent. Simply allow yourself to cry these tears that wash over you, to cleanse you, and to allow yourself to let go. We guarantee you, you will not weep like this for long.

"I have a question about music. I feel like it involves the spiritual world. Nothing else on Earth can make me feel so up, so high. How does music make a person feel good? Is it somehow involved with the chakras?"

It is very simple. Music is sound. Sound comes right before light. Light is the ultimate inspiration. Music cuts through everything that goes on in your conscious mind and goes directly to your soul and joins—makes one with you. Music makes you reverberate.

You listen to music, music is reverberation, and you become the music and so you are then merged with that. It is a very intimate experience and it serves to lighten and illuminate from a place well beyond your conscious thinking. There are more detailed explanations that we do not feel we can give you at this time because of your development, but suffice it to say that music indeed is the voices of the angels and you are merging with them. That is why you become so moved by what you hear.

Teresa: *"Speaking of that, has Randy had any reaction to Sarah's song?"*

☆ ────────────────────────────

Not in his conscious mind. You should not expect it to happen. You are not going to find his transformation coming from that event. It is essential for his transformation, but it is not as if it will be imminent because of that. It is something that down the road he will be able to look back at and when he does his jaw will drop when he finally understands.

For now it pains him, but he must honor his pain and learn to articulate. That is his mission also. In that sense, it is a powerful magic that is working on him. But just as one who is suffering from a serious disease, perhaps cancer, going through treatments, chemotherapy; it is not for some time that you actually see that they get better. In fact, while they are going through their treatment, their hair is falling out and they are losing weight and they look close to death's door. That is like Randy; it is hurting him, so his conscious mind is putting up all of its defenses. But when we say it is hurting him, we mean it is cutting through, right to his heart, which needs to be healed, but cannot be healed as long as he does not honor himself and articulate. It is serving to remove those blocks.

This is not something that will happen quite quickly. It is not something that will happen overnight. In fact you, like your friend, Kim, are still invested. And you, like your friend, Kim, can hear these words and understand. As long as you wait, he will not come. You know you are not waiting like you used to, but it is still there for you. It does not matter that you wait, because he is not ready to come. He will come, though.

"Why do I feel so scared and agitated when I feel you, especially when I feel you pulling me in my dreams and I wake up and I am almost agitated that you were there?"

You have a very large block within you filled with anger. This anger is disguising your pain. You have expressed your pain as anger for so long that to finally get beneath it to that vulnerable young child hovering in the corner is terrifying. It is easier for your conscious mind to point its finger at us and say, "Look you, you are the cause of my fear." That is the way your block is protecting its life. Your anger has been so intensified that it has a life of its own.

What we see with you is this beautiful young child, filled with light in her eyes, ready to face the world. But hovering above you, almost like a cloud, is your anger.

☆

At this point you cannot even remember what caused you such pain to begin with, that then made you so angry. Each time we try to help you to see, through lessons, through dreams, even through the sound of our voice, you hear yourself, your own mind. It does everything it can to wander, to deny, and yet, when you hear us speak of that young girl who sits, longing to connect with everyone around her and yet feeling so isolated, it makes you well up, does it not?

"Yes."

You do not know how to get by your anger. It is okay to feel afraid. It is alright to let loose of your grip on your anger one finger at a time. But do not believe that it is because we come. It is very much like Teresa's friend, Randy. He received the music of his children, the music that caused tears of awe and joy, and yet, when he heard the music, he became angry. His mind said it was because his child was being led down a path of destruction, but that was his anger. The music cut straight to his heart and showed him his pain, and his young boy who is calling out to be held, and no one is coming.

It is the same with you, dear child. You are sitting, crying with your arms out for someone to come. When we come, it is not the right person to come. We come to help, but you ultimately must be the one to sit down and find yourself. Sit down with your fear and invite it to tea. We see you with a little miniature tea set that a child has as she pours air into the cups and talks with your fear. In the next two weeks you will have a major breakthrough with this. Then be very sure to connect with your dear friends, for they will help you. They will also celebrate with you as you relinquish your fear one finger at a time.

"Can you tell me what my block is?"

You lean towards wanting to secure yourself by thinking that you are already complete. You think that if you do not convince yourself that you are already complete, that will mean that you are nothing. This is a tricky explanation because it is a psychological trick that you play on yourself.

You know that you don't know, yet you insist that you do know. On top of that, then you know that you don't know. It is an interesting layering—like a maze for the little rat. The little rat ends up bumping his head on the wall and thinking, "I knew, but I must not have known."

☆ ————————————————————————

So your block is simply time. You need not worry. In fact, like your friend, Kim, you think not doing is not doing. But for you, not doing is doing a great deal. You have a way of wanting to try so hard and make things work, to create this for yourself. If you would surrender to the workings of your soul and simply admit you may know, or you may not know; it does not matter. You are going to simply sit and wait for power to come to you. Then go about your business.

You will find it to be a bit less chaotic in your mind to do things that way rather than constantly thinking that you have to know more, even though you know so much, because there's so much you don't know. We can understand why you are dizzy!

We would like to leave you with a thought about your angels. In this time of great fear, of confusion and anger, of all of your earthly struggles, you must always know, your angels surround you and love you and guide you and protect you. The more that you can see them there, the more that you can feel their presence, even if you cannot see them in a personified way. The more that you can trust in this beautiful, brilliant, unconditional love that shines down upon you, the more courage you will have: to go forward, to become friends with your anger, to invite your fear in, to sit and talk to it as if it were your friend, not something to push away, not something you are ashamed of. And as you do, you honor and thank it because it is teaching you. Then you [will be] able to release it.

With that love filling your heart, you can then turn to your sister, who may be struggling also, and stretch out your hand and allow her to lay her forehead on your lap and stroke and reassure her and surround her with that love that emulates from within you. In this way, dear children, you are going to save the world.

☆

Meet me in the darkness, we can sit for awhile
Tell me of your torture, child, and what still makes you smile
If you show me that you love me, we can go another mile
Feel me there inside of you, now rest for awhile
You're no different, child, you're a lily in the field."

Lily In The Field © 1994 Barbara Lee With

Kim: I'm really upset. We've been told there's going to be readings for each of the positions of the triad. "Compassion" has already been scheduled for this Saturday. "Vision" is suppose to be the big climax of the book.

The reading tonight was beautiful, but Barbara sure seems to be treating it all like an afterthought. If we're going to have a reading about all three positions of the triad it seems like they should all be treated equally. We did the Honor and Articulation reading on a plain old middle-of-the-week night with only two other people there. Does she enjoy adding to my feelings of lack?

February 24, 1994
Barbara: A woman from our group who is a professional photographer has agreed to take the picture for the cover of my CD. She has a huge studio with all sorts of toys and gadgets, and the most gigantic camera I have ever seen. She seems to be as excited about doing the shoot as I am.

I'm exhausted. These past few months have been the most amazing roller coaster of discovery, fear, awe, mystery, logic, insanity and inspiration I have ever experienced in my life. And now my girlfriends are backing away from me, telling me I'm crazy. There seems to be no way to make them understand how lost my mind is trying to figure out what is going on. Not just "We are God" but everything! The way we came together in the first place *and* how many readings have I done lately? Since we started, in about two months, I have done fifteen group readings, lately three times a week, sometimes two in one day … and countless private sessions.

☆ ────────────────────────────────

Then, as we listen to the angels, transcribe the tapes and watch what happens, the prophesies unfold in ways we cannot imagine.

Let's not forget the session with Sherry about the murder, the Purple Jacket Day, mixing the music, the visions, the Circle of Souls. And now, "We are God." Yikes! I feel like I am disintegrating. Some days it feels like all my cells are getting further and further apart, until some day I might end up just a ghost. And it's this ghostly feeling that makes it hard to function.

Kim: I am worried about Barb. I wish I wasn't such a wimp about standing up to her when she claims that we are God. I would come right out and say, "Barbara, this doesn't make any sense at all and it's making you crazy!"

This feels like the Green Shirt Day all over again. I guess we haven't been calling Teresa "The Peace in the Middle" for nothing. Is it always going to be this way? I don't want to go on forever with Teresa constantly keeping Barbara and me from fighting. How are we supposed to teach anyone anything when we can't stop fighting with each other? I know Barbara is better at the metaphysical, but maybe I'm better at the earthly stuff. And maybe the two of us are supposed to meet in the middle—at Teresa: The Peace in the Middle.

February 26, 1994

Teresa: Patti, our photographer friend, offered to shoot some photos of Katie and Sarah. We plan the day, bring along makeup and costumes and have a great time.

At one point, Kim takes a break and calls to check on Barbara. They talk for a very long time. When I check on Kim, she looks like she's at quite a loss. I can tell she's trying to calm Barbara. After a while, I get on the phone with her. She's hysterical. I'm afraid I'm not helping much.

Kim: Barbara is totally freaked out. After two hours on the phone with her, I'm still not sure what she's talking about. She and I have been fighting, so that part is awkward, but that's not all. She's not making any sense and she's really scared. I want to be able to help, but I don't know what to do. Even my old co-dependent traits of taking care of someone in need aren't helping here. I don't know how to comfort her. I'm not even sure what she's talking about. And what in the world is going to happen tonight at the session?

Teresa: After she hangs up, Kim and I talk at length about how worried we are about Barbara. We truly don't know what to do. Things are getting out of hand. We don't understand what she's feeling or the kinds of visions she's having. We're new at this and at times I think we're all ready to call it quits.

The angels once said, "As the channel goes, so go you." I'm pretty sure I don't want to go where she has been lately. It's all getting too intense, and yet we know there's no turning back. I guess we're ready, but some days, you sure can't convince me of that.

Kim: A few of us gather at Teresa's before heading to tonight's session. At one point something is said about the fact that Barbara and I have been fighting and one of the group members asks, in a very surprised tone, "You guys fight?" Geez, of course we fight. We're human, remember. What do people think, that when all this started happening to us, we stopped being human, stopped dealing with all the everyday junk? This is exhausting.

Well, one good thing that has happened lately is that Clay and I are doing better. It's been over a year since I "checked out" of the marriage and he's been working really hard on getting his own life together. We'll see...

Barbara: In preparing for tonight's session, the angels have asked Kim and Teresa to tell their story, and said I should sing a song before we begin to listen to them speak. I am very apprehensive about seeing Kim again. I feel so judged by her. I get the feeling she thinks I am crazy. I can't stand that.

How can I convince her that what I have been saying is true? How can I make her understand that we really are all God, and we really do have the power to create our lives the way we want to? I don't know if I can pretend that we are this spiritual group when I know she is judging me so.

Well, I guess I will just show up and hold my head high and try to believe, without her support, that what I am perceiving is not just the rantings of a lunatic. Tonight the message is about compassion. Surely, that will help us to come to a resolve about these misunderstandings.

THE ANGELS
February 26, 1994

"Compassion"

Kim: The angels instructed us to tell our story tonight, of what brought us together and what brought us to where we are in undertaking this mission, of sorts. I guess when I look back, my transformation began long before I realized. I had never done anything like this in my life. I never wanted to do anything like this!

I got to a point in my life where I was in crisis and needed to do something. So, at the same time as I made an appointment with a therapist, I made an appointment with Barbara for the first time. I really just wanted any kind of answer about what might be going on in my life. I never expected to come away and, within the next few weeks, find a peacefulness I had never known in my life.

I then came to find that I was on a journey back to myself.

I was an angry, bitter woman. The only voices I listened to were the bad ones; the ones that told me I wasn't doing it right. And I believed them!

Through our union, I found out that I have other voices, that we all have other voices and that, if we listen to them, they bring us together, they bring us love, they bring us compassion, unity and honor. Most importantly, I think, for ourselves. It's always been easier to understand how to love someone else. But I think that until you truly, really learn how to love yourself, with all of your flaws and all of you questions, you're really not even able to give everything you can to other people.

And so I started to discover myself. I discovered these two women who have come to mean everything to me in my life. And through them I've discovered so many other new friends and I receive gifts and miracles everyday now. I find myself saying thank you a lot.

I was afraid. I had a lot of pain and I was afraid of that pain, and yet, through that pain came my transformation, my understanding about where I'm going, and where we're all going, and it looks like a lot of us are going together. And so I come to this now with great joy.

The self doubts nag at me a little bit but I'm here and I know I'm here and I know the angels are here every minute of the day, whenever I need them, whatever the question. Those are the voices that I now choose to listen to. I hold on to that peacefulness and the love that God put inside of me.

Teresa: Like Kim, I also came to Barbara looking for answers in my own life. Suddenly I found myself thirty-six years old, with two children, separated from my husband that I'd been married to for fifteen years. I didn't have a clue what to do with myself. And I also listened to those bad voices.

I grew up in the south going to a Baptist church. Every Sunday I was told I was a sinner and doomed to Hell. I came away feeling scared to death and thinking *that* was my spirituality.

What I've found out is that *this* is my spirituality. It has been inside me all the time, but I was looking for it somewhere else. I have never felt closer to God than I feel right now. When people talk about being "reborn," this must be what it feels like, only I'll bet a lot of those people don't feel like this.

It's so wonderful just knowing that you're not alone. I spent the entire summer last year sitting on my sun porch crying my eyes out and wondering why this was all happening to me. After talking with Barbara and learning about my angels, that they are with me all of the time, I knew I could sit out there and talk to them. I knew they were there and would comfort me.

Now my husband—we're still not divorced—just looks at me like he doesn't know who he's looking at because of all the changes in me. I went home to North Carolina last Christmas and everyone there did the same. They had never seen me like this, so peaceful.

It's true, and it's wonderful. And, it's a part of me that I will never let go of again because now I know.

☆ ────────────────────────────

Angels: We tell you greetings and ask you to take note of the weather. [It was a beautiful winter evening.]

Tonight we want to speak with you about compassion. We have asked Barbara to share with you our words through the power of music. It was not an intentional "show" to make you think what a grand performer she is. She understands the purpose behind the use of music. This is not an accident. This is a metaphor. There is so much to speak of when covering the subject of compassion and yet, it is relatively simple, is it not? There are many great spiritual teachings about such a subject. Yet, all that have been given, while for purpose, have a missing link.

Until you interject what we shall call the fourth dimension into those teachings, they are often times only words on a page and concepts that exist outside yourself. They are great words of wisdom filled with power. But without you and your full participation, they are helpless.

The information has been laid out in a specific order to follow a linear line because linear is an idea you understand. You can simply open up the transcripts and find words of wisdom applicable to you anywhere. But if you look at our teachings as a whole, you will see a particular logic that runs through the format.

Understanding that you are "victims of culture" is the first piece of relinquishing control held by your ego and your selfish motives.

You have chosen to be born human at a time when technology seems to have gotten to the forefront of progress. You don't have to quit using the telephone or watching television, but do not allow culture to define who you are. When you do that, you limit yourself to what culture dictates. We have often told you this is the least spiritual culture that has existed on the Earth plane in a very long time.

This first aspect is what begins to shake loose your grip. We see you gripping the table for dear life, clinging to your definitions of what is and isn't. We are prying your fingers off to allow you a bit of "levitation."

Part of letting go of the cultural aspects is to replace any judgments you may have on the process [of listening to the angels speak] that you are witnessing at this moment. Communication from the guides and celestial beings is going to become much more acceptable. People will not be so quick to tell you that you are crazy.

As you know yourself, you have been drawn to this power. You want to know how to hear such divine wisdom clearly through yourself. You may feel there is a certain insanity to it. But do not listen to your conscious minds. If you are not sure which is your angel and which is your conscious mind, ask a stranger, they will know.

Every human being carries the messages of the angels, whether they are aware or not. Throughout your lives you are being divinely guided. This is not some wild revelation you have not heard before. It will only become stronger. This is why we speak to you about letting go of what your culture tells you. This is not just that you are not as beautiful as the woman selling toothpaste. This is not just the fear generated by the reports on the news of how many people have died. This is not just classical religion telling you you're not good enough. It is the culture of the mind. It is the way society has created a voice within you that says that you are not good enough, full enough or rich enough.

Once you begin to shake away from this culture, you can then begin to hear very clearly what your ego voices say. When you hear the voice of your own ego speaking clearly, you begin to realize what it is really saying. When you hear it say that you are no good, wrong, bad, or less, it creates a conflict with the voices of the angels.

This simple place of conflict is where all of the conflict of the Earth plane lies.

But no, it is far too simple. You say, "If I quiet my ego voice and align it with the voice of the angels, how will that stop the war in Bosnia? How will that feed the children? How will that stop the crime downtown?"

It may not stop that particular crime, but it will stop the crime that might be committed against your children. This is what it's all about in space and time for you. If you resolve the conflict within you, if you align your ego voice with the glorious voices of the angels, then you allow peace within. How can you give peace if you do not have peace to give?

☆ ───────────────────────────────────

Once you remove the conflict and create the space within you that fills you with peace, you are then able to turn outwards to those around you. You learn that they are not the source of your conflict and you are not the source of theirs. With that great relief, you are able to turn and give peace. You are not afraid of being rejected. No one can reject you but yourself and you have filled yourself with peace.

You have learned to love yourself. That is when you turn to the world and give inspiration instead of constantly demanding that the world inspire you.

We asked you to stand up, get up off the couch and turn off the television set, but we know it is not fully effective until you have found your peace. But do not wait until you have fully perfected yourself to turn to help those around you. If you have found your peace, you are a million times more powerful. You choose. You choose how much power to take into the world to make it better, to make sure your children never grow up thinking they are less.

You can make those choices and you do that through commitment.

We do not necessarily mean commitment to your family and husband. Commit yourself into the moment. Take the moment, only the moment in front of you. If you are in so much conflict in your mind and you don't know what to do, look at what is in front of you. It might only be a telephone or a child. What does that present moment say to you?

Perhaps you are alone in your bed, or sitting at work surrounded by people. When you are lost in your mind, come back to the moment. It will guide you. You don't always have to know what's going to happen next, or the meaning. All you have to know is how you feel. If you know you are not the source of their conflict or them to you, you don't have to worry about becoming entangled in a web of verbal sparring to try and prove who is the source of the conflict. Even when you do, you hear yourself talk and you think, "This is so silly!" It is a sign. Even you are giving yourselves signs, guiding yourself.

Hear yourself saying, "You did this to me! You did that to me!" Then stop and laugh because you know it cannot be so. This is a dance of great cooperation we are doing here, you as human beings and we as the angels. You cannot fool yourself into thinking you are victims. You are creating. To align yourself with the voices of the angels, you have to commit to the moment.

When you commit to the moment, you can know who you really are. Then you can turn to those around you and express who you really are, not who you think did this to you, or how you feel badly because you did that to that person. Who you really are, what you really think, what you really feel.

When you know who you really are, you can honor that part of self and tell the person who is sitting next to you.

Honor and articulation go hand in hand. How can you possibly articulate who it is you are if you do not honor and embrace the part of self that is angry, sad, even the part of self that is joyful and filled with magnificence? You must embrace all of it. Then you are able, very specifically and with great thought and concern, to turn to those in your world, in your work situation, in your family life, to the strangers on the street, in the super market, in the grocery store, in the restaurant, in the car wash. You think it's absurd to tell the man at the car wash how you honor your feelings and articulate them. What you fail to remember is that you could be giving him a message from his own angels.

You can never discount how much power you have and what it can be used for. It cannot be used unless you can articulate, unless you can sing the praises of your own life. The voices of the angels cut through your conscious mind. You do not have to believe this is happening. You do not have to believe it is true. You can listen to that part of self that says, "Oh my, Barbara is so well versed at the language, isn't she?" But you know that would be silly. This is not her conscious mind speaking. These are the angels. But you do not have to believe. If you listen long enough, even in disbelief, just like music, our words cut through and go straight to the heart.

This brings us to love.

You can understand why all these steps are needed to come before love. Love is something you prepare yourself for, although it is there all the time. It fits right in with all of the paradoxes we are asking you to live with.

Love is not just a concept. Love is not just a feeling. Love is a power. It is where all of the power lies. Only through love can you evolve. This is what the purpose is here, not necessarily just ascension. You are growing in the Earth plane beyond the three dimensions and soon the fourth dimension will be an everyday occurrence. You will all work much more telepathically than you have in the past. Many of you feel this already. It's going to be a given.

It would be very easy to learn the lessons and leave the Earth plane, to ascend and go on to another level of evolution. But you have come here to hear the words back to your conscious mind that have been the whisperings of your soul. You have chosen to be here on the Earth plane in order to put the power of love into use.

All of the predictions of the Armageddon, all of the prophets for years who said "Change your ways or be damned," all of the indications that the world is coming to an end have been based on a prophecy of technology. Those who lived in the times that came before gazed ahead and saw your technology. They saw the movies and the news reels. They saw a very great possibility. But what they did not see was the power of love.

Each of you have that power. Love is the ability to heal instantly. Love is the ability to release. Love is the ability to turn to the one next to you and hold out your hand and pull them up. But you cannot do this, children, until you love yourselves. And how can you love yourselves if you are constantly being bombarded within your own head by voices that tell you otherwise?

This is a time of great awakening. The world is not going to come to an end because you are not going to let it. You have asked us. You have prayed for many, many hours, each of you individually and the world as a whole. We have heard your cries for a very long time. We have been throwing things in your path and dropping hints. Now it is time for us to put our foot down. Now it is time for us to intervene in this way so that you can then go into your world, which is very much like a war zone, and change it, one person at a time.

☆

This is not some pie-in-the-sky desire. This is not some theory or concept that looks ideal but cannot be put to work on the Earth plane. This is quite necessary for your survival. It is also quite pressing. We do not say that in a sense of fright. We say it in a sense of urgency, as if the train were leaving.

The metaphor of the leaving train is not the destruction of your Earth, it is your own personal train. When it is time to go on a journey, you are hopefully prepared with your bags packed. You have your ticket in your hand and you leave at an appropriate time. If you are driving at rush hour, you leave earlier to make the train. You do not drive to the train station in utter fear that you will miss the train. You know you are prepared and have taken every step you can. This is what we are doing with you. We are helping you to get your bags packed and are going to take you on a beautiful journey.

The ironic and paradoxical thing is that you are coming whether you want to go or not. But we all know that you want to go.

Compassion is a word that is illustrative of how it sounds. Compas-ion. Or, "Come, Passion," as if you have a dog named Passion. You want passion to come within you so you can then turn around and give it. Passion is not an emotion. It is the state of an emotion. When you see passionate people, you see them full of their life, even if they are sad. Passion means to throw yourself in to whatever it is, however you feel, whatever you're thinking.

If you are so bored you cannot stand yourself, the first reaction is to push yourself away from yourself, to deny yourself, to judge yourself. If you can love yourself when you are at your worst, if you can throw yourself into being your worst, short of actually trying to hurt someone else purposely, you can get to know yourself very well. It is not the only thing that needs to be done. It certainly is an element.

So you say, "Come, Passion, to me. Let me be passionate. Let me not care what people think if I'm too passionate. I make love passionately. I argue passionately. I cook passionately. I throw myself into the moment and I live my life passionately. So yes, come to me, Passion." As you follow these steps and embrace the lessons, when you turn to someone and give them your hand, think of how much more powerful it is when you do it with compassion.

You can stop by the side of the road and help someone change a tire. You can complain the whole time, thinking you are late, telling them they should have had a better jack. Don't they check their tires before they go? That is not compassion.

Compassion would be to stop and see your own self standing there. See your own heart in that person and truly help that person with all of your heart. Your appointments will wait, this person needs you. Even if they do not need you, you help pass the time with them. You commit to the moment. The act of helping change the tire becomes something much greater.

You have that power and that power is love.

We have said many times (too many times perhaps) that it is all so simple. But you need to hear it over and over and over again. Do not ever assume that you already know. Listen, always listen over and over and over. When you do not need to hear it anymore, it will not be there for you to hear. As long as you are hearing it, it means you need to hear it. In that way, it cuts through you like music.

There is an often overlooked element of love. If you turn to the person beside you and instead of treating them angrily or with indifference, you treat them with love, you set off a chain of events. Each and every time you choose to love, you set off a chain of events that makes a ripple effect within the world. Every time you choose to give less than love, you diminish the chances of changing your world.

We simply want to impress upon you how very important each and every one of your actions is. There has not been a time like this on the Earth plane. Every movement, every thought, every word is very important. If you have an angry thought or word, you don't have to crawl into bed and feel you are personally responsible for the demise of the Earth plane. But you can make a choice. Know you can make a difference.

And we tell you this because we love you.

"A lot of people have many misconceptions about love that are culturally ingrained in us. What is the best thing we can do to let go of some of those misconceptions?"

Let go of the idea that love is outside of you or enters you from someone else. This is the most common and most important misconception you have. This is particularly true of you and everyone here. If you see love as an eternal, endless supply of power within you, it replaces the need to look outside yourself, to grab onto something and hold it tight to feel safe. You are never alone. To access the love, you need to quiet the voices within telling you that you cannot love, that you are not worthy of this great experience.

The paradoxical thing about love is that although you cannot get it from an outside source, you can give it away eternally. It has power when you give it away. When all are giving love, it is not to endlessly fill a bottomless hole in the ground. When you all give love outward, the love joins together and joins you all together. Then you can generate peace amongst yourselves. What happens when you achieve peace globally? Have you thought of this? That is the next chapter.

"How can we make sure our children get these messages?"
By living them yourself. We do not ask you to be perfect, because all of you are perfect the way you are. We ask you to commit yourself to every moment with your children, guiding them with love with the steps we have given you. These simple steps can be used in any situation, in any "movie." The outcome will always be the same. If you put love in, you will make love grow.

"In all the meetings I've been to, you're always talking about how we're all one with everyone here, including the coffee table and the carpet and whatever. Then why do you find yourself attracted to certain people and instantly disliking others? If we all are one, why don't we all get along?"
That is the question for you to answer. We will give you a hint: It is a configuration set up for you, dear children. It is something of a test. Your higher power, along with us and our higher power, which leads into infinity, into the very eye of God, has set up this lesson for you for purpose. Let us assure you, the universe is watching. Earth is not some little planet off in the corner of the galaxy, hidden by large comets and black holes, out of the way. It is the main attraction.

You may have a feeling of being manipulated. We are not cruel overseers dangling you like puppets. You have chosen to take on this challenge in order to transcend it. We have given you the information and told you the answers for a millennium. Your conscious mind has been anesthetized by money, television and technology for a long time. You are paying for the sins of your fathers (and we use that term figuratively) when you embrace technology. Life is so easy now. There was merit in having a difficult life. Now it is time for you to get off the couch, put down the book, and go out into the street.

Find out why that person makes you so uncomfortable. What does that person mirror in you? If there was no conflict with that person, you would have nothing but love for them. You may still have nothing but love for them and be in conflict while you are with them. But do not under any circumstances think that any other human being causes you to feel what you are feeling. Each and every feeling is of your own making.

This is not to say if you feel anger in your conscious mind, you need only sit down and think, "No, I am not angry. I will think my anger away." That is not the answer. Nor do you have to yell at everyone in your path because you are angry. Your conscious mind must figure out the workings of your soul, which have long been unknown to you. You have to find out what your feelings are and articulate them. This is all part of the process of learning to love.

When you find someone who mirrors back to you something you don't want to see in yourself, ask them to come over and have tea. Literally. Have courage. Commit to the moment. Don't tell them they should stop doing this and that. Tell them, "I know because I feel this conflict when you are here, there's a lesson for me. Can you help me?" Talk and listen. More than anything, listen. Listen and put your conscious mind to rest. Let their words reverberate through your being and sit with them for a while. Ask for the answer to come. It always will. But you have to invite that person over to your house and put on the water.

"How can we overcome the fear to love?"
The fear you feel is not outside yourself. Your mind tells you that you're going to screw up again and hurt them. If you listen to us in your other ear, we say you already love them. No one can take that from you. We say you are very capable and very powerful. If they hurt through an experience with you, or vice versa, that is a beautiful mystery given to you to overcome. That leads you back to the beginning, which is what love will do.

☆

"I'm not talking about romantic love."

Neither are we. We are not talking about romance. If you want to love your neighbor, your conscious mind may say, "You'd better not display love to him. What will the other neighbors think?" That is your ego voice, not the voice of the angels. If you listen to the angels, they will say, "It does not matter, you love everyone." What stops you is your fear.

Your fear is not what you think. You are not afraid of what people will think. That is what your conscious mind says. Your fear is your fear. The fear must be detached from all of the conscious reasons you have for why you are afraid. If you commit to the moment and accept the mystery that you do not know why you are afraid, then you honor your fear. That means you invite your fear into your life and embrace it, make friends with it, sit it down, tell it jokes, make it laugh. Get to know your fear. Then it is not fear any longer.

The greatest fear you have is to be separated from yourself. But that is impossible, dear child. It is only an illusion to be separate from yourself. You can be angry and still love yourself. You can be afraid and still love yourself. Do not think that being afraid is not loving. Do you have a specific situation that we could use to illustrate this?

"A lot of people are afraid to stop and help a stranger change their tire or pick up a hitchhiker."

It is not always wise to pick up a hitchhiker. Because you have love, you don't necessarily invite criminals into your life to kill you.

It is not that, when you were young, you saw your parents help someone change a tire and they were attacked. There isn't necessarily a direct correlation. It is the culture that defines you and gives you that voice of fear.

When you drive down the highway and see someone who needs help, the voices in your head may say "Stop and help." Do so immediately without thought. Perhaps you sense danger. You will drive by and keep going. Perhaps it is the time for them to change their own tire, and that is alright. Do not think you are bad, or that the reason you are not stopping is because you are afraid. You think it is, because the voices in your head think this way. But it is not.

When you are in the safety of your home, and you are still afraid, allow the voices to rattle off all the reasons why: because you might get hurt, because you have never done any good in your life, blah blah blah. Let your conscious mind ramble on. Then step back into that place of peace. Watch and listen and just be with your fear. Your fear will turn into an energy, more like electricity than bondage. That is how you transcend it. You will not transcend your fears by ignoring them, nor by assigning a meaning to them. The only way to move fluidly through your fear is to simply be with it, lock, stock, and barrel. Just be with it. We guarantee it will change.

Teresa: *"I have a great deal of anticipation about the trip that I'm going on this week. Can you give me some insight into what I'm feeling so nervous about?"*

You have a sense of anticipation because we are going to meet. It will not be a dream. I will come to you in physical form in the body and the soul of a native. When you look into her eyes you will recognize me. She will not know who I am. Listen to what she says. The veil between the worlds will lift and you will see what Barbara has been trying to tell you, interpreted in your own way. She chose the swimming pool on a winter's day. You chose a tropical paradise. That alone says something about your power.

The friend we are bringing to you is going to greatly alter your perception of yourself. When you leave, you will look back out of the plane and wave. You will leave your old self down on the ground in that beautiful paradise. You are through grieving her disappearance, because you have left her in good hands.

You must put on your new floral power suit and take up the mission in a way that you have not felt so far. When you return, everything will deepen. Everything will move faster and you will be less fearful. It will be the same for your friend Kim, who will go through the same lesson in her own way. So when you get there, you will see me. We will talk.

Kim: *Why is it that they're going to be in Hawaii and I'm going to be in Minneapolis?*

You will see the circle. It will be in a situation with people who love you. You might as well be off on some tropical island. You will feel distant from what you have been in the past. When you arrive where you are going, you'll shed the same skin as your friend Teresa. You'll be hearing us in the same way, through human beings. You must always look at where you are, and draw a correlation to the changes you are going through.

There is great purpose in sending you to Brainerd. It is not what your conscious mind desires. You think you would rather be sitting by the waterfalls in the jungle. On some level this is true. But there is something about the barrenness of the situation that will be very profound. You could not get the lesson you will learn through that barrenness in the lush tropical place. You will claim your power there.

When the three of you reunite, it will be completely different. Because of your perseverance and courage, going into the barren area to learn your very profound message, you will win a trip to a tropical island.

"You mentioned the weather when you started. Why?"

Every time we have gathered tothese three women tried to bring you all in, the weather has been challenging. And still you drove all the way from your destination. Tonight the weather is beautiful. This is no accident. This is an exclamation point. Speaking of weather, how did we do?

"Good. How about future weather?"

Do you have a specific time?

"The next few years."

Yes, there will be weather.

This is a good time to say goodbye. We thank you with all our hearts. There is a brilliant light shining down on you from the heavens, and up on you from the Earth, and from the light of everyone who is sitting around you, and from your own hearts.

What does that make us? Beings of light. The more you can see yourself as energy and light, the more you will save your world.

Simply watch and be amazed.

☆ ───────────────────────────────

"Life is just a runway, access to the sky
The key to your survival, the meat of your surprise"

"Turbulence" © 1994 Barbara Lee With

Later that night . . .
 Teresa: We decide to go back to my house and order pizza after the reading. To me, it feels like a celebration is in order. This was our biggest group yet: twenty-two people came! Kim and I even spoke to the group prior to the reading about what all of this means to us, and Barbara sang a song. And, of course, the reading itself was more than beautiful.

Things have been intense, to say the least, over the last few weeks. Now the three of us are about to be separated for the first time since we came together. A little down-time with a pizza and some gentle conversation sounds pretty good to me.

No way! We no more get the pizza ordered when the battle ensues once again about if we are God or not! I want to scream and run out of the room, out of the house. I don't want to be here. I want to celebrate and eat and bask in the words of the angels from the reading we just came from on Compassion. But here we go again. They each are digging in their heels on their individual positions and no one is giving an inch. God, I'm sick of it.

Barbara: I have every intention in the world to not fight about this, but every time I try to make a point, if feels like, instead of listening to what I am saying and thinking about whether it might possibly be true, Kim just takes the other side and insists that I am wrong. Then I get angrier, and want to make my point all the more.

Kim: Everything in my upbringing tells me that she is wrong, absolutely wrong. It strikes fear in me to even think the words "We are God." The old Baptist voice screams, "How dare she? Blasphemy! Who does she think she is?" I didn't consciously realize until now how deeply this old teaching goes.

Who taught me this fear? Who taught me to believe that thinking we humans are *nothing* somehow elevates God? How do I break through this irrational fear? I didn't even know I had an "old Baptist voice" in me.

Teresa: As I just sit here between them, I'm totally disillusioned. I listen to them go back and forth, each trying to prove she's right and the other is wrong. I can't even say anything, because once again, my position on the subject is smack in the middle.

On one hand, like Kim, being raised in a Baptist church makes me a little uneasy about thinking "We are God." Who the hell are *we*? On the other hand, what Barbara is saying rings with truth from somewhere inside me, so I have to pay attention to that, too.

The angels always said one of the reasons there are three of us is so there can never be a tie. Oh God, please don't ever make me be the tie-breaker between those two! I'll just sit and let them go on...

Barbara: After an hour of volleying back and forth about if we are God or if we are separate, I pose the question: Where in the universe is a place where God isn't? What part of you is *not* God?

This seems to bring a moment of reflection to the argument. Finally! I have made my point! We *are* God! There is no other substance of the universe but God. Gosh, maybe now we can admit that I've been right all along.

Kim: Stop! I never thought of it this way before. I didn't realize until this moment that I have lived my whole life feeling unworthy of God's love. How can I believe I am divine when I believe I am worthless? It would take much processing for me to come to a comfortable understanding of this startling new realization. But the corner was turned when she said, "If God is in you, then what part of you is *not* God?"

Teresa: We are God? I don't know; that's a big one. Although, it does sort of scare me to think what God might be saving my tie-breaker skills up for.

Something finally gives. Pressure has been released and there's once again movement in the air. It's not over, but at least we can all go home and sleep now. I'm thankful Barbara and Kim have gotten to this place without me personally having to become involved in the conflict.

Barbara: I am too tired to continue this conversation. I decide to leave. As we stand in Teresa's kitchen, knowing that in one more day I will be leaving for Kaua'i, Kim looks at me and asks, "Barbara, what

☆ ———————————————————————

do you want from me?" I can only hear the words of the angels from the previous day: "Hold tight and the answers will come."

Standing in the middle of Teresa's kitchen, we put aside our differences for a moment to wrap our arms around each other, three mere mortals, strong ordinary women who have looked into the eye of God and now stand humbled, frightened, inspired and weary, clinging to each other in hope that somewhere, somehow, we will find our way through this mess and come back together, united, inspired, filled with the hope that was once the basis of our work: our hope to bring peace to the world. We could see no possibility of that, as long as we continue to fight like this.

In that moment of the three of us clinging to each other in Teresa's kitchen, a light descends upon us and envelops us in peace and unity. It lasts only a moment, while we are hugging, but it's enough to re-fuse our perception of the one being we have become.

Working together over the past months has indeed bound us together in a way we know we can never un-create. We are one now, whether we like it or not. There is no going back to our old lives. There is only going forward with the commitment we have made to ourselves and each other, and to the angels: We have volunteered, and have been chosen to take this mission across time, to be an important and essential part of bringing peace to this planet of ours. In this moment, as the light descends to envelop us, we remember the sacredness of this journey, and hold very tight.

Just as quickly, the light is gone. We are standing apart in the harsh fluorescent light of Teresa's kitchen. While some of the anger and fear and sense of separation have returned, it's softer and quieter now. We're ourselves again, alone, apart, yet strangely connected.

February 27, 1994

Barbara: I get up early, thinking I will spend the morning packing, but end up with my laptop on the couch, asking the angels what is happening between the three of us. I don't understand everything they say, but their words are oddly comforting.

THE ANGELS
February 27, 1994

"Unity"

What is happening with the three of us now? We appear to be in so much conflict and I am not sure what to do to resolve it. Can you give us some guidance on this?

What is happening is that the three of you are experiencing the world in microcosm. You need to feel this kind of derision in order to be able to come back from it and then turn to the world and show them that it really is possible. This is an important chapter in your story. It is the ultimate heroic drama unfolding before your very eyes. You feel as if you are pawns, as if no matter what you say there is no resolve. This is a misconception. There is always resolve if love is applied.

In terms of the derision of ethics, there is no truth greater than the truth in unity. In this way, Barbara is correct in saying that you are never separate from God. But for the two of you to feel as if it goes against your beliefs is not something that is hers to be concerned with. Her problem is that she demands for the world to know she is right. It is not that her problem is that she is wrong, but her insistence for you to see and understand this truth at this time is a drain of her personal power.

She is coming to terms with this by trying to apply love to the situation. It seems as if no matter what she says, it is thrown back in her face, so to speak. She is creating this for herself to strengthen her in times when the throwing back is being done by someone she does not trust so much. That is why she creates the feeling of mistrust among you. Clever, aren't we?

We realize it seems somewhat cruel to make you go through this sort of transformation. We understand that you so long to be together in each others arms in love and compassion. We need to tell you at this time that you still are together in love and compassion. Do not be fooled by what your psychology has told you about being together. Sometimes there are times when love

☆ ———————————————————————

is so passionate that it swings the other way when things come into disagreement. The reason Kim and Barbara "go at each other" is because of their deep and unending love for each other that has spanned many lifetimes.

Kim, you are correct in your feeling that she is "in your face," but do not be fooled into thinking she is commanding you not to speak. There are times to speak and times to listen. You need to distinguish between those times and learn which is most effective for your personal power. Last night she needed to tell you her story and yet each time she reached a point where you disagreed, she "shut you down." This is not a message to tell you to completely quit offering your insight into the situation. It is an indication for that moment, you need to hear her, not comment. This is a major step in any conflict resolution.

She was essentially doing the same thing with you. She tried to speak and you shut her down. She is fully and completely aware on some level that all this has to be, and yet she does not know how to explain what she saw and derive from you what she thinks she needs.

Within the first conflict resolution *[The Green Shirt Day]*, there was a need to express to her the need to be loving. She heard you clearly. She changed her behavior to accommodate, not because she was responsible for your feelings, but because it advanced her in being responsible for her own. Now there is a different lesson than that day. For her, it is to understand that you are not here to save her, and, yet, paradoxically enough, you are here to save her. But she, like you, needs to know when to look for salvation and when to stand on her own and feel independent.

So you see, this explains the difference in your philosophical views of God. You are essentially both right. What she is saying is something Kim will experience in the next two weeks. The idea that you cannot be separate from God has been what we have been telling you since the beginning of this mission. This is the lesson the world needs to know. And yet, in the same hand, you need to know that you can stand alone and independent from each other and essentially, then, from God. You need to have a sense of being able to assist God, so to speak, in this mission. To that end, what you feel, Kim and Teresa, is correct. But do not be fooled into thinking that ultimately God is outside yourselves. This is not so.

☆

It is much like parables and dreaming in symbolic gestures. Those are displays being put on, filled with imagery and symbolism. Your dreams are specific to each of you. Not everyone interprets a house to be what a house means to you. If you could see without the symbolism, you would not need to have dreams. They are a language to speak with you to make you understand what is happening.

In the same way, the images and rituals of spirituality and religion are meant to be a language accessible to humans to put them in touch with the divine. For the divine is so large and wide and infinite, that to really look into it at this time would make you insane. Barbara has the courage and experience to go to a higher level and *see*. This is not to say that you will not, or do not, but at this time, you are not ready to look in that way. You look in other ways that are equally beautiful and important in their interpretive way.

What you need to understand for this conflict resolution is that, if you were to speak the language without using symbolism that gives you comfort and makes you feel connected and yet humbled (and we use this term as we did in "Inspiration," not smaller but different), you would begin to see as Barbara does. There is no point in eternity where you are separate from God. The connections that are made, one to the other and to the other and on out into eternity, that is what God is all about. That is what we are asking each of you to accept in full faith in order to then turn to the world and make a difference in the outcome of the fate of future generations.

There is a piece within you that blocks this. It would then mean too much responsibility in your conscious minds. You have been trained through media and watching others who have made this claim and carried it out erroneously that you would then be saying something sacrilegious and damning. But this is not so. There is not a place where you and God separate. Together, all human souls, all angels, all guides, all entities that work together in love and light are completely and irreconcilably connected. Together all of this energy makes up the energy that you call God, the creator, the Higher Power. It does not mean that you do not feel that "small" feeling, but it means that you are never separate from God and from each other.

Do you see how that plays out in your conflict? You cannot be separate from each other. In your fear, and in your ego state, you think you will only go so far with this idea of unity, but you will stop at a certain point. You are creating your own self-fulfilling prophecy. It is a lesson that must be played out. There are no accidents in this physical separation that you are involved in right now. It is meant to illustrate the division of your *thinking*. Barbara can go on without you theoretically. You two can form your own organization and teach what you feel is the "correct" way of thinking. But by doing that you defeat the purpose, the reason we have joined you all together at the hip.

There is something being shifted here, and you need to know that your free will is very important in this part of the path. This is what we have been trying to tell you, what you have to bring to the world: that you can stand up and make a difference.

There is no blasphemy in the fact that all of the universe together makes up the collective conscious mind of God. There is not an outside entity: It is indeed you. But for so long you have labored (and we say this quite literally, for it is indeed laborious to think you are separate from God) under these assumptions of separation.

This is a time of awakening to the true nature of self and understanding that your power is much greater than you have ever imagined or been told. That is why you have this fear. You have this fear because you are ultimately afraid of standing up and seizing power. You have so long been told that it is a bad thing, that you will get lost in it and it will overcome you. But that is not what is happening here. You are not trying to control the masses or each other, you are trying to understand the best and most loving, efficient way to utilize this power that you have been invested with, that is your birthright.

If you need to feel yourself separate from God, then that is the way power will play out for you. It is not a bad or good thing. We are saying, as we have often said in the past, it is not the most efficient use of your power. It is not less or bad, just that it is not as evolved. You have seen this in others around you and thought that you were more evolved. Yet, when push comes to shove, you are sitting here with all the others, fighting and crying amongst yourselves, wondering why it is so difficult. You will find the answers to these questions next week. You will each individually have the experiences that lead you to understand the answer to your particular situation.

☆

Kim, when you go through this, you need to know that even though they are not with you physically, Barbara and Teresa are always with you in mind and soul. You will feel as if you are on the edge of a barren plane, as if you have lost your mind. This is the effect of taking that quantum leap. You will say you do not want to go there, and we say, with all the love in our hearts, that we are with you every step of the way. You will see how your isolation is a necessary step to learn what you are about to take in. Barbara and Teresa cannot be there with you in body for, shall we say, the "shock value" of the lesson. This arguing and fighting has been preparing you to be even more alone. It is for purpose.

Teresa, you do not need to create this kind of barrenness to learn your lesson of the impossibility of separation. You will hear our voices and know. You will discover the voices have deepened and will provide you with more information about what it is you are supposed to do in order to unite the masses.

You will find that your meditation was actually an out-of-body experience. It was not a mythical precipice, it was an actual physical place where you went that exists on the Earth. When you get there you will have a realization that will come from within your body, somewhat of a shock, and you will understand more of what Barbara experienced that day she came to you and Kim at your office.

Barbara will begin to understand that her anger is a bad habit that is not needed anymore. She struggles hard to relinquish it, but like old gum on the bottom of her shoe, the more she tries to get rid of it, the more she becomes stuck. The trip will be as if someone comes with a strong disinfectant and washes not only the bottom of her shoes, but her mind and spirit as well.

She needs to understand more than ever that her part of the mission is dramatically different than the two of you, and that there are certain circumstances that she must face alone. In that way, she understands the concepts that you have been talking about, about unity and separation, but she will also be reinforced with ideas that will help her understand more than ever what she saw and how she perceived it to be true.

Do not be hard on each other. You need to have conflict but it is essential that you learn to deal with each other in complete love. This means you must learn how not to snip and argue as little children. But again, the great paradox, the only way you have to do this is to do it with all of the passion in your hearts. In that way, you have indeed been true to the process.

Dear children, you must credit yourself for undertaking a great and noble journey. When you say it is where no one has gone before, you do not even comprehend the depth of the meaning of those words. You have little inkling how true they ring. Just as before, when the concepts were palatable as long as they were concepts and you began to see the true nature of the self, you will be equally awe-inspired and terrified. To be terrified does not mean you are not safe, or that you are separate from your soul or the souls of those who are with you here in the ethers. It is a necessary part of evolution. You should give yourselves credit for attempting to consciously make such a leap. There are many who will not wake up until it is too late, and their fate will be different than yours. Much like the difference between your friends Patti and Alice. Alice waits to release her burden that she could not let go of in her lives on Earth. Patti is free to go on to higher planes. She has fulfilled her commitment and is ready to move forward. But she stays with her mother's soul out of deep and abiding love. This will make a difference in her path also. She knows she needs to not move quickly now.

This is Barbara's lesson. She needs to understand that love is more important than evolution. She needs to stay for love. This is tied into your lessons as well. For you need to understand that, too. And you will, soon, from your own healing, and all will be united again.

You will see in due time what Barbara has seen. Ignore her human voice that feels left out. Ignore her sense of vindication. Know that without a doubt, when you return from that journey that takes you to places and feelings that you have never seen before, indeed, that few humans have ever seen with human eyes and lived to tell, then she will be here for you. She will have made up your beds and will tuck you in, and bring you oatmeal, and she will sit quietly on the side of the bed and listen, rapt, to your tales of wonder and glory. You will all come to better understand why you needed to travel as you have, and all will be well.

Epilogue

Tie your camel to a tree, it's full tilt boogie!

"What if everyone was innocent
And sin was just misunderstanding?
Could we then be free of adversity?
Would we melt into the soul of God
Like we were meant to be?

"Gravity" © 1997 Barbara Lee With

April 30, 1997

Sitting in the very room where our journey began more than three years ago, the three of us take our seats as we have on so many nights together, plug in the tape recorder, and set about to listen. It is almost impossible to believe that we three women, sitting in this room tonight, are the same ones who sat here on December 14, 1993 and did our first group reading. On that cold December night, we had no idea what the repercussions of that group, and all the others that were to follow, would be in our personal lives and our perspective of ourselves and our relationships to each other. We were truly naive.

Little did we know that our gathering that December night would sweep us along into a magical journey, like some kind of action/adventure movie, complete with passionate love affairs, fierce fighting on the jungle floor, very high cliffs in thin altitudes, where planes almost crashed and angels feared to tred. We lost the lottery, in a big way, all the while surrounded by the ghosts and apparitions of just about every dead person any of us ever knew, and we met almost as many more new ones. We suffered through the deafening silences of separation, had near-death experiences, were married twice and once divorced, all amid tidal waves and fireworks, prisons and parades.

All three of us were driven, each in our own way and time, deep into our own recesses, hurled into a training program so immense and spontaneous that no one could have predicted the outcome. The mission: to learn the most empowering, energy-efficient, *compassionate* way to resolve conflict in order to learn how to love ourselves.

☆ ───

We continued to fight, but remained committed to extending love. In fact, *because* we allowed ourselves to fight so passionately and compassionately, we learned to love ourselves and each other all the more.

In committing so thoroughly to each other, to the moment and to the mission, we made the choice to go as deep together as Spirit would guide us. From the outside, our friendship often drew remarks about how liberal we were with talking behind each other's backs. But we knew that we *needed* to talk, to process, to use the details of why we were mad at each other to work our way inward to find the real root of the conflict. It was the hardest work of our lives. It drew out of us humility and equality, as we would slowly turn from blaming the other person for our hurt, to seeing where we were perpetuating the very thing in our own lives that we were so angered by in the other. Those moments of recognition were very moving and highly contagious.

One of the most important aspects of our mission together has been learning how to celebrate taking even just one baby step towards choosing love in a moment of conflict. Each time we do, we've just made one more choice that contributes to world peace. Even the smallest bit of progress towards learning self-love has become very precious to us now. Because we appreciate the small things, we no longer see only the extremes of black and white. We can now perceive all the colors of the rainbow that fall in between. That makes every moment a "masterpeace," as Kim would say, deserving to be honored by a choice of peace.

One more thing we have clearly learned: We write the script, we direct the action and we star in the drama. No matter how intense the pain discovered in our darkest caverns and subterranean enclaves, we know that we can always choose to write a happy ending. In the darkest of nights, sometimes separated by thousands of miles, we always found our way back to each other, no matter how far away we were taken or tried to get.

Barbara: The events that took place the year after those first few months of our association literally drove me insane. Our wedding in northern Wisconsin in July 1994 revealed submerged reefs with harsh and jagged edges, and a cavern of pain so deep within that I didn't even know existed, much less how to heal. I'd find myself in the bathroom in the afternoons, smearing my body with clay brought home from up north, squatting in the shower, crying and howling like a wolf as I watched streams of red water run down the drain, imagining it was my blood. Watching the wedding video made me weep uncontrollably. I did not know who I was anymore.

No place on the planet felt safe. I retreated to northern Wisconsin to hide out, crying myself to sleep at night and waking in the morning screaming from nightmares. Back home, I might have been put in a hospital. In Wisconsin, I stayed with friends who took care of me, made sure I ate and gave me a place to live. But leaving Gary so quickly after the wedding scattered my identify to the four winds and the seven spirits.

My behavior was driven by my unhealed pain and a knee jerk reaction of flight. On one of the worst nights, somewhere deep in the cold of November, I considered flinging myself off a friend's third story balcony, but instead wrote a beautiful song called "Innocent Future":

Wherever there is darkness simply shine your light
Whenever anybody's wounded, tired or blind
Whenever anybody's needing a reason to keep fighting for their life
Shine your light, simply shine your light.

Even in my darkest hour the angels were prodding me to write! I guarantee you that was not "me" talking in that moment.

Somehow I knew I was suppose to focus all my energy on my own healing. As I feverishly prayed for guidance, two different but reciprocal paths were revealed to me. From a psychological point of view, the wedding revealed a segmentation within me that been dormant since as far back as early childhood, the apparent result of being sexually abused at a very early age. From a shamanic point of view, parts of my soul had fled and were still hidden somewhere in the underworld, waiting to be found. The answer for my healing was found in combining both points of view.

☆ ────────────────────────────

Researching my own remedy, I read everything I could about both soul retrieval and multiple personality disorder. I concluded I needed to find the lost parts of me and bring them back to consciousness, then integrate all the aspects of my personality. Shamanically, I had to die in order to create a sacred space for the power to enter and work through me. Psychologically, the challenge would be to identify and teach these parts to work together. A shaman conducted a soul retrieval, and I then took that information to a psychologist and slowly began to piece myself back together.

Gary, Kim and Teresa somehow managed to hold on to me through the deepest and most complicated time of my life. Struggling through my own illness, I often blamed my malaise on my husband, the angels and my antics with these two women. In the spring of 1995, when I went on a singing tour to Japan for two months, I swore I would have nothing more to do with these two insane women ever again for as long as I lived. Upon returning to the states, I once again fled to northern Wisconsin.

During this serious and befuddling period, I stopped channeling altogether. I felt the angels had led me on with great promises of grandeur, only to leave me sick and fragmented. But they hadn't. It was all part of my healing. I was forced to come face to face with my deepest fears in order to become balanced and whole. Little did I know how far my ego had to shrink in order to truly heal.

On this most glorious Spring evening in 1997, I celebrate my integration. Not that it was easy, but I believe with every fiber of my being that each turn and tumble was completely orchestrated for great and divine purpose. I see now that each step was indeed "a beautiful dance of great cooperation."

The challenge of finding the pain and healing it brought with it a deep and lasting peace. A day doesn't go by when I don't awaken in my beautiful home, look at my husband who stood by me every step of the way, walk into our gardens that we began planting over seven years ago and thank my lucky stars. Those gardens reflect the maturity grown in me. This is what it must feel like to have had a Near Death Experience. Every day is truly a miracle.

How can I ever thank my two sorority sisters, who were walking through their own fire the whole time they were holding so tight to me? There has been no greater honor than to be a part of their journey as well. Through it all, we have always found a way back together. Since last March, I have been allowing the angels to speak through me again. The joy of this process is indescribable now. Kim coaxed me out of retirement for her 40th birthday party to channel "Vision," what we always thought would be the last chapter of this book. Little did we know, it was not the last chapter of our first book, it was the first chapter of our third book. Go figure!

And what about Hawaii? Well, the Goddess smiled upon us all through that trip. Guided by Teresa's dreams and meditations, apparitions of ancient Hawaiian warriors, dolphins and whales, wild dogs and lighthouse keepers, we found our way to the Sacred Valley of Creation, where Pele herself resided at what is now known as our "First Wedding." Under the waterfall at Limahuli we gathered at sunrise: Gary and I, Beverly (our Pele Incarnate), Luddy and Teresa, and a hierarchy of angelic guests from all across the Heavens who came to witness our union. There happened to be an angel convention on Molokai during our ceremony on Kaua'i! What a coincidence. Suffice it to say, that story shall be another book entirely.

Teresa: The events of the last three years have been nothing less than mind-blowing. When I think about how the three of us were brought together and how fast things began to change for each of us as a result of the union, it's like watching a baby as it takes in everything it can, observing and learning, and then putting everything it learned into immediate action. That's what we've done, all in blind faith.

As I've learned and worked the concepts the angels have taught us about resolving conflict, loving the Self, and how much our culture influences us every day, I am awed by the truth that rings so clearly within me. I can see where I have perpetuated conflicts in my life, especially with my ex-husband. I can see how I NEVER had a clue how to love myself and honor me for who I was. Now, after all this training we've been through together, I immediately feel a jolt in my body when I find myself fallen prey to one of culture's dictates, one that lies to me about the divine child of God I really am by trying to tell me I'm not good enough. But most of all, I am continually amazed at how quickly the space within me opens simply by contemplating these ideas. And, once the space is opened, there is finally room for movement and change.

Kim and I have often said that giving up an old behavior or way of thinking is hard. There you are, left with this hole where the old way once resided. Now you have to find a new way. You have to figure out what to fill the hole with that doesn't make you feel bad, treat others badly, or perpetuate a way of being that no longer serves you. Somehow, with the grace of God, we're all three learning to do that.

We decided that all you can do is fill that space with God and love, hope and faith, and a willingness to let go of the old for the promise of the new. And with it, the new brings peace and a sense of self about who you really are, not based on who you happen to be standing next to at that moment, comparing yourself to, either thinking you're better or worse, or that you have more or less than them. There is magic in those moments when we can still our minds long enough and just *be*; and we all could use a little more magic in our lives.

I still struggle through my own healing but I've learned that if I just stick with the processes the angels have taught us, sooner or later I get it. Sometimes it takes way longer than I'd like, but when the revelation comes, oh my, you can't imagine the peace it brings.

I want to share what I've learned with everyone. I want every person I know, and those I don't, to understand that they are divine too. I want people to see how they are being influenced everyday by old wounds that really can be healed. I want them to see their own divinity and love, for how could someone who loves themselves shoot down a stranger in the street? Who could beat a small child senseless or even to death if they see their own divinity and the divinity of the child? Who could break another's heart with their words if they understand they can choose peace and they don't have to prove they are right?

I don't know, it may seem like a stretch, but I'm not giving up on saving the world. I have felt the power of healing things in my own life that I didn't even know were there and I'll never stop believing that peace and love are the birthright of every person on this planet. But *we have to choose.*

Kim: How do you sum up three years of miracles? My journal alone is in its third, three-inch, three-ring notebook. If I told you how many fights the three of us have had over these years, you wouldn't even believe me! Barbara and I once spent an entire week screaming at each other through e-mail on the Internet. We never even spoke on the phone. We just slammed e-mail back and forth over the airwaves as we each tried to be right . . . couldn't even remember what the fight was about by the end, but, by God, one of us had to be right. Teresa and Barbara didn't speak for months because pain and fear and doubts got in the way. Teresa and I worked our sick, co-dependent patterns on each other for so long that even we were bored to tears by the time we finally gave it up. What I know now is that every one of our fights was a miracle. Not that they weren't difficult and painful and filled with dread, but we made them miracles because we chose to see them that way.

I have always said, "What is real is not what matters. What you *believe* is real is what matters." Are you wondering what happened to the awful voices in my head that told me all of my life that I was not good enough? They are gone. I do not believe them anymore and so they stopped.

A couple of years ago I had a breathtaking dream. I was watching God weave the tapestry of our lives and the beautiful fabric stretched out into the distance, as far as the eye could see. Up close, it was as though God's hands were in the act of creation as I looked on. There were golden threads woven in everywhere. I heard the words, "God weaves the fabric of our lives with baby's breath and angel tears." Under the spoken words, I could hear God explain, "You see, as I weave, it goes up and down. If it doesn't go both up and down, then it's not weaving. It's just running thread across thread. It will not hold together. You must understand this about your lives, about the tough times. If it doesn't go up *and* down, it's not weaving. It will not hold together." I have retold that dream countless times and its message always brings renewed hope. Life is bittersweet because it is meant to be that way and we learn amazing lessons when we make it over the rough spots.

Do you see the paradox here? We still fight, I still have doubts, Clay and I are not yet sure of where our relationship is going and some days my three wonderful children hate me! But I have made a million baby steps toward wholeness and I learn more each day about how to stay in Love. I believe that's all there really is in this world: learning to Love. Start by learning to Love yourself. Celebrate even the smallest victory and turn the toughest trial into a miraculous lesson, instead of letting it become the end of the world. Begin to recognize God in you, and you will learn to see God in every single living thing around you.

When my son was five years old he drew a picture and scrawled on it the words, "I am Scott. God is in me." I learned a lot that day! When I accepted the fact that God is in me, working through me, every moment of every day, my life took on a whole new meaning.

That's what I have learned about the barren plane. It's about making a choice. It's about perception: what you believe is real. I had to go out on that barren plane alone because it was *my* barren plane. I created it and only I could recreate it. I have to face my doubts and fears with Love every day.

On April 26, 1994 I made the trek out onto the barren plane alone when I almost died from complications of a tubal pregnancy. I saw then, with my own heart and spirit, that God is Love and Love is about Completeness. Love includes everything! All That Is. The Angels say, "There is no place where there is not God." God is in our darkness as well as our light. It's not about looking perfect; it's about being perfection, in this moment, right where I am.

When I recovered and told the story of seeing that white light and standing in the Completeness of Love, Katie said, "Mommy, you mean you didn't miss us?" My answer was simply, "Honey, I couldn't miss you, because you were there too." Completeness, Love, Peace: It's hard to explain in words.

I once wrote a poem about "I am becoming." If I could share only one thing with you it would be to hold that statement in your heart everyday and allow God to direct you to who it is that you are becoming. We each have the choice every day to become Love. To forgive. To be Peace. To free ourselves from the voices, inside and out, that tell us we are less than perfection. God's thoughts, as angels, have come to guide us.

Become like a child again. Little children don't know all the "stuff" that grown-ups know. If you catch them early enough, before the voices around them convince them otherwise, they still talk directly to God, so they still believe they are the center of the universe. We come into this world as the perfect reflection of God. That is reality. When we lay our bodies aside and leave this world, we return to that perfection. That is reality. What we create in between is a choice. Living in Love creates heaven. Anything else is hell.

At Easter in 1996 "the box" I used to live inside transformed itself into a beautiful Lily. I am now Lily and I have found a Peace I never knew existed. It grows each day.

Reality is free. It's the illusion you have to pay for.

☆　☆　☆

Tonight truly seems like the end of an era. They told us it would take three years to lay the foundation of our Foundation. Three years of intensive, one-on-one training. Three years of intricate mirroring between the three of us. Three years of cementing our souls together to become one, larger-than-life, limitless being of the New Millennium. We have become Synergy. We have become ourselves. We have come to realize that "We" truly are God, reflected through our relationships, first with ourselves and then with those we love, and on out to even strangers on the street, to the clouds and trees, the sky and the water, to everything in God's creation.

Each time we commit to becoming Love, we can see a whole new range of possibilities on how to live our lives each day. But there are a few "catches" that come with Love.

☆

The first catch is that we have to be patient. There are often many layers of pain, guilt and doubt to work through before we find the innocence inside. This process takes time. Amazingly, though, it doesn't take as long to heal as it took to create the mess in the first place.

The second catch is that we have to shift the focus from the outside to the inside. God gave us all the tools and all the instructions we need, all inside us, accessible any time we choose. And there are no shortcuts. Nobody can pick up your power for you.

The third catch is that we have to stay in the present moment. Our lives have ceased to be about who we've been before and who we're going to be someday. Instead, they are about who we are right now, in this moment, in *every* moment. Nothing is needed except a shift in perception.

A sunset is now a special event, instead of something rarely noticed. The next time you see a beautiful sunset, say to yourself, "That sunset is just for me." Now, this is not to say that the sunset is *only* for you. But when you take the time to really experience the sunset and take it as your own, something changes. Not because you own the sunset or because the sunset changes. You change. You visit eternity in that moment and take the sunset with you. It expands who you are at that very instant and changes your outlook on the world. It's a miracle. Try it. You'll understand.

Albert Einstein once said something to the effect that we will never heal the problems of our world from the level at which we created them in the first place. Perhaps this new level he's referring to is the shift in perception back to the innocence of a child.

A child will find joy and laughter in a flower growing up through a cracked sidewalk even though she may not eat today. A child will smile at a sunset even though he will be beaten by someone that same night. A child will dream of carrying a white flag out into the middle of the battlefield to help the adults understand, even though she has awakened many times to the sound of her parents screaming at each other in the middle of the night. Children can do this because they have an intimate and active relationship with the Divine on levels that we, as adults, *think* we have outgrown.

Become a child again. Open to the possibility that love will heal you. Trust yourself. Listen carefully. Be patient and live in gratitude. God's thoughts, as angels, have come to guide us all.

It is the journey, you see, that you don't want to miss. Peace be your journey.

THE ANGELS
April 30, 1997

"Graduation Day"

This is a very auspicious occasion. Many have gathered here to look upon the reconstruction of a perspective of the journey of three women, through the deserts, the mountains, the oases; through the heat and the cold and the dead of night and the early dawn to sit in the forest, to sit by the ocean, to go to the mountains: to heal.

The journey that you have been on since your inception is about to come to a diminutive close. We sat before you over three years ago, the first time you met only as three *[January 1, 1994]*, to begin what we told you was a three-year cycle. This day, somewhat passed the actual anniversary that was assigned because of other numerical values, directly ties back into the dates of the past.

Now you are experiencing the fourth spring together. Each time that spring has come for you in this cycle, you have made spiral steps into the actualization of all that you have set out to do. As you look back upon all that you have been through, you can see a rainbow of changing perspectives, each step growing deeper, richer, fuller, each experience between you individually adds itself to the broadening prospect of your deepening self-awareness.

As you sit here tonight on a somewhat casual yet very intense evening, you are about to be regarded with the completion of a promise, a promise that was made to you before you came into this life. A promise that you made to yourselves and a promise that was made amongst the three of you to see come to fruition a particular influence that you have chosen to carry.

Up until now your influence has reached very broadly in your local universe. You took this information and immediately began to offer it to any who were interested around you. As you yourselves took in this information to see exactly how it fit for you, you broadened its influence onto your family and the other friends in your life who may not have come to see this information as specifically as you have. As your growing sense of self-love touched those closest to you, they, too, were influenced beyond their thinking minds, to turn and touch others in ways that were more loving.

Understand how all of the people have been influenced who have been brought into the modest comfort of your home, into your presence to experience the delivering of information. Begin to see how far your influence has stretched already. It is much, much broader than you can perceive it to be. You would have to draw many, many circles.

This mission, to expand your circle of influence in these past three years, has been a great success. You are international in that way, because you have been experienced in other parts of the world through varying methods of communication. This reach that you have is just the tip of the iceberg.

This growth is much bigger than any of you could have decided to do. Where you are about to head is so much grander than you could even begin to imagine at this time. Just as when you first sat before us as a triad, you could not conceive of how far-reaching the messages would be in only three years.

The *[live talk show]* broadcast that you sent from Seattle *[in November 1996]* was beamed all across the planet. That was the beginning of a kind of firming up and reaching far of the message and the mission and who you are.

The past three years are like no other three years that you will experience again. From here on in, you are now headed to the last two years of the five-year cycle. These two years are meant to be very specific training that will involve making deeper, stronger, more secure footholds all across the world so that the airplay will increase. The live contact through the groups will be able to be far-reaching. The information that has been printed will increase and multiply. You will open up the channel to begin to receive the kind of support from the universe that you yourselves have purpose-fully deferred for three years. It wasn't that you weren't working hard enough, or were over-indulgent when you shouldn't have been. Those things may have been true, but the overall timing was not going to deviate.

All things will be divinely timed. If you find resistance to moving ahead, do not resist the resistance.   Resistance is the braking for the stop sign. That is a good thing. Surrender to the resistance, thereby removing it. Then simply acknowledge with your conscious mind that there is divine timing.

Quit assuming that there is a shortcoming within you because you have not achieved the future that your conscious mind sat and imagined. Also, now is the time to eliminate punishment. Punishment is an obsolete form of waking up. It's hard to miss when you're draining your energy away beating yourself over the head with a stick. Punishment served its purpose but is no longer applicable. It is for you to now, in these months ahead, to train yourselves to put the stick down. It's very simple. In fact, it's much easier than you make it. Flow freely and breathe through whatever turbulence might be involved in the decision that you are making.

Settle into the divine timing and make sure your garden is properly watered, fertilized, trimmed. Your mission here is to be the gardener.

Because you cannot predict futures, we would like to steer you towards the conditions that will be most efficient in order to live as a healed human. Because you have never done so, it will seem quite foreign. This time period is one of adjustment, of acclimating, taking baby steps and acquainting yourself with how it feels to be healed. When you don't have the stick in your hand to beat yourself up, what is in your hand? A paint brush? A pencil? The beautiful brow of your child? What are you going to pick up instead of that stick? It may be that now your two arms are free to embrace someone and thank them and bless them.

You have, through the course of these three years, been attended by who we have often been referred to as the Counsel of Nine. We insinuated of their presence in a casual way three years ago as we coached you as a triad on Tuesday Nights. We said that each of you had three that worked with you and then moved to the next. The Counsel of Nine is actually three triads that, together with you as the fourth, make up the Party of Twelve.

In the past, they revealed themselves to you as an ancient counsel from beyond the threshold of time and space who had a very specific and far-reaching influence in the universe who had come specifically for you. This still holds true. But on this, your Graduation Day, you see that they, too, are graduating.

☆

Perceive yourselves to sit equally in the Party of Twelve, as opposed to the Counsel of Nine being a wiser, more divine, more intrepid congregation. The difference is, they are in the crow's nest with the capability to see more far-reaching than you can. That does not mean upwards is better or more divine or more knowledgeable. It means that this is their position.

You, on the other hand, as there are nine of them and three of you, have had to provide the details and the detailed perception to three of them at a time. They have been very specifically working with you. You've received three times the amount of information. You have received more information than your human mind can grasp in these past three years.

You sit on this day in equality, all of you come to receive your wings, the symbolic and official gesture of completion and speculation. Completion of a learning process that has solidified and integrated you. And speculation of where it is you are going to steer the power that is you.

From above comes an energy, an influence from the stars, as you can hear the hierarchy of heavens applauding. This is not the first counsel of nine nor party of twelve and it will not be that last. But it surely is one of the most wide awake that we have seen.

The future is a place of great promise. You have been gifted with the knowledge to understand how to make all of your heart's desires come into physical reality. The next two years is about sending you off to experiment with how far you can take that knowledge. How much are you going to change the physical details of your three-dimensional world? How many of your deepest dreams are going to surface and push through the construct of the coordinates of your three-dimensional living? You can almost see them rising up, molding themselves out of the flat terrain into mountains and oceans and forests. It's as if you are creating your own planet. You have come to the time of Genesis. You have come truly to the beginning.

As you walk from here, hold tight to the very apparent responsibility that you have and the commitment that you have made to creating the details of love. Love and honor, expression and feeling.

In these next few years, there is going to be a change in each of your individual pathways. The clarity between you, the differences are going to rise to great heights. You will be able to celebrate the diversity as all find a path now outward of each other, attuned to the singularity of the dream. The dream that the three of you create will be the basis of an association that will be eternally interconnected and yet, equally as free. Do not be afraid of that freedom. You have settled into a being that is quite complex, that functions very much as a unit. Now is the time to go back, go back to your homes. Do not stop being together or working towards creating the future. But allow yourselves the freedom and the comfort, like a good marriage, to know that you can go off and fly free without losing any of the connection. In fact, as you indulge yourselves in the freedom of your dreams, you only strengthen what is already there.

On an intricate level, you are in the midst of another nine-month birthing cycle. When you come to the end of the nine months from the first of the year, a very dramatic change comes about. You'll see it coming for a long ways, but when it actually transpires, the movement, and the input and output are going to help to come into fruition the short term dreams of solidification.

This summer is a training ground on all levels: personal, physical, emotional, intellectual, business, pleasure, energy, every pursuit that you undertake, you will observe and watch as an experiment. Find the places within you that you want to strengthen, and use the circumstances to be the actresses that would channel forth those particular sets of desires and emotions and thought patterns.

The groups that you are going to be hosting (as you have an inkling already into understanding) are for you. Use the interaction with the people and the opportunities to practice your presentation. Not just what you say, but make sure every word that you say is accounted for. Do not be extravagant. Be efficient with your words. Also experiment with the energy of the people moving around before, during and after. Use the opportunity to create yourselves into different beings. Use the opportunity to make the learning exciting and fun and unpredictable. Use it to experiment.

At the end of this series of groups, each of you will be more well-defined in terms of what direction you're going to go with your personal stake in Synergy Alliance. You will be able to create a business plan and a visualization of your dream through the course of what you learn in these next four months in a way that never before has been so clear and so supported from within and without. You find the strength to become individual sole proprietorships in ways that you can't even imagine at this moment.

Use that time, and all of the other things that transpire. It's not going to be just groups. There will be people coming into all three of your lives who are going to draw you into a bigger influence and seem to take you farther away from each other. You begin to see just how you need to structure Synergy Alliance in order to accommodate the terrain of each of the three of your hearts desires. You don't want to be over-committed, or under-committed. You don't want to be overlooking or exaggerating the potential. Use this time period, don't think you have to rush out and create a business, "or else." Use the time to straighten up the business amongst you.

You have already been given inklings into that work also of cleaning up your communication and opening yourself up to even deeper self-examination, using each other to be the "bad cops." Instead of just going through life and using your random emotions as you have for the past three years, get together for the sole purpose of revealing and critiquing and bouncing things off each other, so that you know it's safe. You all understand the need to be compassionate and you're all on equal footing.

In real life, you often have waited until the other person is ready to take their share of the responsibility. Now we want you to have an agreement: no matter how you feel at the moment, you must process instantly, as it were, amongst yourself, to practice, to strengthen. We guarantee, you're going to be faced with having to communicate with many, many people at one time in situations that are nerve racking. Test your ability to present yourself and be composed.

We want you to not overlook this opportunity to use all of these details we're bringing you until the end of summer to do that. Once you have done that, you will be sufficiently prepared to face the lights and the camera and the action, however that shows up for you individually.

☆ ───────────────────────────────────

The composite of your lives together, your history, is about to make another great turn. All the things that you have been through are about to change, too. As you evolve the present, the past grows richer also. All the things that were judged in the past are going to look brighter and more meaningful. All the times when you thought you fell short are going to suddenly be smart moves. The embracing of the gateways to deeper and higher perception is going to help move you along the course, point the way, lend the strength and open the door to your greater tomorrow.

After the session, the three of us hug one more time, holding on for dear life, not sure what's in store for us as we say goodbye to the beginning. It feels like we are preparing for another separation. We aren't sure when we will be able to get together again for our regular Wednesday night Psychic Sorority meeting. One thing we are sure of, though. The next time we meet back here in this room, as we have for over three years, everything, once again, will have changed.